LIVING ETHOS

Living Ethos

Exploring the Heart and Practice
of Catholic School Ethos

Edited by
Denis Robinson

DOMINICAN PUBLICATIONS

Published (2025) by
Dominican Publications
42 Parnell Square
Dublin 1
Ireland

www.dominicanpublications.com

ISBN
978-1-905604-49-4 (Paperback)
978-1-905604-53-1 (E-Book)

British Library Cataloguing in Publications Data.
A catalogue record for this book is available
from the British Library.

Copyright © (2025) the Contributors and Dominican Publications

All rights reserved.
No part of this publication may be reproduced,
stored in a retrieval system or transmitted by any means,
electronic or mechanical, including photocopying,
without permission in writing from the publisher
or a licence permitting restricted copying in Ireland
issued by the Irish Copyright Licencing Agency Ltd

Origination by Dominican Publications

Cover design by David Cooke

Printed by
Sprint Books, Tallaght, Dublin 24

Contents

Acknowledgements	9
Contributors	11

Prologue

Where There Is No Vision, People Perish *Denis Robinson*	15

Ethos from the inside out

1	Basic Convictions: Faith in God and Faith in People *Denis Gleeson*	25
2	Leading from within: the Inner Dynamics of School Leadership *Denis Robinson*	37
3	Leadership, Ethos and Catholic Social Teaching *Michael Shortall*	50
4	Building Bridges: Inter-religious Dialogue, Inclusion and Diversity *Aiveen Mullally*	63
5	The Role of Ethos in Relationship and Sexuality Education *Vivek da Silva*	75
6	Ethos as a Sign of Hope and Uncompromising Love *John McHale*	90

Ethos Is for Life

7	It's Everyone's Business: a Whole-school Approach to Ethos *Katherina Broderick*	101
8	A Question of Identity: the Contribution of Teachers to Living Ethos *Michael Hayes*	115
9	A Culture of Care: the Quality of Relationships *Marian Farrelly*	125
10	From the Floorboards up: Ethos and Adolescent Faith Formation *Orla Walsh*	134
11	Learning for Life: Ethos and Life-long Learning *Gene Mehigan*	146
12	Creating Good Memories: Ethos and School Gardens *Sandra Austin*	156
13	Ethos in School Traditions, Symbols and Rituals *John-Paul Sheridan*	167
14	Creating a Sacred Space: Reflective Practice *Gerry O'Connell*	178

Ethos and the Wider Community

15	Parents as Partners: Ethos at Home *Rosaleen Doherty*	191
16	Ethos at Play: Extra-curricular Activities *Aodán Mac Suibhne*	199
17	Going the Extra Mile: Afterschool Support *Máiréad Minnock* and *Siobhán Shovlin*	208

Contents

18	Ethos in the Wider Community: Community Service *Tom Ryan*	218
19	Being Stewards of Creation: Ethos and Caring for the Earth *Paul Whearty*	226
20	Politics and Ethos in Irish Primary Schools *Clare Maloney*	236

Epilogue

Love Comes First: Reflections on Catholic School Ethos   245
Denis Robinson

Notes   257

Acknowledgements

This book would not have been possible without the support of many people.

I am especially grateful to faculty members of Marino Institute of Education and MA students in the Leadership in Christian Education programme for sharing their research on the different aspects of school ethos presented in this book. Marino Institute has been running an MA in Leadership in Christian Education for the past 10 years, previously in collaboration with Mary Immaculate College, Limerick, and now receiving accreditation from Trinity College, Dublin. This programme is designed to prepare participants for leaderships roles in all levels of Catholic education. This book is one way of sharing the rich insights and disseminating the research of the faculty and MA students to the wider public.

Special thanks must be given to the leadership team of Marino Institute of Education for their unceasing endorsement and encouragement of this project, in particular Professor Anne O'Gara, former president of Marino, and the current president, Professor Teresa O'Doherty, for their unwavering support.

A word of thanks must also be given to Wesleigh O'Hagan who completed her MA at Marino Institute on the study of ethos from an intergenerational perspective. Her research contributed significantly to the original inspiration for this book. Wesleigh is currently principal of a community college in Dublin.

Many thanks to all the students of the MA in Leadership in Christian Education programme. Though only a fraction of the research is presented in this book, they each in his/her own way have contributed to a growing body of research into the power of ethos to significantly and positively impact people's lives and engagement in education.

A book does not come to life without a publisher, so I am particularly grateful to Dominican Publications, for their patience, guidance and able assistance in editing and producing this book. It would not have been possible without their commitment to and belief in this project.

Contributors

Sandra Austin (PhD) lectures in social, environmental and scientific education, and is head of the Department of Global Diversity, Sustainability and Intercultural Education at Marino Institute of Education. She has published in the areas of inquiry based learning; the environment and sustainability.

Katherina Broderick (MA) is principal of Presentation Secondary School, Listowel. She is a qualified educational leadership and life skills coach and mentor for newly appointed principals with the Centre for School Leadership. She has published in the areas of religious education; curriculum development.

Rosaleen Doherty (MA) is a teacher of music, history, is a learning support co-ordinator and year head in a secondary school in Dublin.

Marian Farrelly (PhD) is a former primary school principal and currently lectures in sociology of education, philosophy of education and education policy at Marino Institute of Education.

Denis Gleeson is a Christian Brother and former Headmaster of St Mary's Christian Brothers Grammar School, Belfast. He served on four boards of governors, the Council for Catholic Maintained Schools, Northern Ireland and the Governing Body of the Marino Institute of Educatio. He has published in the area of spirituality.

Michael Hayes (EdD) is a retired primary school principal and former primary inspector. His research areas include teacher identity; reflective practice.

Clare Maloney (PhD) has taught religious education at Marino

Institute of Education. She has published in the areas of poetry; children's books.

Aodán Mac Suibhne (M. Litt.) has recently retired as principal lecturer, head of the Department of English and Roinn na Gaeilge, and co-ordinator of Irish-medium Bachelor in Education at Marino Institute of Education. He has published in the areas of the Irish language learning, Irish history.

John McHale (MA) is Principal of St Finian's Diocesan College in Mullingar.

Gene Mehigan (PhD) is Vice President for Education and Strategic Development at Marino Institute of Education, Dublin. He lectures in the area of literacy. He is past president of both the Literacy Association of Ireland and the Irish Learning Support Association, and former chair of the Standing Committee of Heads of Education and Teacher Unions.

Mairéad Minnock (PhD student in the School of Education, Trinity College, Dublin) is school placement coordinator at Marino Institute of Education. She has written on school placement and co-teaching during school placement.

Aiveen Mullally (EdD) is a lecturer in religious education, course leader of the MES in Leadership of Christian Schools Online, and director of the Centre for Religious Education at Marino Institute of Education. She has published in the areas of teacher identity and religious education; belief fluidity; and religious diversity in Catholic schools.

Gerry O'Connell (EdD) has recently retired as a lecturer in Religious Education at Marino Institute of Education. He has published in the areas of religious education; religious imagination; and reflective practice

Denis Robinson (PhD) recently retired as director of the Centre for Religious Education and Course Leader of MA in Christian Leadership in Education in Marino Institute of Education. He teaches in the areas of theology and spirituality. He has published in the areas of spirituality; leadership.

Tom Ryan (MA) is deputy principal in Blackrock College, Dublin. He is a teacher of religious education and English. He is also involved in the pastoral care programme. He has published in the area of religious education.

John-Paul Sheridan (PhD) lectures in religious education, catechesis, and liturgy at St Patrick's Pontifical University, Maynooth. He has published in the areas religious education; catechesis; liturgy.

Michael Shortall (STD) lectures in moral theology and ethics at St Patrick's Pontifical University, Maynooth. He has published in the areas of human rights; Catholic social thought; ministry.

Siobhan Shovlin (MA) is a sixth class primary school teacher in Dublin.

Vivek da Silva (PhD student in DCU) is an assistant professor in religious education at Dublin City University. He is researching in the area of relationship and sexuality education in post-primary Catholic schools in Ireland.

Orla Walsh (EdD) taught religious education, was previously a deputy principal and is currently a part-time educational consultant at Mount Sackville Secondary School, Dublin. She has published in the areas of Catholic identity; child poverty; catechetics.

Paul Whearty (MA) is a class teacher and assistant principal in a national school in Drogheda.

Prologue
Where There Is No Vision, People Perish

DENIS ROBINSON

The rationale for this book is to provide a practical exposition of the nature, meaning, inner dynamics, and practical implications of an intentional Christian school ethos. It explores, from different perspectives, the heart and soul of ethos, particularly highlighting the necessity of having a comprehensive Christian vision of education, and understanding the implications of this. It recognizes the fundamental role education plays in helping us realize our innate capacity for the good, the true and the beautiful, for right relationship, for growth, and transformation in preparation for total engagement with all facets of life.

This entails operating beyond a narrow image of the person to appreciate and promote the extraordinary potential that exists in each individual student, be they persons of faith or not. Fundamental to this vision is acknowledging our relationship with the Godhead as the infinite horizon against which we interpret the dignity of our individual lives, the deeper significance of life and learning, and how education prepares us for the grand purpose of human existence. This vision helps us discover the depths of possibility that exist in the education of the entire person, incorporating body, mind, heart, soul, social, cultural and economic reality.

A basic assumption is that a Christian school ethos is based on:

A set of beliefs, convictions, principles views that permeate the heart and mind to positively impact one's life, not in an unconscious way, not subservient, compliant submissive passive way but with conviction as to the merits of these beliefs to promote a holistic vision of life, a way of being that humanises and divinises, that provides a vision and a way to fully engage in life and become all that is possible for us as individuals and as a learning community.[1]

As has been noted by many, the vision behind school ethos can never be perfectly realized; but it is, still, a vision worth striving for. At its most essential, ethos it is a pointer to the possible. A school ethos is never intended to be the expression of a once-for-all vision but rather, with faith in God and with core values as guides, it is expected to dynamically mature and judiciously adapt in response to the development of experience, insight, new knowledge, and the challenges and opportunities presented by education, Christian faith, society and cultures.

Acknowledging the evolutionary nature of school ethos will allow it to grow organically in response to the desire to promote the individual flourishing of all students while also responding to the needs of society. Such a comprehensive perspective is at the heart of a Christian school ethos. Its primary objective is to promote all aspects of the life of a person, the sacred and the secular, the ethical and the spiritual, the mundane and the mysterious. A Christian school ethos is underpinned by a theology and philosophy to which nothing human is alien. Such an approach implies that in the pursuit of truth we are not afraid to ask any question or confront any issue. It means not longing for some future utopia but preparing students for the real world and, not being passive participants in life, helping them become proactive and motivated to change self, society and the world for the better.

This requires educating students to be responsible for the knowledge they gain and conscious of the power this generates. It entails being unafraid of life and its challenges and, not expecting a perfect world, equipping them to embrace the good and confront the bad, to dream new dreams and, as Ghandi advises, be the change they envision. To do this necessitates providing them with the necessary education, faith foundation, freedoms, skills and ability to imagine and be creative.

Prologue: Where There Is No Vision, People Perish

A Christian school ethos aims to educate, not for subservience, but for independence; it advocates a spirit of caring and solidarity as it tries to help students see the world beyond their own needs and personal perspective.

To achieve this, means that leaders and educators be responsible for the values they engender, be responsible for the role models they present and mindful of the memories they create which will guide and influence students for the rest of their lives. This perspective on Christian education demonstrates how faith is both vision and practice; it illustrates how religious belief becomes personally meaningful and thoroughly pragmatic. This vision champions the education of the inner and outer person, with an emphasis on the unique, personal development of each student. It advocates education for emancipation from whatever dehumanises, from selfishness, from apathy, from being drawn into self-indulgence and blind materialism. There is no apology for advocating a reverence for the nobility of the human person and allowing the religious spirit permeate and advance the holistic growth and development of pupils. There should be no apology for operating out of this affirming and enlightened perspective of humanity, and no apology for wanting to teach faith, promote core values, and actively foster the type of formation which contributes to individual development, human prosperity and the advancement of peoples and civilisation.[2]

Such education is not intended to be a form of programmed character engineering – for there needs to be great respect for the dignity, individuality and uniqueness of everyone in the context of their own life and culture. Dermot Lane suggests that such a vision 'is a central conviction of Catholic education, that humanity learned something decisive about itself in the story of Jesus of Nazareth, crucified and risen. Catholic education, therefore, is committed to keeping the disturbing, liberating and healing memory of Jesus alive in our world.'[3] The 'good news' is as much good news today as it was 2,000 years ago! The Christian school and its ethos is meant to reflect this Good News in all its ramifications.

We want the best for our children. We want them to live both the mystery and ordinariness of life in its fullness. We want them to achieve all they are capable of and to have educators who do what they can to make this possible.

To this end a Christian school purposefully advocates the holistic education, the personal development, and moral formation of each student, not in a prescriptive or doctrinaire manner but rather with the intention to create what could be called a Kingdom of God experience where they, be they people of faith or not, are valued, genuinely loved and cared for, where they are nurtured as individuals and know compassion, where personal dignity and respect for the uniqueness of each is guaranteed, where they experience friendship, acceptance and support. The community life, the learning that takes place, the different relationships, and rituals of a school are the means by which this becomes possible. A Catholic school is meant to be a place of encounter where faith, life and culture are brought into dialogue through responsible and systematic discourse; it is meant to be an environment which offers guiding principles, provide necessary life skills, a sense of justice, and a critically reflective orientation toward life.

It is also the mission of Catholic schools to propose faith, but never to impose it. The dream is that a school be an opportunity to experience the best a Christian ethos can offer, whether as staff, students, or parents. The intention is not to proselytise but for students of all faiths and none to encounter core Christian values, to experience Christian love, justice, inclusion and genuine care that can be accepted and assimilated and contribute to their own personal development without the necessity for assent by way of faith for those who do not believe or belong to another faith tradition. This affords a way of knowing, exploring, celebrating, and transforming our common human nature for the betterment of all. We thus live the Christian ethos, not as an imposition but in search of a way for all of us to appreciate and live life in all its sacred and secular potential.

In seeking a more authentic way of living the Christian ethos we need to be open to share with those of different faiths or none their own understanding of faith, their experience of transcendent reality and the meaning the world holds for them. In this way we want all members of the school community to experience what it is like for a school to be inspired and touched by the love of God and how this is made visible on a day-to-day basis. This must include being open to help others pursue their own faith or philosophy of life. The goal is to translate Christian belief into vision and practice for the benefit of all, for the school ethos to be inspirational and aspirational, and, in the school setting, to reflect what the Kingdom of God looks like for them.

What should be evident in the internalisation of the school ethos is the development of a culture of genuine reflection where faith and belief is not just something one endures, or learns about, or learns from, but rather a way of being together which is an affirmation of each person by the way they are loved and cared for, by the way they are respected and cherished, in the way we help them become all they are meant to be.

Advocating a faith-based school ethos means accepting that education is an organised and pragmatic way of learning and preparing students for life, and acknowledging that there is no value-free education. Whether people are conscious of it or not, all education is value-based. It has a philosophical underpinning and adopts a particular vision of what it means to be human and what education is about. While education involves the provision of knowledge, life-skills and how to use these effectively and for the common good, it also influences, directly and indirectly, personal and value formation. The formative effect of education takes place in what is said and how we teach, in the presentation of values, in our educational aims and objectives, and in our understanding of what it means to be a person and a learner. Whatever is taught reflects an underlying anthropology, and presents what we consider to be essential for a fulfilled life. For better or worse, all education is a type of simultaneous education in that it caters for the education and personal development of the student at many levels at the same time. In operating out of an intentional Christian ethos, we try to purposefully hand on what is needed to live a full, good and flourishing life that fosters authentic human development in all its aspects, as well as facilitating the spiritual and religious growth of those who believe, and those of a different faith tradition.[4]

It is a truism to say that no one is an island and that we always grow in reference to someone or something outside ourselves. We need others to help us discover who we are and imagine what we can be. There are many models and personality theories in existence advocating what it means to be human and how this can be expressed. How do we decide as an individual, as a school, and as a society what is the best anthropology to help us understand ourselves and guide us towards the realisation of what it means to be human and live a fulfilled life?

The media are currently deemed the main influencer of values. This means that the ethics and morals of many are now acquired, or hugely influenced, primarily by the television and the various forms of social media. It seems that many of our young and not so young, especially in the West, are engaged in the process of trying to self-invent, re-create or remodel the self at a fundamental level. The idea of self-sufficiency and autonomy is so valued that we witness in societies across the globe how easy it is to be influenced by the principle of consumerism and the implied endorsement to isolated, autonomous self-actualisation where competitive behaviour and individualism so readily replaces community, solidarity and collaboration. The end result is that many will come to believe they are the final arbiter of what is right or wrong without reference to anything or anyone outside the self.

To forfeit belief in someone or something greater than ourselves is perilous because without a belief and vision, as history repeatedly shows, people will be driven by self-interest and, consequently, develop a very limited self-understanding and often selfish, myopic view of reality. We are led by some to believe that we can be masters of our own destiny and able to take control of our lives. Yet, in reality, we are not the source of our own being, we are not the origin of meaning, we are not the measure of life, nor are we the foundation of our own happiness. We need others, benevolent, caring others; we need to love and be loved to uncover the best in us, we need a lot more than ourselves to find meaning and fulfilment in life.

A defining moment in the history of our self-understanding as human beings is depicted in one of the most iconic paintings of all time, the *Creation of Adam,* a fresco painted by Michelangelo which forms part of the Sistine chapel's ceiling and at its focal point illustrates the creation narrative in which God gives life to Adam. The image of the nearly touching fingers of God and Adam is considered a depiction of the fact that God did not just create humankind but sought to forge a relationship with us. It captures and illustrates why we are fashioned in the image and likeness of God, that we are created for companionship with the Divine. In this one painting Michelangelo epitomises the essence of what it means to be human. It portrays God, the source of life, reaching out to share his life, through Adam, with all humanity. It implies that we are drawn by love, not driven by fear to believe in God. It expresses the nearness and accessibility of God. The intensity of the gaze and imminent touch are intended to signify the mutual desire for connection, for union, for relationship.

However, it is not a relationship of equals: God gives, Adam receives. It is rather a relationship of love whereby the wonder, beauty, and life of God is offered across the practically indiscernible gap between their almost touching fingers. The spark of the Divine bridges this gap to give life, to divinise what is so obviously human. It offers a relationship to sustain us as we try to humanise the Divine in us, as we strive to grow from being a created image to evolve into the more noble likeness of God. This painting represents the essence of everything we believe about ourselves as Christians. It represents the heart of our soul-searching, our self-understanding, the meaning for our existence, the hope for our final destiny, and so much more.

Can a greater dignity or a more magnificent life-purpose be imagined than to be the beneficiary of the total self-donation of God as a Trinity of persons dedicated and committed to the transformation of our humanity for the benefit of self and the wider community? The great theologians and philosophers teach that to know what it means to be truly human is found in discovering the divine within, and, just as importantly, they teach us that we can become someone we could never have been except through this relationship with God. This reality is both humbling and awe-inspiring.

To have the opportunity to experience this truly transformative and life-giving relationship with the Divine is what we want for our ourselves and our children, not as a burden but as possibility, not as imposition but as openness to a caring transcendent reality, not as a limitation but as the ultimate horizon against which we can dream and imagine a better future. It means to have a vision of ourselves as desired by God who alone can fulfil all our possibilities in the present and the future. We believe that what was offered to Adam can come to realisation in us – that each one of us, in our own unique way, touch the finger of God, make the connection, experience the love, live this love in everyday life, and allow the liminal image that we now are to grow into a closer likeness of God to be lived just as fully in the sacred as in the secular dimensions of life. This invitation and possibility are at the core of the human story and the heart of our relationship with God. Michelangelo brilliantly captures this defining moment in the self-understanding of humankind in its relationship with God.

Christian education, likewise, aspires to make our own encounter with the creator God an equally defining moment and bring to realisation our innate capacity for fullness of life in a real and intimate relationship with God. This is the ultimate vision which inspires and guides Catholic school ethos and is the 'good news' that will be told and retold until it is fully realised at the end of human time.

Ethos from the inside out

1 Basic Convictions: Faith in God and Faith in People

DENIS GLEESON

Ethos and education go hand in hand because both are about naming reality. In support of parents and guardians, and in response to their trust, education and ethos are concerned with identifying what life is really about and exploring what is of the essence. If content is all that is held to be essential, for example, then education is reduced to preparation for the workplace and the development of productivity. If this is the case then the focus of ethos centres on maximising future earning power. If on the other hand, education truly is about human flourishing, then ethos will be inclusive of the *more* there is to life and will be about revealing life's purpose. It will be about spiritual depth and the understanding we have of creation, humanity and the divine.

All Christian spiritualities are based upon interconnected concepts of God, humanity and creation. These concepts add their own colour and tone to a spirituality and can be either positive or negative. As a consequence, not all spiritualities are healthy. In fact, we have had many examples in the past of spiritualities that were decidedly unhealthy and caused suffering and harm. My contention is that for a Christian spirituality to be healthy and authentic it must be founded upon an unwavering faith in God and faith in people. By faith here, I mean trust. If I declare that I have faith in someone, it means that I believe in them and that I trust them. I believe that they will be present for me when I need them and I trust that they will never intentionally do me harm. The double foundation that I want to build on is my firm belief and experience that God is indeed a God of infinite and unconditional love, and that human beings are, in essence, good and always will be. Into the future, I can trust in both. Do the Scriptures support my belief and experience? I am convinced that they do.

There is genius in the first three chapters of the book of Genesis. With their two accounts of the creation of the world and their story of the events in the Garden of Eden, they set the scene for all the sacred scriptures that are to follow. The first creation story has God creating the world in six days and resting on the seventh day. Two key verses are in chapter one. The first of these recounts the creation of humankind:

> So God created humankind in his image,
> in the image of God he created them,
> male and female he created them. (Genesis 1:27)

The other makes the emphatic assertion that all of God's creation is good:

> God saw everything that he had made, and indeed, it was very good. (Genesis 1:31)

The second creation story has God taking dust from the ground and breathing life into it. Man becomes a living being, is placed in the Garden of Eden and is told not to eat of the tree of the knowledge of good and evil. Later, from the side of man, God creates woman as man's partner. Of course, we know what happens. The serpent appears on the scene, the man and the woman do eat from the forbidden tree and their eyes are opened to the reality of good and evil. They become ashamed of their nakedness and they try to hide from God. God reprimands them and they are driven out of the garden.

The first thing to recognize here is that, as often happens in the Bible, the two different accounts are allowed sit side by side. Their difference is simply not seen as a problem. Both accounts are seen as treasures of the oral tradition and both accounts are preserved as a result. Their genius is their recognition that God is indeed the sole Author of all life. We encounter a God who is dynamic, whose very presence is creative, whose existence demands an outpouring of the divine nature because the nature of the divine is to care and to share. God breathes, as it were, and things happen and what happens is good. The breath of God is life itself. Light is separated from darkness, the sky is separated from the earth, vegetation is abundant, the sun and the moon are put in place and birds and animals of all kinds come into being. Finally, God creates humankind, male and female. Humankind is created in God's own image. The breath that we breathe is God's own breath of life, breathed into us. Crucially, however, the garden story is a recognition that when humankind experiences itself apart from God, we struggle with aloneness and incompleteness, death and change, desire and the choice between good and evil.

Unfortunately, we have often tended to bring a literal and fundamentalist mind-set to these chapters and even to the Scriptures as a whole. We try to read them as we do a newspaper. So, the story of the Garden of Eden has been interpreted as a tragic story,[1] as a fall from grace and loss of innocence. In large measure, this has prevented us from viewing it as an evolutionary story, as an invitation from God to grow towards the type of world and the life-giving relationships that he wishes for us and has wished for us from the very beginning. The genius of the first three chapters of Genesis has actually proved beyond us. We prefer, it seems, to grieve for a paradise that we see as lost and a humanity that is fatally compromised, rather than envision a Kingdom of God that is creation in the making and a humanity that is evolving and invites completion.

Despite the daily unveiling by science of the evermore complex and spectacular glories of the creation that surrounds us, we find ourselves almost immune to the presence of God and deaf to the music of the universe. We then compound our misery by immersing ourselves, by the hour, in news and stories of human evil while neglecting the inspiration of human goodness that is before our very eyes. Yet, in human goodness we can find our way to God, but it is to a God who is love and, who will not, therefore, impose upon us if we choose to reject his invitations. God, however, will never give up on us and will constantly invite our trust and will continue to offer us the promise of the fullness of our humanity.

Ultimately, we know this because of the mystery of the Incarnation which is the extravagant fullness of God's revelation and God's intimate embrace of creation in the person of Jesus. The good news that Jesus brought was that God, whom he named as Father, is in all of life and that the fulfilment of human life is to be found only in God. Our nature is the nature of God. God is love, therefore, our nature too has a great capacity for love. But God's love is perfect, pure and unconditional love, whereas we frequently make the mistake of thinking that God loves as we love. The fact is that we just cannot imagine the depth of God's love for us. It is truly beyond us. It knows no limits, it sets no boundaries, it has no horizon, it is generous beyond all human comprehension.

As human beings, we are called to grow into and reflect our own true nature of love. God's love dwells within us and it is to this love that we have to give expression. Love gives freely and because of our free will, we have to learn what it is to choose love and to live in love. We have to learn to love ourselves, to love others and to love God's creation. As we do this, we come to realise that our journey to love is our journey into the fullness of our humanity and into a deeper consciousness of the truth of who we are. It is a journey to God who is love and who created us in love. As Genesis poetically illustrated, however, it is not a straightforward journey. There are obstacles.

Though creation is good and we ourselves are made in the image of God, we can make bad choices and live in a selfish and individualistic way. We can turn a blind eye to exploitative economic policies that keep people in poverty and maintain a consumerist culture that is founded on excess, waste and greed. We can play high stakes roulette with the environment and our nuclear capability, with the destruction of our planet and leave humanity itself hanging in the balance. We are, in fact, at a stage where if we do not challenge our mind-sets and encourage our children to challenge them, we will be faced with potentially disastrous consequences. Yet, rather than make the hard decisions that need to be made in order to take control of our future, we seem to be in denial. We hope that, somehow, science will bail us out and relieve us of our moral responsibilities and the necessity to change the way we live.

From the beginning, the Old Testament insists that history is a journey forward.[2] It is at God's request, for example, that Abraham and Sarah leave their home and it is at God's command the Moses leads the Hebrew people into the wilderness and towards nationhood. The prophets continually challenge the nation to take the next step, to reach for more. This is the theology of journey and of pilgrimage, it is the theology of evolution. God is asking his people to go forward, to accompany him on a great adventure. In the New Testament, this message and invitation does not change. In fact, it is given spectacular momentum in the person of Jesus. The Incarnation is God's embrace, not just of the people of Israel, but of all humanity. It is an invitation to evolve, and to take responsibility for ourselves and for creation. It is a renewed challenge to realise our essential nature, which is our potential for love. Our task is to give expression to what Jesus calls the Kingdom of God, everything that God wishes for us.

In the person of Jesus, God offers us a model of how we are to live and love. The incarnation, God's embrace of humanity in Jesus, was always God's intention. It is the Divine nature to give of itself and to give with breath-taking generosity. The Incarnation is simply the supreme example of this giving. Jesus is the human face of the Divine and the Divine face of the human. In him we can see what a human being can become. He is good news and he brings good news, reminding us that God is in all of life and that our happiness, the fullness of our humanity, can only be found in God. In Jesus, in fact, we are empowered to claim this fullness.

Everything that Jesus does and says proclaims this message. His is a message that empowers the poor, offers sight to those who cannot, or will not see, allows those who are crippled to get back on their feet again, opens the ears of those who are deaf or who have closed their ears, and banishes all of the many demons that possess us. Enthusiastically acclaimed by ordinary people, the message of Jesus was, to put it mildly, less warmly received by religious authorities who sought to control access to God's mercy and forgiveness [3] through control of the rituals of the temple and its sacrifices. Likewise, the provincial Roman authorities would not have been impressed by the authority of Jesus and his popular support. They ruled by cruelty and oppression and through the imposition of taxes that were collected through the temple. [4] They also held their own emperor to be divine.

Jesus knew that the powers of the day would eventually catch up with him and that he would be put to death. But, he could not compromise on his commitment to the Father and on his message of hope and abundant new life. Both his integrity and his experience of himself are at stake. It is not a loving Father's will that Jesus necessarily has to die on a cross, but it is the Father's will, that through the Incarnation and through the life and death of Jesus, the power of evil, and of death itself, will be forever broken, the kingdom will be initiated and humanity will be given new hope into the future.[5]

The resurrection is the Father's confirmation and vindication of Jesus. In Jesus, who is now the risen Christ, a new creation has unfolded. Evolution has taken a major bound forward. The love that animated Jesus when he walked among us can now animate us and transform each one of us. The law of love can now be written on our hearts (cf. Jeremiah 31:33). We are encouraged to put on the same mind that was in Christ Jesus until we can say with Paul, 'it is no longer I who live, but it is Christ who lives in me'. (Galatians 3:20). There is a new world order. Christ, risen and ascended into heaven, is now a cosmic figure. He is the beginning and the end, the alpha and the omega, the first born of all creation.

The journey forward for humanity, in Christ, is both a collective journey unhindered by boundaries of time and it is also a personal, lifelong journey inward for each one of us. However, it is not a given that any one of us will take responsibility for this personal journey within. Understanding the stages and the nature of this journey is a decided advantage. Modern psychology comes to our assistance here. Thomas Keating[6] is a spiritual writer who has done much work in this area. Keating says that the only thing that separates us from God is really the thought that we are separate from God.[7] This thought is the major obstacle that we have to overcome on our journey towards growth, maturity and wholeness. This is a self-made obstacle. So, imagine if we could just get rid of that one thought! Our lives would surely be transformed. However, letting go of this thought usually pushes us to the limits.

In the first instance, we insist on entertaining all kinds of strange ideas about God. We imagine God to be all-powerful when clearly that is not the case. God cannot change the past, cannot force us to respond to the love bestowed upon us, and he will not deprive us of our free will. We can choose, for example, to banish God from our lives and from society and yet, in a moment of crisis, angrily demand an explanation for God's absence. Then, if we do decide to look for God, we invariably look in the wrong places. This means, of course, that we also tend to look for happiness in the wrong places. So, obstacles that we face on our journey to God and on our journey towards the fullness of our humanity, are often fashioned by ourselves, with the seeds of our inevitable confusion sown very early in life, taking our cue from the dominant culture.

As well as having physical needs, every new-born baby has very basic emotional needs that have to be met. These emotional needs are threefold. The child has to feel that they are loved and accepted. The child has to feel that they are safe and secure. Finally, the child will, gradually, have to develop some measure of power and control in their life. To the extent that these needs are appropriately met, the child should flourish. If they are not met, there will be problems either in childhood itself, in adolescence, or later in adulthood. However, due to the human condition, social circumstances and cultural context, there are problems even when these needs are appropriately met.

The problems begin with the emotions and feelings that cluster around our human experience and are further complicated by the complexities of temperament and personality.[8] Then, encouraged by society and in competition with everyone else around us, we begin to invest in the satisfaction of our basic needs. Failing to look beyond them, even when we come to adulthood, we convince ourselves that if these needs were met in full we would be happy. We tell ourselves that if we were perfectly safe, if everyone loved us and if we were in total control of our lives we would want for nothing. Even as we realise that our basic needs have been sufficiently satisfied to guarantee normal psychological and emotional development, we find that these needs are actually insatiable and we cannot help ourselves as we pursue them relentlessly.

Sucked down by the quick sands of introspection and selfishness, our only hope is that we will come to see that God alone can satisfy the depth of the longing for love and need for fulfilment within us. Only in God can we find total security. Only by surrendering to God's power and control in our lives, can we achieve the freedom to become the person that each of us was born to be. When we grow through childhood, adolescence and into adulthood and are without conscious awareness of the presence of God in our lives, we are incomplete and we run the risk of having resorted to substitutions, addictions and a variety of false gods.[9] We will also be operating with only a partial sense of our own identity, a self that is fabricated by the need to survive in society, a false self. Frey offers us a disconcerting picture when he says that:

> Our false self is an incomplete self, a needy self, an unevolved self, and a temporary self. It's a spiritually ignorant self, trapped under the hypnotic spell and illusion of absolute ego-identity. This illusion of ego identity is generally accepted as a given fact of human life and is supported by cultural conditioning as 'consensus reality' in human society and relationships.[10]

This is not a pretty picture and it does not take much reflection to see how devastating this can be both individually and collectively. But there is an alternative, if we accept it. We need to face down our out-of-control ego and consciously develop a trusting relationship with Ultimate Reality, or that Higher Power which we call God. By this means, we can access our truer self, our deepest self. Loosening the bonds of an unconscious over-identification with the culture in which we are immersed,[11] we can give expression to that absolutely unique reflection of the Divine that the Book of Genesis reminds us is within each one of us. Thomas Merton addresses the situation well when he says:

> We are what we love. If we love God, in whose image we were created, we rediscover ourselves in him and we cannot help being happy: we have already achieved something of the fullness of being for which we were destined in our creation. If we love everything else but God, we contradict the image born of our very essence and we cannot help being unhappy, because we are a living caricature of what we were meant to be.[12]

If only God can satisfy our search for happiness then, it is only by connecting with God, by communicating with God, that we can individually allow this to happen. This means that we have to learn how to relate, communicate, and pray. We have to pray in a way that acknowledges the presence of God all around us and in every moment of our lives. We have to pray in a way that indicates our consent to God's transformation within us. In other words, we have to learn to pray in silence, accepting God as God is, in contrast to how we may perceive God to be. We have to open ourselves to God on God's terms, avoiding any temptation to control or manipulate the relationship. If we are able to do this, we will be led into growth and a more genuine life. Gradually, we will divest ourselves of our baggage, our emotional, psychological and spiritual shortcomings, as we allow ourselves to be led forward. The God, who is love, will facilitate us in reining in the false self and giving expression to our deepest self, to our true self, which is Christ within.

When considering the journey within, Bruce Sanguin reminds us:

> Our lives are not our own, meaning that they are not simply for the realisation of our personal goals. Our lives are for the realisation of the *universal* goal of evolving deeper expressions of what it means to be fully human, fully divine, and fully cosmic. We

are the presence of the universe evolving in and toward a divine promise of greater freedom and greater love.[13]

It may come as a surprise for many to find that even Charles Darwin, the 'father' of evolutionary theory, acknowledged that our evolution as a species was dependent on much more than competition and aggression and our need to survive. Love, according to Darwin, was for humans the more significant driver.[14] Even in Victorian times, he was not alone in his conviction, and other significant factors that were identified included concern for others and the pursuit of beauty, truth and goodness. Cleary, this is entirely consonant with the teaching of Jesus in the Gospel and absolutely central to the question of ethos in education.

When Jesus was asked by one of the Pharisees (cf. Mathew 22:35-40) to name the most important law of all, he answered by combining two passages from the Hebrew Scriptures. The first passage exhorts us to love God with all our heart and soul (cf. Deuteronomy 6.4:5) and the second tells us to love our neighbour just as we love ourselves (cf. Leviticus 19:8). On another occasion, Jesus repeats the so-called Golden Rule which encourages us to treat everyone else as we would wish to be treated ourselves (cf. Mathew 7:12). Throughout the Gospel, loving and just relationship is at the heart of the teaching of Jesus. He asks us to be generous, compassionate and non-judgmental. We are to put others before ourselves, even if it means taking risks. Sin is actually our failure to allow ourselves to be loved by God and our failure to reach out in love to others. Simply put, it is a refusal to love and, therefore, a reluctance to allow ourselves to grow and to evolve, personally and as community.[15]

As educators we are conscious that we live in a materialistic, excessively individualistic world. For many, everything including truth, is held to be relative. Relationships can be virtual rather than real and social media can offer a screen to those who wish to demean people they may not have even met by subjecting them to the language of violence. The young need to be helped to acquire 'a sense of purpose in their lives, something to give a shape and objective to their personal existence.'[16] They need to feel that they are part of something greater than themselves, something that is evolving, something that is profound, rich and positive, something that offers them a challenge. Educators are perfectly poised to make this known.

So, it has never been more important to consciously initiate the young into the Christian way and into concern for and the service of others. A Christian ethos within education can provide us with the means to do that. It can also provide us with the context and opportunity, as well as the language, concepts and understanding that are needed to engage in self-reflection. Adolescents, in particular, benefit from hands-on experience in the area of justice and need to be taught how to reflect on their experience in the light of the Gospel. The exploration of our own inner experience is a critical element in life's journey. Without investment in the conscious, deliberate and skilled facilitation of such exploration we cannot flourish and we cannot fully make our unique and irreplaceable contribution to the upward evolutionary thrust of humankind.

Hunger, food and nourishment are ever present biblical themes and, today, there is no doubting the spiritual hunger that exists, especially perhaps, among the young. Jesus offers us food and nourishment in his Gospel message of love, in his presence within our deepest selves, in the sacramental life of the Christian community and in the unfolding of the new creation that he referred to as the Kingdom of God. But, as well as the spiritual hunger, there is a spiritual poverty and I would suggest that spiritual poverty is the most widespread poverty in our society. It is spiritual poverty that allows us mistreat the refugee and the asylum seeker, tolerate the scandal of homelessness, constantly ignore an expanding gap between the rich and poor, disregard inequality in the workplace, belittle those of a different sexual orientation or political point of view, subscribe to accepted prejudices, and devalue even life itself.

In this second decade of the new millennium, to be a Christian and to accept God and humanity as defined by love, is certainly to be countercultural. Uncomfortable as it may be, this must also be the case with an educational ethos that is driven by an evolutionary approach to knowledge, spirituality and the quest for the deeper meaning of life. Let me end with the words of Pierre Teilhard de Chardin, a French Jesuit priest, whose life's work was the articulation of the presence of God, and of the centrality of Christ, in the evolutionary process.

> Someday, after mastering the winds, the waves, the tides and gravity. We shall harness for God the energies of love, and then, for the second time in the history of the world, man will have discovered fire.[17]

2 Leading from within: The Inner Dynamics of School Leadership

DENIS ROBINSON

Being a leader in education is one of the most important professions in the world. No two days are ever the same. For the leadership team of any Catholic primary or secondary school in Ireland, or any part of the world for that matter, each day is filled with a plethora of challenges with the unexpected, the humdrum, and the endless paperwork involved in policy and procedure implementation. There are the struggling students, the absent teachers, the needy staff member, and the worried parent to contend with. This can, and does, exact a tremendous physical, psychological and emotional toll. In spite of this, education leaders continue to be dedicated and committed people with the vast majority well qualified, having the requisite personality skills, professional qualifications and leadership competencies to lead both students and learning. These school leaders tend to possess enough of the emotional, relational, psychological, pedagogical, and character traits to be effective leaders able to engage proficiently with staff, students, and parents. What more can we expect of these remarkable people who play such a significant role in the education and unfolding of countless lives?

The essential role of school leaders is to help facilitate and co-ordinate the holistic education of students, which is to animate and bring into being the potential that is already nascent in the body, mind, heart, and soul of a student. The tried and tested means to help learners recognize and achieve their potential is through the process of imparting and acquiring knowledge so as to help them develop the ability to reason and make good judgements, develop reliable life skills, grow in character and wisdom, pursue truth in all its manifestations, develop physically, intellectually, personally, morally, socially and spiritually in order to be the best integrated and fully alive person they can be. The question explored here is: how can a Catholic school ethos facilitate this, particularly from the perspective of school leadership?

THE CENTRALITY OF RELATIONSHIPS

One of the least appreciated aspects of Christianity is that it is primarily about relationships. The heart of Christian theology and spirituality is essentially about the nature, quality, and meaning of our relationships. This is evident within the entire corpus of the bible, from the book of Genesis to the book of Revelations and is simply but appropriately summarised as the love of God and love of neighbour. From a Christian perspective, you cannot have one love without the other. The two relationships are meant to be integrated, lived alongside each other, and perhaps, better still, lived to the point where one love is indistinguishable from the other!

We are relational creatures, we do not thrive in isolation. We need other people to help us discover who we are and what we can be. Relationships tend to define and characterise us as nothing else can. We are told, 'That our very constitution as human beings is our capacity to relate….that we are our relationships.'[1] Relationships give us a sense of identity, they help reveal us to ourselves, situate us in a community with its values, hopes and dreams, with its myths and culture. Relationships give us an orientation to life and its meaning, they give us a sense of our duty and responsibilities towards others. This is particularly well expressed in the South African Bantu proverb, popularised by Desmond Tutu, *ubuntu umuntu ngabantu*, which means: 'I am because we are.' This implies that my life is inextricably bound up with yours, that together we find our humanity, that there is an essential interdependence between us, and although we have different gifts they need to be shared for the common good; while we are different personalities this can be experienced as complementary, as an appreciation and celebration of difference for the benefit of all; and in the effort to work together as community we discover the foundation and means of our mutual human flourishing. It is self-evident that this approach to relationships helps promote what is most authentic and noble in us as individuals and community.[2]

From a Christian perspective the experience of relationship with God raises the significance of relationships to an entirely new level. At the heart of the life, death and resurrection of Jesus is the unambiguous invitation to relationship with the Divine. In Jesus we discover how God communicates his understanding of relationship with us, and how much it means to him. This is apparent in the many ways Jesus demonstrated God's desire to share his love, life and all he is with us. Whenever Jesus encountered people, especially those in need, he expressed God's relationship through his love, mercy, compassion, healing, wisdom, truth, through sharing food and drink, in forgiveness, companionship, promising life beyond death, and imparting a dignity and nobility to all. This is confirmed again and again as he reached out to all regardless of social status, faith tradition, or gender to present the ultimate meaning of life, to offer freedom and truth so as to eliminate division, hatred and violence, to abolish fear of life, fear of God and fear of death. In doing so he revealed the nature and consequences of God's relationship with us. In essence, Jesus' primary message was to proclaim in word and deed the presence and reality of a God who cares, who is totally committed to us, who wants the best for us now and into the future.

We witness Jesus challenge the religious and civil leaders of his time precisely because they failed to adequately facilitate genuine relationship between God and his people. Rather, they essentially reduced relationship with Yahweh to the observance of rules and regulations. When Jesus was condemned to die for challenging this he did not recant, he did not deviate in any way from his trust in God, he did not resort to violence or power to defend himself or his message. He choose to love as the Father loves and elected to demonstrate the Father's commitment to us regardless of the fact that he was being denounced for expressing the love and loyalty God for his people. He choose to live to the end the meaning and implications of God's relationship with him.

In an astonishing affirmation of Jesus' message and trust in God we find in the resurrection that death, no matter how cruel or unfair, does not end or interrupt God's relationship with us, that rejecting God does not prevent him from caring for or loving us, nor does it mitigate God's desire to be life and give life to us. We see in Jesus' identification with humanity, even in this saddest and most heinous act, one who experienced the meaning of this marvellous relationship with God: he conquered the apparent finality of death to make immortality real, he defeated animosity, did not resort to hatred or revenge in the face of evil but choose to trust God's relationship with him. In him we discover God's absolute commitment to us. The central message is that nothing will separate us from God. It is God's nature to relate, to love unconditionally, to share himself completely and have us know and experience the import of this relationship in this life and its culmination with our face to face encounter with God in the next. As Andrew Llyod Weber suggests in a song from his musical, *Aspects of Love*, love changes everything. In the case of this relationship with God Jesus showed that everything is not just changed but totally transformed, it transcends and transfigures everything about us – this relationship is so powerful that death leads to new life, isolation to union, despair to hope, wounds are healed, sins forgiven, reconciliation offered, and this life-giving relationship will never end, no matter what. This fundamental Gospel truth impacts every dimension of the life of a Christian, from the way we understand who we are, to a revision of the essential meaning and potential of life itself, to a renewed concept of what relationship is and how it can be so transformative. There is no other relationship that can offer and achieve so much!

What is also truly remarkable about this relationship is that it is a boundless, gratuitous gift of God's self. It is humbling to realise that we have absolutely nothing to add or contribute to God. No matter how good we are, there is nothing we can do to embellish God's nature, enhance his being, or add to his existence. God as Creator Father, Jesus as Word, and the Holy Spirit as empowering love utterly transforms the limits of human existence to make of us a new creation, giving us the potential to mirror God in ourselves and all our relationships. God, as Trinity of persons, is the ultimate model of relationship. They are inseparable in being and action, each unique yet one, giving and receiving in total self-donation, living a life of mutual indwelling, sharing equal and reciprocal love, completing and fulfilling each other so as to be eternal life for each other.

This is indeed an extraordinary relationship and we are not naturally capable of relating at such a level. It is only by way of participation, in and through the human and divine Jesus, that we have the possibility of such a distinct and real affiliation with God. From as early as the second century the Church preached that God became human so that humans could become divine! It is astonishing to realise that human beings are invited to share divine life. This is not something we could attain by our own means, no matter how hard we try or how virtuous we may be. It is an undeserved, unmerited gift, so that now and forever heaven and earth, humanity and divinity are united and exist in an eternal inseparable bond. This is a truly remarkable relationship. Bringing out much more than just the best in us, it heals with love, it empowers with friendship, it is faithful and committed for all time, it seeks only our good and the realization of our ultimate destiny. It gives endless life, it utterly transfigures.

For Christians this capacity for relationship with the Divine is meant to inspire and guide our relationship with others and the world; it provides us with a model of the possibilities that exist in us as a consequence of relationship with God. This life-sustaining, freely-given, committed and transforming relationship is meant not just for each unique individual but to be reflected in our relationships with others, with nature and all that exists. In reality ours is not generally a loyal and committed 'I-Thou' relationship of mutual regard and reciprocity with God. We are well aware of the darker, fallen side of our human nature. More often than not we bring very little to our relationship with God, or with others, because of our tendency to be inherently selfish, persistently egotistic, ever pleasure seeking, and engrossed in the attempt to make of ourselves demi-gods in our own little worlds. Notwithstanding our self-centred nature, we are recipients of a relationship which offers real, enduring love, compassion, forgiveness, patience, and so much more. We are first loved, even while we are undeserving and incapable of knowing and appreciating how much we are cared for and how truly transformative and devoted this relationship is.

This makes God's relationship with us truly selfless and caring beyond measure. It is beyond logic, beyond reason, beyond what we understand to be fair, it doesn't make sense, it's not rational. It is a true, divine, unending, unchanging love relationship and all we can do is let ourselves be loved, be healed and given new life – and, perhaps, learn to relate in the same way.

So, what can school leadership learn from God's relationship with us? The universal truth of the *ubuntu umuntu ngabantu* reflects how to flourish as a human being, how to be a successful, integrated individual in community and demonstrates how genuine human relationship are good, life-giving and sometimes life-changing. However, relationship with the Divine, as we have seen, takes us to a new stage of awareness. It revolutionises the way we see and think about relationships, it completely changes everything. It unveils the power of a human-divine relationship that is entirely different from any other relationship. It generates a paradigm shift from the *ubuntu umuntu ngabantu*, 'I am because *we* are' understanding of self in relationship to the more profound awareness that 'I am because *you* are' which makes relating more personal, more dynamic, more enriching, and, simply put, more divine. In this relationship we are invited to move way beyond the old primal image of self to become a closer likeness to him who loves us. A saying, attributed to St Clare of Assisi, illustrates this when she said: we become what we love and who we love shapes what we become.[3] In other words, we become like those we love! Such a transcendent participation in the Divine makes us more than just good people or useful participants in community, more than economic units, consumers, cogs in production, tax payers, even more than male and female, or whatever our gender designation. It takes us into another realm of existence.

It is beyond doubt that we need others to help us discover who we are and what we may be. In a relationship with God we have the opportunity to discover a truly human, transcendent and transcending self capable of flourishing in ways almost beyond imagination. In this relationship we get a glimpse of how we might believe in people as God believes in us, how we might be truly free and responsible, compassionate and caring, givers of life and sharers of love, capable of genuinely contributing to the unfolding of others, re-imaging the world, and living our individual lives to the full. Jesus is the example, par excellence, of what we might be. This Gospel truth is meant to be at the heart of our relationships, with its potential to inform, influence, inspire, motivate and shape how we think, feel and relate.

HOW DOES THIS INSIGHT INFORM CATHOLIC SCHOOL LEADERSHIP?

So what does this understanding of relationship teach us about Catholic school leadership? Trying to embody this essential Gospel truth will, undoubtedly, influence the perception, practice and quality of school leadership, hopefully to give birth to a significant change of consciousness and a distinctive way of understanding to inform and transform the interpretation of school leadership. In a brief overview of the research into the connection between leadership and relationship we have Cowley and Purse confirm that leadership is essentially about relationships and emerges from within the person.[4] Bolman and Deal attest, 'The heart of leadership is in the hearts of leaders. You have to lead from something deep inside.'[5] To live and lead from within also reflects Parker Palmer's enduring insight that school leadership mirrors and projects the condition of one's soul onto those one serves.[6] Ultimately, 'Leadership is not simply what we do, but who we are, and what we do because of who we are.'[7]

The research is unambiguous. Authentic leadership emerges from the inner self, rather than from a set of techniques, traditions and strategies, from inner conviction rather than external authority. This is a central truth around which the lives and values of leaders are crafted, their core commitments formed and quality of presence achieved. This is what generates a deep conviction and enriches one's personal and professional life. This form of self-transcendence, the move toward a dynamic personal transformation to a truer self, is also the gateway to a more developed social awareness, becomes a positive source of energy, a change of heart, and spiritual growth. Dolan and Altman's research has shown that there is a direct correlation between spiritual values and effective leadership because they form and transform the depths of one's inner being to have a direct impact on how one leads.[8]

Leaders, like everyone else, rarely change unless their hearts are touched. So for any significant change of understanding or belief we look for a change in the inner depths of the person where one's perception of the world is shaped and the motivation for action and external behaviour arises. Trying to live Gospel values and striving to embody a school ethos are not merely notional concepts; they emerge from insight and personal conviction, they are the direct fruits of one's eyes being opened and heart enlarged to become a critical source of certainty, confidence and practical wisdom. Everything about authentic leadership flows from this. A positive experience of the significance of relationships can become the reason why school leaders are motivated to cultivate good relationships and promote community building whereby each person is valued, has the opportunity to develop their own identity, is respected and belongs, where a culture of care and compassion is nurtured, and the holistic unfolding of students and staff is considered essential to school leadership.

SOME IMPLICATIONS

Those in educational leadership, by virtue of their position, inevitably influence others. While insight is first personal, it is never private; and although each leader's inner journey is unique, it will nevertheless be shared; the consequences of inner conviction and personal growth has both an individual and community dimension. When a school leader changes, even a little, it is enough to modify perceptions and encourage some transformation. This is what persuades and leads to action. Any change of mind and heart, triggered by a deeper understanding of the nature of God, affect's the leader's way of relating. Value systems change. One becomes more altruistic. It is such moments of insight that pave the way for an appreciation of the heart of a Catholic school ethos and the efficacy of a service oriented school culture.

The movement from mind to heart to action is expressed within a school community when one starts to nurture and cherish others by protecting diversity, ensuring equality, being ethically responsible, seeing power in terms of servant leadership, having the courage to care, be fired by concern for others, not ignoring the wrongs foisted on people, seeing beyond legal, cultural and stereotypical definitions, helping people live to their fullest capacity free from fear or the threat of neglect.[9] This is what a commitment to interpersonal relationships looks like after the example of Jesus, and in imitation of God's relationship with us. This is making transcendent insight real, this is how one begins to implement Gospel values and embody them in the culture and ethos of a school. Richard Kearney, writing about the incarnation of transcendent insight by people such as Dorothy Day, Gandhi, and Jean Vanier, wrote:

> [E]ach restored, in specific ways, the bond between the secular and the sacred, challenging the tendency to oppose inner and outer, private and public, human and divine. Living in the creative tension between sacred and secular, they are not diametrically opposed, but two sides of the same coin.[10]

Coming to an appreciation of the centrality of relationships as a crucial Gospel value does not deny the challenge of trying to live what is truly authentic, dynamic and generative about Catholic school education and leadership. From both a professional and personal perspective this can be quite demanding, and even countercultural. For some the values and orientation advocated here run counter to mainstream thinking. Nowadays, being committed to the ideals and practice of Catholic school leadership is akin to a public declaration to live a radical way of life in the attempt to reflect the tender graciousness and human expression of God's concern for people. This kind of leadership is a very specific way of being committed, inspirational, invitational and, perhaps, even prophetic, particularly in the context of contemporary postmodern Ireland.

CHALLENGES

All leadership involves change and the ability to deal with change is a critical challenge. Change is not always easy or predictable; it can be complex, sometimes painful, but it always involves a process of self-discovery that is not meant to be so much revolutionary as evolutionary. Everyone has their weaknesses and shortcomings, their inner conflicts, aspects of personality and thinking that need to be healed and transformed; and we all have our fair share of toxicities buried or repressed in our unconsciousness which control or influence us without our conscious awareness.[11]

The opportunity for the inner self to emerge speaks of the need for school leadership to consciously engage with the still-forming, evolving self. Inner growth is a necessary aspect of authentic leadership. Learning, growing and maturing through interpersonal relationships happens gradually over time. As relationships teach and challenge, as they smooth the raw edges and allow new insights to emerge, they makes possible the genuine transformation and flourishing of a leader. Being able to let this happen in one's self leads to the possibility of letting it happen in the lives of others. So, for school leadership to be authentic it must be open to growth, change and new learning, making it possible for a truer, more authentic self to emerge. Becoming the best school leadership one can be at a personal, professional, and community level is an ongoing process. It is out of such experiences that one develops a sense of the living, dynamic heart of Catholic school ethos. Leonard Doohan suggests that

> growth in leadership means turning toward the world in its dis-

tinctiveness and towards others in appreciation and desire for greater relationship. Such leaders are collaborative, value the authentically human in self and others. For this kind of person, leadership development, spiritual growth and human maturing all wax and wane together. So leadership development is ultimately self-development; it is a way of spiritual growth.[12]

To be committed to this process can be, for some, a move beyond social and personal expectation. The model of Catholic school leadership presented here can be daunting for some since it may require a shift in expectation and understanding of school leadership. There will be those who find themselves uncomfortable with concepts such as the 'need for ongoing change', 'conversion of heart', or 'transcendent values' because these terms are generally outside their understanding of the requirements for school leadership.

This discomfort is expected given the fact that there are some Catholic school leaders who are not people of faith or who have little faith. Their faith may not have matured enough to deal with the vicissitudes of life; some may have lost their faith because of the impact of our postmodern, secular culture which does not support a Christian vision of life; and then there are those who consider faith and religion to be a largely private affair making the invitation to integrate one's inner life with school leadership unthinkable. There may be some who see school leadership primarily as an attractive possibility for power, prestige, personal gain or as a means of building a positive self-image. And then there are those few who have a narrow concept of school leadership that is more akin to management and policy implementation and find irrelevant any willingness to explore a deeper inner life in the service self or others. So, for some, to engage in a personal journey of inner growth, and be open to relationship with God for the benefit of self and school community, may be a step too far for them.

MANAGING EXPECTATIONS

The ideal and aims for school leadership outlined here are well supported by faith, experience and research. This being said, no one is perfect, and no one can completely embody a Catholic school ethos. We have our good and bad days. With the best of intentions we will fail from time to time. But this should not prevent one from trying to create an environment where Gospel and educational values are integrated, where the inner and outer life are equally important, where personal and professional aspirations are amalgamated to incorporate the practice of Gospel values into school leadership. A leader embracing the vision and ethos of Christian education is grounded in two worlds: one is the external world of education with all the skills and competencies this requires; the other is the inner world of self that is open to dynamic and ongoing inner growth. The creative tension that exists between these two worlds is meant to dynamically influence and complement each other.[13]

School leadership is a life of witness. It is a way of being. It is a lot more than just a job. School ethos provides both a vision and the context for leadership to learn, to grow, to be dynamically involved in a school community. The genuine transmission of ethos can only emerge out of inner conviction - inner conviction is necessary in order to take personal ownership of the ethos - to live it from the inside out. It is only when leaders in Catholic schools embrace and embody an ethos and vision, that they can call others to share the vision and live the ethos. In this sense the school leader is the most vital resource to illustrate ethos and articulate vision. It is out of such leadership that a learning community is animated and holistic education can take place. In the final analysis

> Our fundamental affiliation is to humanity itself and to God that made us, and without attention to our spiritual core we may serve well neither God nor humanity.[14]

Striving to achieve excellence in education is not incompatible with trying to embody a Christian school ethos. Bringing ethos to life in one's self will have an impact on those entrusted to your care. Many people in Ireland think and operate out of a 'neck-up' model of education. How then do we educate the whole person? How can head and heart, the cognitive and affective, the inner and outer world of each person be integrated? Implementing ethos is the means through which we can explore and discover what it means to be truly and fully human. It is the lens through which we interpret reality and what is valued, it offers a positive perspective on life, provides a language to transform how we see, feel, and engage with the world. Ethos is meant to enrich our experience of life, nurture the human spirit, contribute to the culture of a school through its emphasis on quality relationships, its commitment to empowering students and providing a quality education open to critical engagement with the world of learning and ideas.

CONCLUSION

Leadership has never been more critical in education. This has given rise to a shift in emphasis with the focus now on who the school leader is rather than what the leader does. Leadership is best understood from a personal perspective, at an individual level, where heart and mind, body and spirit, history and culture, hopes and dreams interplay to make a leader the unique individual he or she is. It is through this unique person that leadership happens because this is where convictions live, resilience waxes and wanes, moral consistency or inconsistency resides, beliefs and doubts manifest themselves, power is exercised or denied, relationships created or avoided, where fears and anxieties secretly dwell, where competing challenges vie with each other, where values are born and decisions are made. The individual school leader is the most powerful instrument in any school. This is why a commitment to one's ongoing personal, professional and inner development is needed for effective and caring leadership. This is why a Catholic school ethos, and the Gospel values that underpin it, need to be appropriated and integrated into the life of a school leader for that individual to develop a discerning appreciation of the power and potency of ethos to generate life and animate a school community from the inside out.

3 Leadership, Ethos and Catholic Social Teaching

MICHAEL SHORTALL

The ethos of a school is not solely dependent on leadership and management. Yet how educational leaders act is vital in sustaining ethos. This chapter explores what guidance may be offered to those in formal and informal educational leadership about ethos and Catholic Social Teaching.

VISION

There is a story often recounted in the kind of leadership and management books that fill the shelves of airport bookstores. Although it can be set at any time, it is regularly told of Christopher Wren, the architect of St Paul's Cathedral in London, rebuilt after the Great Fire of 1666. The story goes that Wren visited the construction site and came across three people working. It continues:

> He asked the first, 'What are you doing?' and the man replied: 'I am laying bricks.' He asked the second, 'What are you doing?' and the man responded: 'I am building a wall.' As he approached the third, he overheard him singing to himself as he worked, and asked, 'What are you doing?' The man stood, looked up at the sky, stretched his back, smiled and said, 'I am building a cathedral!'[1]

The short tale is traditionally constructed: three characters, a repeated question, and a punchline that induces a smile of recognition. It suggests, and we are encouraged to acknowledge, that it is possible to see a final vision that can inform and motivate someone, even in the most ordinary of tasks.

What if the story was reimagined in an educational setting and, in particular, a Catholic school?

> You walk along of a typical school corridor. Three doors are ajar, revealing three teachers busy at the most mundane of tasks. You ask the first, 'What are you doing?' She replies: 'I am cleaning up for the weekend.' You ask the second. 'What are you doing?' He replies, 'I am preparing a lesson plan'. You come to the final room. You hear a teacher singing to herself as she works. You ask, 'What are you doing?' She stands, looks up, stretches her back, smiles and says ...

Let us pause the story here. How would you imagine the final line? To follow the dynamic of the original story, the answer should name the final purpose or goal of the common project. What, then, is the point of education? Some answer that it is about passing on values and ideals and building character; others that it draws out innate curiosity, gifts and interests of individual students. Some argue that it is ultimately serving the good of society or indeed the national interest; others that it is facilitating critical thinkers capable of challenging society. Some say that it is about preparing young people for life; others are more specific by naming careers and success in the job market. The answer we settle upon is vital. As the story suggested, the greater the vision, the more power it has to motivate people beyond the obvious. It implies that education can be enlivened by ownership of a common vision, ideal or goal.

EDUCATIONAL LEADERSHIP

The airport bookstore paperbacks that tell the opening story go on to compare the builders: the first had a job, the second a career, the third had a calling. Often, they conclude that while management can direct the first two, it is leadership that generates the third. Tony Bush, in *Theories of Educational Leadership and Management*, characterises the difference between management and leadership: while the former stresses maintenance, procedure and policy, the latter emphasises change, values and vision.[2] Bush's comprehensive text refers to an extraordinary variety of theories. Theory can be off-putting. Yet, although it can become very abstract, the intent is either to depict or to direct our experience and context.

Let us say that a group of teachers are speaking of the school administration. They begin by referring to a structured hierarchical system, with positions of authority, marked by managerialism and policy. Broadly, they are naming a conventional model of leadership. But as the teachers continue to reflect, they are likely to speak about how the administration functions in more complex ways. They may point to interest groups that continually negotiate and bargain, effecting those who are the formal leaders. They may also describe how individuals can be influential by investing in their priorities, whether in self-interest or for a greater cause. Finally, they could admit that, despite all the efforts at organisation, the system is in fact unpredictable and ambiguous. Such may be called descriptive models of leadership.

Through the course of the conversation, the teachers also imagine future possibilities. They propose that decisions should be made through discussion and consensus, drawing on the wisdom of everyone. Or they articulate basic beliefs or values that ought to direct the decisions of everyone. These approaches are normative (directive) models.[3]

If leadership stresses change, values and vision, I would suggest that it operates in the complex world between what is described in conventional and descriptive models on one hand, and what is proposed in normative models on the other. It navigates a to-and-fro movement between the realities being described and futures being visualised. In this space in-between, can social ethics in the Catholic tradition provide some guidance?

ETHICS

To begin an answer, let us return to the story. There is an even more basic reason for identifying our goals, not accounted for in the story.

What if, in the original story, the characters had actually been asked to lay roads. Building walls in London after the Great Fire would then make no sense. To use an ethical term, goals are normative; they guide our action. Purposes help define what should be done practically. It may be argued that in each of our actions, or certainly those that are freely chosen, there is always a goal or purpose that is intended. If an action accomplishes the purpose that is intended, then we can call it appropriate or evaluate it as a good action. On the other hand, if an action falls short or brings about the opposite of what is intended, we call it inappropriate or evaluate it as a bad action. Purposes then are criteria by which we can appraise our actions. It is essential then that we know what they are.

It prompts the question: is there a final purpose by which we can evaluate all our actions, as we navigate through this experience we call living? Simply put, and echoing the question of education, is there a point to life? While some argue it is a false or impossible question, others return to observe the experience of being human. They argue that there are certain basic purposes towards which people are always and everywhere inclined to strive. These basic purposes can be called fundamentally good because, ultimately, we recognise that they facilitate the experience of a life lived better. Examples of such basic requirements necessary for a life well lived include life itself, relationships, knowledge, personal integrity. When they integrate well and come together, life is experienced as succeeding. It flourishes. This, in the end, is what we aim towards; it is the point of it all. Ancient Greek philosophy, influential on the Catholic tradition, called this happiness. By happiness is not meant simply pleasure; rather it is a sense of fulfilment, becoming the person we deep down desire to be. As a result of the need to become who we are meant to be and the desire for fulfilment, we are profoundly restless. This is most aptly illustrated in the often-quoted words of Saint Augustine, 'We are restless until we rest in thee.' To this desire for happiness Christianity announces that ultimate meaning and final fulfilment is found in God. We cannot attain this happiness by ourselves. However, God has taken the initiative, has already invited us into a life-fulfilling relationship in Jesus Christ and continues to do so in the Spirit. Happiness, in the Catholic tradition, is termed *beatitudo* and this becomes the ultimate criteria for our actions. For example, *The Catechism of the Catholic Church*, before it ever turns to regulations and obligations, begins its exposition of morality with a section entitled 'The Desire for Happiness'. It reads:

> The Beatitudes respond to the natural desire for happiness. This desire is of divine origin: God has placed it in the human heart in order to draw man to the One who alone can fulfil it ... The Beatitudes reveal the goal of human existence, the ultimate end of human acts: God calls us to his own beatitude.[4]

SOCIAL ETHICS

But, what concretely – in the here and now – makes for a meaningful and fulfilled life? Perhaps the most famous categorisation of the requirements necessary to live a flourishing life is Abraham Maslow's Hierarchy of Needs. At the bottom of the pyramid are elemental needs, such as water, shelter, food, sex. Building on this foundation are further needs that concern safety, belonging and self-esteem. All are required, to some degree, if a person is to achieve self-actualisation – a contemporary term corresponding somewhat to the notion of fulfilment. Furthermore, these basic requirements mutually reinforce one another in what we may describe as an 'integral human fulfilment'. For example, the basic requirement of knowledge is furthered by shelter, while advances in knowledge can advance how shelter is created.

The basic requirements can be made concrete in a myriad of ways. For instance, the basic need for belonging can be fulfilled in a marriage, in friendship, or in a football team. It is possible, for this reason, to say that we are all the same in our basic needs while also acknowledging that there are seemingly endless choices available in how to attain them. Importantly, if one of the basic needs is missing the capacity for fulfilment, or true happiness, is significantly curtailed. This we experience as suffering and evaluate it as bad or evil. In short, our moral code arises out of this fundamental dynamic – do that which is good and avoid or do not do that which is evil.[5] In other words, always act in ways that concretise the basic requirements in ourselves and others, and never act intentionally in a way that opposes them. To do so is always wrong.

Striving for happiness is necessarily a common project. As social animals, we require each other to succeed or be fulfilled. We need to interact with each other in a manner that facilitates another to achieve their basic requirements or, at very least, not be an obstacle in their way. This we may describe as the common good. The common good consists of those social conditions that allow groups and individuals access to concrete requirements necessary for their fulfilment; examples include peace, law, good governance, and support structures such as health and education systems. The common good we may say is the purpose of common living. At the heart of living together are the attempts to live in right-relationship, or what we might we call justice. If we are to live in a way that supports, at least not hinders, the flourishing of another, then we may define justice as 'doing right by someone', that is, 'to give someone their due'.[6] Justice then is directed towards the individual needs of another. It is better described as being proportional than just being equal. Social ethics is more than an attitude of respect to another. It describes the responsibility to provide the concrete conditions that will allow the other to attain their flourishing. In turn, human rights are the fundamental demands that such responsibilities be lived up to and the basic requirements be secured.

In 1967 Pope Paul VI stressed the central place of an integral human fulfilment. It may 'be said to sum up our obligations'. He said:

> In God's plan, every one is born to seek self-fulfilment, for every human life is called to some task by God. At birth a human being possesses certain aptitudes and abilities in germinal form, and these qualities are to be cultivated so that they may bear fruit. By developing these traits through formal education or personal effort, the individual works his way toward the goal set for him by the Creator.[7]

CATHOLIC SOCIAL ETHICS

Pope Paul was moved to write *Populorum Progressio* after visiting the Holy Lands and India in 1964. It became a key document in the legacy of social reflection within the Catholic tradition. Social reflection in the Catholic tradition has its roots in the prophetic witnesses of Scripture, Jesus himself, and the early Church. In specific terms, Catholic Social Teaching refers to the contemporary Church and papal documents and encyclicals that address the social problems of today's world. The first of such documents was *Rerum Novarum*, written by Leo XIII in 1891, in response to the widespread deplorable conditions resulting from the Industrial Revolution. By reflecting upon social conditions, affirming certain basic principles of justice, and exhorting the building of a better society as a necessary element of faith, Pope Leo began a body of social criticism that continues to this day. There are many taxonomies of the central themes of Catholic Social Teaching, including a comprehensive *Compendium of the Catholic Social Doctrine* (2004).[8] Daniel Groody in *Globalisation, Spiritualty and Justice*, cleverly organises the principles into an acronym – A GOD OF LIFE.[9]

The Catholic Social teaching documents do not offer a blue-print or detailed map for how to organise a more just society. In the words of John Paul II on the one hundredth anniversary of *Rerum Novarum*, Catholic Social Teaching

> has no models to present; models that are real and effective can only arise within the framework of different historical situations, through the efforts of all those who responsibly confront concrete problems in their social, political and cultural aspects, as these interact with each other. For such a task the Church offers her social teaching as an indispensable and ideal orientation.[10]

Catholic Social Teaching, then, is a tapestry of overlapping principles that provide a prism through which we consider concrete ways to develop a better society. Donal Dorr describes the approach as heuristic.[11] The term is derived from a Greek word meaning 'to discover'. It refers to a method whereby rules or principles are discerned through experience that can help further deliberation on a problem. In a rudimentary way, they could be called 'rules of thumb'. They direct and guide rather than provide final conclusions. It remains the responsibility, and hard work, of the different forms of leadership to continually act in ways that advance society. So, we return to the question: Can Catholic Social Teaching provide some guidance?

CATHOLIC SOCIAL TEACHING AND EDUCATIONAL LEADERSHIP

The central intuition is that principles of Catholic Social Teaching can also be applied to leadership in education. In what follows, an implication for educational leadership will be drawn from some of the central principles. A few of these principles have been unearthed already: the quest for meaning, integral human fulfilment, and the common good; others include social cooperation, preferential option for the poor, solidarity, subsidiarity, gift, and joy.

Meaning

The dynamic and foundation of ethics is intimately linked to the question of the meaning of life. The question is better described as a quest – the reality of living for something or someone. Therefore, morality is not foremost about rules and regulations. John Paul II wrote:

> ... the question is not so much about rules to be followed, but about the full meaning of life. It is an essential and unavoidable question for the life of every person ... there is a connection between moral good and the fulfilment of his/her own destiny.[12]

The first implication for educational leadership is attentiveness. An educational leader, when pondering on the question, 'What should I do?', is, in fact, part of a greater question and quest. The answer should not be reduced to, or looked for, in rule or regulation. Rather it is first found in attentiveness to the lived reality of people who are searching for meaning in their lives. Such attentiveness implies that leaders are committed to developing conscientious relationships by being transparent, approachable, open-minded and striving to build a sense of community.

Integral Human Fulfilment

The question of integral human fulfilment is a fundamental aspect of reaching out towards happiness. In a Christian perspective, it is to be found in our relationship with God and others. In the context of social ethics, this is facilitated by meeting the basic requirements necessary for life to flourish. To return to the words of Paul VI, 'Endowed with intellect and free will, each man is responsible for his self-fulfilment even as he is for his salvation'.[13] Therefore, the second implication is person-centred purpose. As a final goal of living itself, it encompasses the purpose of education and therefore leadership within it. Integral human fulfilment makes real the notion of human dignity. This implies a commitment to people, and a willingness to be concerned about their personal and professional development. The basic requirements of all must all be met in a holistic manner – or at least none of them must not be denied. Valuing a person is more than an attitude or respect; it makes demands that must be embraced.

The Common Good

Integral human fulfilment can only be attained with others. The good of each can only be achieved through the good of all; that is the common good. The Second Vatican Council, in a document reflecting on the modern world, described the common good as 'the sum total of social conditions which allow people, either as groups or as individuals, to reach their fulfilment more fully and more easily'.[14] Concern for the common good is the measure of authority: in so far leadership fails short in this regard, it loses legitimacy.

The third implication is justice, for it is the means by which the common good can be secured for everyone. Justice is not simply a matter of treating everyone equally but treating each individual in proportion to their needs, while allowing for the common good of all. Furthermore, the judgements of an educational leader cannot be reduced to mere calculation but must take account of the whole person.

The Principle of Social Co-operation

The 1891 encyclical *Rerum Novarum* was written in response to the twin dangers of unbridled capitalism and authoritarian communism. The first sees society as competitive individuals; the second as competing classes. Instead, Pope Leo XIII argued that because people are necessarily interdependent, they are best served by social cooperation. In short: 'Each needs the other'.[15] In this context, he makes an appeal to those in authority and power to live up to their responsibilities in respecting the rights of others.

The fourth implication is responsibility. Catholic Social Teaching supports the legitimacy of authority within a complex grouping such as a school. But with authority comes responsibility, which is intimately linked to the recognition and provision of the rights of others.

The Preferential Option for the Poor

A key moment in the development of the Catholic Social Teaching occurred after the Second Vatican Council, when local Churches reflected on their particular experience. The Latin American Bishops, at a conference in Medellin in Columbia in 1968, shifted the focus somewhat off the tradition. Since *Rerum Novarum* the focus was the powerful in society living up to their responsibilities to the poor. At this time, it shifted decisively towards standing with and empowering the poor through structural changes in society, and a

> distribution of resources and apostolic personnel that effectively gives preference to the poorest and most needy sectors and to those segregated for any cause whatsoever, animating and accelerating the initiatives and studies that or already being made with that goal in mind.[16]

The fifth implication is social change. Educational leadership guided by this principle takes on a transformative character. This principle demands that leadership evaluate the structures that would marginalise students and staff from their perspective. In turn, leadership should work to empower people to rebuild more liberating structures.

The Principle of Solidarity

At the height of the Cold War, John Paul II gave further grounding to the experience of interdependence. Solidarity, he argued, is 'not a feeling of vague compassion [but] a firm and persevering determination to commit oneself to the common good; that is to say, to the good of all and of each individual, because we are all really responsible for all.'[17]

The sixth implication is concern or care. Educational leadership must be marked by real relationships, for solidarity is the bond that creates and supports our mutual obligations and our espousing a culture of care.

The Principle of Subsidiarity

A long-standing principle in Catholic Social Teaching is subsidiarity. It is principle that recognises a power inherent within each level of society, which must not be denied. It is a limitation on the extension of power by those in higher authority. John Paul II defines it as follows:

> a community of a higher order should not interfere in the internal life of a community of a lower order, depriving the latter of its functions, but rather should support it in case of need and help to coordinate its activity with the activities of the rest of society, always with a view to the common good.[18]

The seventh implication is participation. In leadership, power is not simply held centrally and then delegated. Rather it is already distributed across an organisation, such as a school. Subsidiarity requires that the capacity to make a contribution be recognised. People then ought to participate, as is appropriate, in the structures of decision-making.

The Logic of Gift

The deepest recession since the Great Depression struck in 2008. In part, it happened because of a lack of trust within the international banking system. In his contribution to Catholic Social Teaching, Pope Benedict XVI argued that economic and political systems must operate, at least in part, by the logic of gift, reflective of God's grace. He wrote:

The human being is made for gift, which expresses and makes present his/her transcendent dimension ... development, if it is to be authentically human, needs to make room for the principle of gratuitousness as an expression of fraternity.[19]

The eight implication is service, for service is the concrete manifestation of self-giving. It reflects truly God's faithful and sacrificial self-gift in Jesus.

The Spirit of Joy

The first encyclical of Pope Francis is ordinarily not considered part of the documentary heritage of Catholic Social Teaching. Yet *Evangelii Gaudium* (2013) reaffirms the central place of the principles outlined above in living out in a joyful way the Catholic faith. He writes: 'We become fully human when we become more than human, when we let God bring us beyond ourselves in order to attain the fullest truth of our being.'[20]

The ninth implication is hope, because our joy as a Catholic community is based not only on things of the future but salvation that is already won. The encounter with God has already occurred. Therefore, the efforts of educational leadership in a Catholic school are not measured by outcomes but on faithfulness to the One who loved us first.

CONCLUSION

The original question asked what guidance could be offered to formal and informal educational leaders by Catholic Social Teaching in supporting the understanding and expression of ethos. If by guidance is meant a specific plan or blueprint, the short answer is: none. If by guidance is meant a set of principles that can help reflection and engagement and can offer values and inspiration, then the answer is undoubtedly yes.

These principles and guidelines are intended to inspire, inform and help direct the implementation of educational leadership in a faith-based school. In reality, no one is expecting to find the ideal educational leader possessing all the necessary qualities and abilities in equal measure. Some may be stronger in particular areas and certain leadership characteristics but may be wanting in others. This is not to suggest that they are ineffective leaders. Rather it recognises that all leaders are human and each is unique in the way they actualise their vision of Catholic education. This chapter is presented as an opportunity for educational leaders to review their understanding of leadership, to affirm the approach that currently works for them, to acknowledge the leadership qualities they already possess and then, perhaps, discover ways they might develop their personal and professional leadership style.

4 Building Bridges: Inter-religious Dialogue, Inclusion and Diversity

AIVEEN MULLALLY

'Unless we demonstrate that each and every person in our school community, regardless of their faith or orientation, is unique and precious to our school community, we cannot claim to be Christian in the true sense.' This statement was made in a recent conversation I had with a principal of a Catholic school. Two things struck me about the statement. Firstly, the passion with which she said it; and, secondly, I found myself wondering if the same could not be said by the leader of any school, Christian or otherwise, in Ireland today.

Other chapters in this book explore characteristics of school ethos from various perspectives and many of these characteristics are common to all school types, denominational or multi-denominational. Here we consider not only *what* is taught in schools today regarding religious education but significantly, *how* and *why* it is taught. The goal of this chapter is to articulate the conviction and motivation driving an ethos which welcomes and celebrates religious diversity in Catholic schools that respond, passionately, to religious difference and the reality of pluralism.

The population in Ireland has become increasingly diverse over the past two decades. This diversity represents a wide variety and richness of cultures, languages and faith systems. In response to this, public debate has become more urgent on the role of religious education in schools, on religious pluralism, and about what equality in education in Ireland now means. The term 'religious pluralism' refers to the variety of religions and beliefs that are currently practised or affiliated to in Irish schools. It acknowledges the diversity that exists within these religions themselves, and the growth in the number of people who are disengaged from the religious tradition they are affiliated to. It is also taken to encompass people identifying as Humanist or people who do not ascribe to any particular belief system, for example, atheists and agnostics.

Corresponding with the rise of religious diversity in Ireland is an increased disengagement from Church life and practice. The 2022 census highlights the decline in numbers of people identifying as Roman Catholic in Ireland, falling from 78% in 2016 to 69% in 2022, and the 'no religion' category has risen from 10% (2016) to 14% (2022). (CSO, 2023). This reality is brought into sharp focus in our schools and many educators would agree that practising Catholics are now becoming a minoritised group in Catholic schools in Ireland. This growing secularisation and religious diversity have resulted in many changes and challenges in Catholic schools as they seek to adopt more inclusive practices and embrace diversity.

THE CATHOLIC CHURCH AND RELIGIOUS DIVERSITY

One of the characteristics of being a Catholic is to live a life dedicated to inclusivity. The etymology of the word 'catholic' originates from the Greek adjective *katholikos* which means universal. In Jesus' life and ministry there was no 'other'. He emphasised the dignity of all human life and reached out to all, especially those who were marginalised or oppressed due to their gender, religious belief, culture, occupation, or health. He challenged cultural and religious taboos of his time; questioning the Jewish order (Matthew 5; Luke 11:37-54), speaking to the Samaritan woman at the well (John 4) and touching the leper (Matthew 8:3). Jesus demonstrated a profound way of relating to others that offers Christian anthropology and pedagogy a 'grammar of dialogue'[1] that is inherent to Catholic identity.

Church documents speak of the necessity of inter-religious dialogue being at the heart of the Catholic enterprise as one of the means to imitate and live the vision and mission of Jesus.[2] The Church values the 'ray of truth' that is present in the teachings of all religious traditions:

> The Catholic Church rejects nothing that is true and holy in these religions. She regards with sincere reverence those ways of conduct and of life, those precepts and teachings which, though differing in many aspects from the ones she holds and sets forth, nonetheless often reflect a ray of that Truth which enlightens all.[3]

In regard to schooling, the Church offers general principles on how Catholic schools can include and celebrate religious difference while remaining true to its own teaching and vision. Catholic schools are schools for all, and affirming diversity is at the heart of Catholic education.[4] Catholic schools recognise the religious freedom of their students and their families and do not seek to coerce or indoctrinate students with different religious beliefs into the Catholic faith. Rather, the Catholic school 'offers itself to all, non-Christians included, with all its distinctive aims and means, acknowledging, preserving and promoting the spiritual and moral qualities, the social and cultural values, which characterise different civilisations'.[5] At the same time, the Catholic school holds the right and duty to offer faith formation based on the values of the Gospel to Catholic students.[6] So, how do Catholic schools remain true to their Catholic identity and mission while also welcoming and including students with different religious beliefs?

RELIGIOUS EDUCATION AND RELIGIOUS INSTRUCTION

The new reality of pluralism in Ireland has significant implications for the approach taken to religious education in schools. In 2018 the then Minister for Education, Richard Bruton, issued a Circular Letter (0013/2018) to all state-managed secondary schools (ETBs) stating that students who withdraw from religious instruction should be offered an alternative subject in its place. This re-ignited the debate on the nature of religious education in schools and the difference between religious instruction and religious education. It highlighted the need for clarity regarding the language and terms used when referring to religious education in Ireland. These terms are not interchangeable and can mean quite different things.

Historically, in Ireland, the term 'religious instruction' has been used in legal documents to refer to educating into a particular religious tradition, whereas 'religious education' implies a broader approach and is not defined within a particular religious tradition. It seeks to open students to education about different beliefs as well as an opportunity to learn 'from' these different religions and beliefs.

Legislative documents referring to public schools in Ireland (Education and Training Board Schools or Community Colleges) clearly refer to 'religious instruction' taking place during the school day. This was also the term traditionally used in denominational schools. The nature of religious instruction has changed in the last 20 years to reflect the growing diversity of belief of a once relatively homogenous Ireland. At primary level, the Department of Education's Primary Curriculum Framework, 2023, reflects the complexity of that change in how it refers to what was 'religious education' in the 1999 Primary Curriculum. The terminology now used is 'Religious/Ethical/Multibelief and Values Education – The Patron's Programme' (NCCA, 2023), which testifies to the concern of the NCCA to include the various patron bodies at primary level and their different approaches to the patron's half-hour. Interestingly, the term 'religious education' is accepted as an inclusive term across Europe, encompassing ethical and multi-belief dimensions as well as faith-formation approaches,

At secondary level another significant milestone in the development of religious education in this country was the establishment of a curriculum by the National Council for Curriculum and Assessment (NCCA) for the assessment of religious education at the Junior Cycle (2000) and Leaving Certificate Cycle (2003). The Junior Cycle religious education curriculum was revised in 2018 and provides a framework for students of all beliefs to study religion together, exploring a variety of religious traditions and interpretations of life. For denominational schools, two challenges emerge from this approach. How does a Catholic school teach a religious education programme that is inclusive and open to all while at the same time addressing the faith development of the Catholic students? Secondly, parents from a different religion or belief may exercise their constitutional right to remove their son or daughter from religious education (believing that it is educating students into the faith of the school).While this may pose resource and supervision challenges to schools, it should be facilitated positively, as it is a legitimate and important right pertaining to religious freedom. Is it possible, therefore, for Catholic schools in today's Ireland to serve students of all faiths and beliefs while retaining a distinctly Catholic character?

A PEDAGOGY AND CULTURE OF DIALOGUE

As stated earlier, Catholic schools are always open and inclusive. Religious education seeks to foster a space for questioning, exploring, enquiring and reflecting. It is a unique space. It enables students to learn from the wisdom of their own belief and the beliefs of others. It is an opportunity for students to be enhanced by their own convictions, moral values, and an understanding of the Divine in their lives. It seeks to be a source of enrichment and human flourishing. The Congregation for Catholic Education states that teachers

> should be open at all times to authentic dialogue, convinced that in these circumstances the best testimony that they can give of their own faith is a warm and sincere appreciation for anyone who is honestly seeking God according to his or her own conscience.[7]

Religious education that seeks to facilitate conversations between different voices and perspectives calls for a dialogical pedagogy. In the Congregation for Catholic Education's *Educating to Intercultural Dialogue in Catholic Schools'*(2013), schools are called to place intercultural dialogue as an overarching aim of Catholic schooling. It encourages Catholic schools 'to avoid closing in upon 'identity' as a goal in itself'[8] but rather to be spaces of encounter and harmony. An educational pedagogy that acknowledges the growing multi-religious reality of society needs to be fostered where students learn about different beliefs and dialogue with those beliefs and with non-believers.[9] It goes on to recommend that teachers allow students 'to experience real listening, respect, dialogue and the value of diversity'[10] in Catholic schools.

A fundamental principle of inter-religious dialogue is a mature understanding of one's own faith tradition. In his *Global Compact on Education* (2019) Pope Francis states, 'a culture is strengthened by its openness and its exchange of views with other cultures, as long as it has a clear and mature awareness of its own principesl and values.'[11] This calls on Catholic schools to meet their students where they are in their faith or belief journey and to provide space, not only for healthy dialogue between students, but also for reflection and opportunities for the faith development of students who are aligned, however tenuously, with the Catholic faith. Catholic schools 'have the responsibility for offering Catholic students, over and above a sound knowledge of religion, the possibility to grow in personal closeness to Christ in the Church.'[12]

OPTING OUT OF RELIGIOUS EDUCATION

According to the UN Convention of Human Rights, parents have the right to raise their children according to their own choice of religion (1948, art. 26:3). Similarly, the right of schools to provide religious instruction in the Irish Constitution is carefully balanced by the right of parents to withdraw their child from religious instruction (Art. 44.2.4). This is also echoed by the Second Vatican Council (1965) which states that parents:

> have the right to determine, in accordance with their own religious beliefs, the form of religious upbringing which is to be given to their children ... the rights of parents are violated, if their children are compelled to attend classes which are not in agreement with the religious beliefs of the parents, or if there is but a single compulsory system of education from which all religious instruction is excluded.[13]

In 2010 a study on the views of students of minority belief background, regarding their right to opt out of religious education, was carried out through Queens University, Belfast.[14] While this research project was conducted in Northern Ireland, many of the emerging recommendations are relevant to wider national and international situations. Some of the key findings in this report state that the existence of the right to opt out of religious education does not necessarily lead to students of minority beliefs feeling that their religion or beliefs are acknowledged or respected in the school.

The report also acknowledges that while many students of minority beliefs feel supported by their peers and, at times, by their teachers, the lack of attention given to their beliefs in the religious education curriculum causes them to feel that these beliefs are not valued or respected by the school, or, indeed, more widely by the education system. Even when transparent policies and procedures are in place regarding students' withdrawal from RE, the lack of consultation with students of minority beliefs led to a sense among many of them that their beliefs were not of interest or concern to their school. However, the new Junior Cycle framework for religious education (2018) at second level seeks to offer opportunities for all schools to ensure that no students with minority beliefs in a school feel excluded from religious education.

It is essential that dialogue remains at the heart of all interactions in the Catholic school and students with minority beliefs experience a recognition and interest in their beliefs from the teachers and students in the school. An example of this is when students are fasting for religious reasons during term time. This can be highlighted and encouraged by the school principal or year heads. The school community should be aware that they are fasting and why and the students can be supported and commended for their spiritual practice.

ADDRESSING THE CHALLENGES: CURRICULAR ISSUES

It is important that, before enrolment in a Catholic school, the school's ethos, policies and curriculum are clearly laid out for incoming parents. The subject of religious education has already been addressed but some parents may also have other curricular challenges. For example, the issue of physical education (P.E.) at second level for some Muslims, considering their perspectives on gender, clothing, modesty and fasting. Some Muslim parents prefer that their sons and daughters do not mix with one another in sports. They cannot be on the same team, nor can two teams of the opposite sex play against each other. Muslim students may also have difficulty with P.E. during Ramadan, the Islamic period of fasting, due to the physical effort required. Some scholars [15] refute these issues with P.E. and believe that 'religiously responsive' accommodation in P.E. is possible if educators are more aware of the values and stipulations on Muslims regarding sport. It is vital, from the outset, that the school discusses with the parents and student about what reasonable accommodations are necessary and how the school might provide support in such cases.

Similarly, participation in music class or music-related activities in school life can pose challenges for some faith groups. This is usually influenced by their culture and religious interpretation of sacred texts. Parents need to be informed if music is a compulsory subject in the school at second-level and provided with the objectives of the music curriculum which may allay some fears about the subject. However, under Section 30(2)(e) of the 1998 Education Act, no student is required to attend instruction in *any* subject which is contrary to the conscience of the parent of the student – or of the student themselves once they reach the age of 18. Therefore, schools are obliged to arrange alternative arrangements for the student, in dialogue with the parents. At primary level, on the other hand, it is not possible to opt out of music. Music is used as a pedagogy in most classrooms in primary schools and central to the development of the child in the curriculum. Reasonable accommodations can be made around singing in shows or choirs but it is not possible to remove music from the life of the school due to religious objections. Reasonable accommodation entails recognising and valuing difference between religions and cultures and seeking to accommodate difference where possible rather than only focusing on what we have in common or requiring all students to fit into a prescribed norm in the school.

'Multiculturalism and pluralism are characteristic traits of our times; thus, teachers must be able to provide their students with the cultural tools necessary for giving direction to their lives'.[16] This can be challenging for teachers. Studies of Irish schools reveal that teachers express levels of uncertainty and discomfort in the face of diversity in their classrooms.[17] There is an increasing need to adapt teaching styles and approaches when teaching religious education in a multi-belief context. The need for initial teacher education in religions and beliefs and the necessary skills required for managing religious diversity and dialogue in schools is essential for teachers to confidently and competently enable respectful interaction between pupils of various beliefs and cultures. Continuing teacher development also needs to be prioritised by school patrons and trustee bodies as schools become more diverse.

RITUAL AND THE LITURGICAL YEAR

Just as students should be able to recognise themselves in the curriculum, they should also be able to see themselves and others in the religious celebrations of the school community. Class rituals, in particular, can take many forms and offer endless possibilities to reflect the diversity of belief within a class group. Inclusive prayer services can highlight important festivals of Catholic and other faith traditions throughout the school year.

Catholic schools benefit from a rich spiritual and liturgical tradition. Prayer and sacramental experience are a central feature of a Catholic school. The liturgical seasons should be clearly marked and celebrated in the school. Students of all beliefs and traditions should always be warmly invited and welcomed to these liturgical celebrations, but never obliged to attend. Just as respect of their religious freedom and appreciation of their cultural and religious beliefs are shown to them, they too are invited to show a willingness to attend and show respect for practices within the Catholic tradition, albeit in a limited way. Observation of the sacrament of Eucharist can be a rich learning experience for students who do not identify as Catholic; and they can be invited to approach the altar during the distribution of Communion, with their arms folded across their chest, for a blessing if they wish. Inter-religious ceremonies can also be considered for graduating year groups if there is a large proportion of religiously diverse students in the year group.

POINTS FOR REFLECTION

The Catholic Church has a large body of teaching in relation to inclusivity and inter-belief dialogue that offers clear guidelines on how and why everyone is welcome at the table in Catholic schools. The challenge seems to lie in how Catholic schools remain true to the Church's teaching and vision while embracing religious diversity at the same time. Catholic schools are one of the interfaces between secular society and belief communities in Ireland today. Catholic values are at the core of what it means to be a Catholic school. The task for inclusive Catholic schools is not to 'relinquish its own freedom to proclaim the Gospel and to offer a formation based on the values to be found in a Christian education.'[18] The Catholic vision and mission is offered to all students but never imposed. It is always an invitation, not an expectation.

The following reflection points may help school leaders and teachers to hold this identified tension creatively.

Articulate and Live the Mission of the School

How does a school leader or teacher invite a religiously diverse school community into an experience of belonging in a Catholic school? Do all students and staff feel welcomed and valued in your school? Is there an opportunity to invite the different stakeholders in the school to engage in a review of the school mission statement, inviting those who share the values of the school but not necessarily the Catholic faith, to participate in the articulation of the mission? What are the values informing the ethos of your school that you are passionate about and motivated by? Can relationships be developed with parents and students from beliefs other than Catholic, that are based on trust, listening, mutual respect, and recognition?

Acknowledge and Celebrate Diversity

It is important to focus on what we share in common. It is also vital that we do not gloss over our differences and that we see diversity of belief as a value that enriches our communities. Does your admissions policy reflect the diversity of your local community? Do your school activities foster cultural and religious diversity? How do you deal with tensions between different ethnic groups or with parents or students who disrespect the Catholic ethos of the school?

Faith Presence in Catholic Schools

With the decline of the presence of clergy and religious men and women in Catholic schools in Ireland, how comfortable are you as a lay faith leader in your school? With the change in focus from faith formation for Catholics (catechesis) to religious education for all in Catholic schools, could your school prioritise the place of a school chaplain who holds a faith presence in the life of the school and supports students and staff in the growth of their own beliefs?

Reflective Practice for Educators

Are opportunities provided for on-going teacher development regarding cultural and religious sensitivity? Teachers play a crucial role in creating a safe space for the interaction of students with differing beliefs and the facilitation of inter-belief conversation. The skill of reflexivity and reflective practice among teachers on their classroom practice and own identity in relation to the various beliefs they teach, is essential. The same is true for principals and how they interact with various belief groups. Reflective practice involves stepping back and adopting a bird's-eye perspective on one's professional practice by considering one's behaviour, thoughts and feelings in a given circumstance. This can assist educators in fostering an awareness of how underlying cultural or personal assumptions can influence our judgements.

CONCLUSION

Embracing diversity in a Catholic school can be complex. There are no hard and fast answers as to how this is lived out in the daily life of a school. But we must keep asking the questions and encouraging on-going conversations within our school communities.

To return to the principal's voice at the beginning of this chapter 'unless we demonstrate that each and every person in our school community, regardless of their faith or orientation, is unique and precious to our school community, we cannot claim to be Christian in the true sense'. We are only following the example of Jesus if everyone in our school community feels invited and welcomed around the table, recognised and valued for their differences and experience a sense of belonging to the school community. No one should feel invisible.

> When those who have the power to name and socially construct reality choose not to see or hear you, whether you are dark-skinned, old, disabled, female, or speak with a different accent or dialect than theirs, when someone with the authority of a teacher, say, describes the world and you are not in it, there is a moment of disequilibrium, as if you looked in the mirror and saw nothing.[19]

5 The Role of Ethos in Relationship and Sexuality Education

VIVEK DA SILVA

'I don't find ethos and RSE difficult to balance, I just find it awkward.'[1] These words of an educator in a Catholic school shed light on the complexity of teaching Relationship and Sexuality Education within the values framework of a Catholic school ethos. The awkwardness arises from trying to walk a path that remains true at all times to the principles of Catholic education, Catholic doctrine and the reality of contemporary thinking with regard to human sexuality and relationships.

WHAT IS SEXUALITY?

Sexuality includes all aspects – feelings, thoughts, and behaviours of the human person – 'that relate to being male or female and is subject to change and development throughout life.'[2] It shapes an individual's personal and interpersonal relationships. It determines their sexual orientation, gender identity and expression. It concerns sexual activity and procreation, and influences the capacity to give and receive love. Sexuality is an integral part of the human person and is affected by the interplay between biological, psychological, cultural, social, political, ethical, legal and religious factors.

The Catholic understanding of human sexuality is deeply rooted in the acceptance that sexuality, the intimate nucleus that enriches one's personhood and contributes to the development of a person's physical, psychological and spiritual personality, is a gift from God.

With love as its intrinsic end, sexuality is realised in its fullness not only by 'existing with someone but even more deeply and completely by existing for someone.'³ Ronald Rolheiser, observing that the word 'sex' comes from the Latin word *secare*, meaning to be cut off or divided from, says that one's sexuality drives the lifelong desire for communion with something beyond themselves.⁴ This all-encompassing energy for relationships that seeks friendship, companionship, family and generativity, says Diarmuid O'Murchú, is at the very heart of the evolving process of each person seeking to come to a fullness of their being as a human.⁵ The Catholic concept of sexuality is built on this relationality with self, the other and the Divine.

SEXUALITY IS NUANCED BY CULTURAL AND SOCIETAL SHIFTS

The understanding of sexuality is also a product of the social and cultural influences of our time and must be viewed within the context of a particular culture.⁶ Sexuality is understood and expressed differently in different cultures. Legislation, cultural practices and social norms and values influence the understanding and expression of one's sexuality just as much as a person's biological constitution. It is important, in this context, to recognise the changing landscape of contemporary Irish society and culture to grasp its evolving understanding and expression of sexuality.

The lifespan of the Eighth Amendment of the Irish Constitution mirrors the journey of a society moving from being largely conservative and religious to being increasingly liberal and secular. During this time revelations of widespread clerical sexual abuse, abuse of women and children in the Magdalene Laundries and Mother and Baby homes considerably eroded the moral authority of the Church. So much so that Leo Varadkar, addressing Pope Francis in 2018, remarked that the Ireland of the twenty-first century is a different country now than it was in the past. He observed that Ireland remains a country where religion, even though it may not be at the centre of Irish society, still holds an important place.

The pattern of legislation from 1983 to 2018 signposts this shift. In

1983, the Eighth Amendment of the Constitution had recognised the right to life of the unborn equal to that of the mother. Subsequent legislation would chart rapid change: in 1985, the liberalisation of laws regulating contraception; in 1993, the decriminalisation of consensual same-sex activity; in 1996, the lifting of the constitutional ban on divorce; in 2015, the constitutional recognition of same-sex marriages, and the Gender Recognition Act providing for the legal recognition of a person's preferred gender. Finally, in 2018, the Thirty-sixth Amendment of the Constitution removed the Eighth Amendment and associated texts and explicitly empowered the State to introduce legislation for the regulation of termination of pregnancy. The pendulum, it would appear, had swung from one direction to the other, from one determined by faith and belief to one influenced by secular liberalism. This shift has fuelled the debate on school-based RSE as political, social and religious groups tussle to capture the moral and ideological high ground.

DIALOGUE NOT DEBATE

In a society experiencing such rapid flux and a palpable anti-Church sentiment it would be naïve to expect a unified language to exist among the many diverging understandings of the meaning and expression of human sexuality. Deputy Paul Murphy, in moving the Provision of Objective Sex Education Bill 2018, said there was need for 'factual, objective and impartial sex education in schools that caters for the needs and rights of our young people.' He argued that RSE in schools was 'at odds with where society is now' because people are faced with an 'education system that, unfortunately, puts the ethos of schools, largely religious based, ahead of the needs of young people.' Deputy Bríd Smith mentioned that only a limited number of students 'get the delivery of proper sex education through the youth services which includes discussion and non-ethos based, factual, biologically correct education.'[7]

Carl O'Brien questions whether schools should 'be allowed to use their ethos to prevent pupils having access to objective sex education.'

He is of the opinion that if policy-makers show some 'bravery' this 'could signal another major shift in the State wresting back control from religious groups on education matters.' A student at Trinity College is quoted as saying that he was failed by his experience of sexual education in school as it was outdated and focused extensively on abstinence, risks and dangers. He lays the blame for this squarely at the door of religious 'ethos and its incompatibility with modern teaching.'[8]

Archbishop Eamon Martin addressing the JMB/AMCSS Thirty-first Annual Conference (2018), countered these negative perceptions of an ethos-based approach to RSE in Catholic schools as 'unfair, harsh, uninformed and agenda-driven.' He insisted that RSE in schools must address the 'questions and challenges facing young people living their lives today' in both the 'virtual and real worlds they inhabit'; that consideration be given to 'the advances in psychological, pedagogical and didactic sciences (*Amoris Laetitia*, 280)'; and be 'situated within a morals and values framework that is derived ultimately from the life and teaching of Christ and transmitted through the teaching of the Catholic Church.'

The Catholic Schools Partnership (CSP) supports this view and believes there is a 'temptation in contemporary Irish discourse to dismiss religious belief as inherently irrational, divisive and anti-intellectual.' They state that this is 'contrary to the Catholic education tradition which is built on a respect for faith and reason.' Those who dismiss this viewpoint are either unaware of or misunderstand the 'long evolution of Catholic schools over many centuries, the rich diversity within the Catholic sector and the principles which underpin such education today.'[9]

It is in this polarised climate that a suitable school-based Relationship and Sexuality Education is sought. If that is to happen, the debate needs to move towards respectful dialogue which is a two-way cooperative conversation where participants exchange information and build a working relationship with one another. This conversation is mutual, with both genuinely trying to engage with and learn from one another.[10] RSE could well be that opportune place to begin the process of building 'a new relationship between Church and State in Ireland – a new covenant for the 21st Century', as Leo Varadkar advocated.[11] The question then is not whether Catholic ethos hinders an objective and factual RSE but rather how a Catholic ethos can contribute to a relevant, inclusive and effective RSE.

HOLISTIC EDUCATION AND RSE

The Irish Constitution guarantees the provision of educational facilities with due regard 'for the rights of parents, especially in the matter of religious and moral formation' (Article 42). The Education Act (1998), in this context, obligates school education to 'promote the moral, spiritual, social and personal development of students and provide health education for them, in consultation with their parents, having regard to the characteristic spirit of the school' (Section 9, d).

The Early Childhood Curriculum Framework, *Aistear*, clearly states that a holistic education must provide opportunities for all children to develop their cognitive, creative, emotional, linguistic, moral, physical, social, and spiritual dimensions. The Government's Action Plan for Education, 2019, calls for a progressive and equitable education that aims to transform lives by facilitating learning which offers individuals the possibilities to achieve their full potential so that they can contribute to the 'development, cohesion and wellbeing of an inclusive society' (p. 6,7). Likewise, the United Nations Convention on the Rights of the Child seeks an education towards the development of the child to their fullest potential. Accordingly, RSE, as an integral part of holistic education, is designed to promote 'the overall development of the person and which includes the integration of sexuality into personal understanding, growth and development' (Circular 0027/2008).

To accomplish this a plural society must show the will and capacity to hold the tension of the multiplicity of religious and secular views about the complexities of human relationships and sexuality. *Aistear* lays emphasis on the integral development of learners, including the physical, moral and spiritual, to enable them to become 'competent and confident learners within loving relationships with others' (p. 6).

The Action Plan for Education 2019 envisions education as a means to achieve transformation that 'brings important social and economic benefits in the form of self-confident and dynamic communities' by offering every opportunity that empowers learners 'to achieve more and to take every opportunity that arises to be the best that they can be (p. 6).

In recent times the religious and spiritual dimension of education appears to be incorporated under the umbrella of Wellbeing. In 2018, the subject area of Wellbeing was introduced as part of the revised three-year junior cycle programme. The Wellbeing curriculum sets out to be child-centred, inclusive, evidence-informed, collaborative and outcomes-focused. Wellbeing includes Physical Education (PE), Civic, Social and Political Education (CSPE) and SPHE, of which RSE is a component. The Wellbeing Policy Statement and Framework for Practice (2018) identified that wellbeing is present when 'a person realises their potential, is resilient in dealing with the normal stresses of their life, takes care of their physical wellbeing and has a sense of purpose, connection and belonging to a wider community. It is a fluid way of being and needs nurturing throughout life' (p. 10).

Archbishop Eamon Martin (2018), acknowledging the risks to the health and wellbeing of young people in the real and virtual world, envisages Catholic education enabling them to navigate the challenges they face. He proposed an RSE programme, with the active collaboration of parents, as an integral part of the Catholic school curriculum to equip students with the critical ability to debate and discuss relevant issues such as contraception, sexually transmitted infections, same-sex relationships and the meaning of consent in an age- and developmental-appropriate language and manner. This approach to RSE intends to educate young people to take responsibility in making well-informed decisions. It seeks to nurture the skills a student requires to make ongoing value-based lifelong decisions about their relationships and sexual behaviour choices.

Pope Francis supports a Catholic education that offers a fresh experience to learners through a culture of genuine encounter, wide-ranging dialogue, mutual understanding and collaborative partnership. *Amoris Laetitia* calls for sexuality education to consider the advances in psychological, pedagogical and didactic sciences (n. 280). The role of Catholic education has always been to help people discover something of value in their lives as they search for deeper understanding and ask critical questions.[12]

The Joint Committee on Education and Skills (JCES) in their Report on RSE (2019) affirms that RSE needs to be implemented in a manner that is appropriate to the student's age and developmental stage. It recognises that parents are the primary educators and encourages a partnership between school and parent. It endorses the need for a whole-school approach to sexuality education to promote positive values and to facilitate the development of age-appropriate knowledge and attitudes. It upholds the view that RSE needs to support young people to understand themselves and develop healthy relationships with others. It recommends that the current RSE curriculum in schools needs to be updated to reflect the 'significant and welcome changes' (p. 23) in Irish society today. They insist that RSE must reflect the lived experience of students, including the experience of those identifying as LGBT+. It recommends that RSE be taught with 'a mindset of inclusivity which is centred on competence, wellbeing and the development of mutually satisfying relationships' (p. 10). They suggest that the approach to RSE needs to be 'gender-equality based, inclusive, holistic, creative, empowering and protective' (p. 26).

The revised SPHE/RSE specification for the Junior Cycle (2023) is grounded in values of respect, care, compassion, equality and inclusivity. It strongly emphasises nurturing, caring relationships and healthy lives. It focusses on building the social and emotional skills of young people while nurturing their skills of critical thinking so as to interrogate existing social and cultural norms. This revised specification places the young person and their context and needs firmly at the centre of learning.

ETHOS AND VALUES

In the past, the Department of Education and Skills (DES) has largely respected schools' commitment to implement RSE in keeping with their ethos or characteristic spirit. However, Circular 0037/2010 reflected a shift in DES directives on RSE. In keeping with Article 11.2 of the European Social Charter, it indicated that sexuality education must be provided in a manner that is 'objective, based on contemporary scientific evidence and does not involve censoring, withholding or intentionally misrepresenting information, for example as regards contraception or different means of maintaining sexual and reproductive health.' With Circular 0043/2018, it reminded schools that they have a 'duty to protect students in their care at all times from any potentially harmful, inappropriate or misguided resources, interventions or programmes' while promoting the students' wellbeing, and social and emotional learning. While there is general consensus about the purpose of a school-based RSE, a point of contention emerges when considering what values or moral standards frame the teaching of RSE. While most schools have an open-minded approach to RSE, some schools, citing ethos, choose not to address those topics that appear to be incongruent with their values or religious doctrine such as same-sex marriage, abortion, contraception, sex outside the context of marriage, and gender identity.

JCES indicated that ethos has led to inconsistencies between the content taught and the approach taken for the delivery of RSE in schools. It maintains that the religious ethos of a school can be used as a barrier to teaching a comprehensive RSE programme. It, therefore, recommends amending the Education Act 1998 'so that ethos can no longer be used as a barrier to the effective, objective and factual teaching of the RSE curriculum to which every student is entitled' (2019, Recommendation 14, p. 28). This raises the questions: Can education about sexuality and relationships and its provision be value-neutral? Does this recommendation intend to replace one value-system with another? Does it suggest that another value-system is better than a Catholic one?

It is evident that culture and societal values shape the experience and expression of sexuality. Irish society's understanding of sex and sexuality is increasingly more liberal and morally relativist and influences the current call to modify the nature and approach to RSE in post-primary schools. It favours the approach that RSE is simply life-skills orientated and gives precedence to the autonomy and authority of the individual to determine what is morally right or wrong with regard to sexuality, its understanding and expression.

It is equally true that an RSE approach which does not engage with the realities of contemporary life is unhelpful and damaging. In an Open Letter to Religious Leaders about Sex Education the Religious Institute on Sexual Morality, Justice, and Healing stated:

> Education that respects and empowers young people has more integrity than education based on incomplete information, fear, and shame. Programs that teach abstinence exclusively and withhold information about pregnancy and sexually transmitted disease prevention fail our young people. Scriptural and theological commitment to telling the truth calls for full and honest education about sexual and reproductive health.[13]

DIVERGING ANTHROPOLOGIES

The State and the Church differ considerably with regard to approaches to RSE because of their ideological positions and differing values. Dermot Lane is of the opinion that the contemporary self is in crisis because human dignity is undermined by consumerism, market capitalism, and globalisation. This, he believes, has raised significant questions around anthropology which include 'radical individualism, the myth of the self-sufficient subject, the commodification of the self through market demands, the deconstruction of the self by postmodernity, gender issues, the spiritual and cultural isolation of the self in the 21st century.'[14]

The Catholic understanding of anthropology, which finds expression in the ethos of Catholic schools, recognises the human person as ultimately created for life with God, and others. This has extraordinary ramifications for our self-understanding. We are essentially created for relationship. It is with and through others that we come to discover who we are, what we can be, and develop the potential to grow in ways that would be impossible without these other people in our lives. For Christians, the most significant relationship is the one we have with the Triune God. The person of Jesus is the model of what humanity can become. Jesus provides a template for how we can genuinely and inclusively relate with God and others, how we can live in such a way as to transform ourselves, our relationships, and the world. In our relationship with God we discover ourselves to be more than merely human and are invited to experience a truer, deeper, more transcendent self which radically influences the vision we have of what it means to be human. In other words, we are invited to experience the deepest truth and potential of our being, that we are created in the image and likeness of God. Athanasius of Alexandria (*ca* 296-373) captured the essence of this when he said that God became human so that humans could become divine. This is the heart of the Christian message and shapes how we understand and relate to each other. In imitation of Jesus, we try to reflect this understanding in all our relationships. We acknowledge the dignity of every human person as being an expression of God. Sexuality, in this context, is understood as a fundamental means by which the individual can genuinely discover and be a more authentic self in and through intimate relationship.

Quite in contrast, a utilitarian understanding of what it means to be human defines the worth of people by their usefulness to society. It over-emphasises individualism and personal autonomy. It is a perception influenced by the norms of consumerism that create infinite need and encourage constant upgrading and acquisition over stability and durability. It favours convenience over self-sacrifice, and places the rights of the individual over those of the whole. 'My body, my choice' is a slogan that might in part illustrate this understanding. It is a position that reflects the popular understanding of sexuality as primarily for self and pleasure.[15] It allows the individual to express self without reference to any value-system or moral code. From this vantage point the expression of one's sexuality in a more traditional way is sometimes viewed as repressive, guilt-laden and restrictive.

SHAPING A NEW DIALOGUE

With so many 'new ways of living affectivity, and the multiplicity of ethical perspectives,'[16] the Church's stance on such complex and conflict-laden contemporary issues is seen as intolerably intransigent and incongruent with its core message of compassion and understanding. Many would like to see the Church more empathetic. The Church, however, remains steadfast in 'obedience to the truth which is Christ, whose image is reflected in the nature and dignity of the human person,… interprets the moral norm and proposes it to all people of good will, without concealing its demands of radicalness and perfection.'[17]

This steadfast stance can create an awkwardness for those entrusted with the teaching of RSE in schools as they attempt to balance accurate, factual information and the lived reality of their students with the moral code and doctrine of the Church. The Church is aware that its teaching regarding human sexuality is not universally accepted. However, it is convinced that, like Jesus, in challenging the prevalent norms of society, it strives to be careful 'not to break the bruised reed or quench the dimly burning wick' (Isaiah 42:3). In this, the Church, following the example of Jesus, is invitational in its approach and does not seek to impose any one set of beliefs. The Catholic school, animated by the Gospel spirit of freedom and love, is leaven in the human community.[18] It is aware of the living presence of Jesus in its midst. Through its characteristic spirit it nurtures the personal development of every student, fosters their sense of values, encourages robust dialogue between culture and the Gospel message, promotes a spirit of mutual understanding, illuminates all learning with the light of faith, develops a collaborative partnership with families of the students and forms good citizens with respect for the observance of just laws.

Pope Francis believes that Catholic education fosters a Gospel-centred anthropology for contemporary culture. He invites all educational projects to expose learners to more than just one form of thought. This will allow initiatives like RSE to challenge societal stereotypes and biases that influence student attitudes and assumptions. This requires a deep listening and respectful attention to the lived experiences of the young people so that a Catholic ethos will encourage inclusiveness, respectful engagement with the other, care for those marginalized, and dialogue with secular ideological structures, and propose transformation of attitudes and behaviours.[19] For instance, when it comes to the issue of consent there is the implicit understanding in society that sexual intercourse is acceptable outside the context of marriage or intimate long-term relationships. The Catholic understanding of sexuality challenges behaviour that encourages casual or random sexual encounters. It proposes attitudinal transformation that respects the dignity of each one's personhood, a commitment to the relationship and an openness to life. Catholic understanding also challenges the perception that sexual intercourse is appropriate solely because it is consensual and pleasurable.

Religious patronage and the ethos of schools have persistently been identified as challenging for young LGBT+ people because of 'the impact of unsupportive attitudes towards homosexuality and transgender issues.'[20] However, many Catholic schools are taking considered steps to address LGBT+ issues to promote respect, compassion and sensitivity towards others irrespective of their sexual orientation or gender identity. Catholic schools strive for a balance between affirming Catholic teaching and pastoral concern. This balanced approach, first and foremost, recognises every person as created in the image and likeness of God as 'it is fundamental for human development that dignity, freedom and autonomy be acknowledged and respected.'[21]

It is a misconception that the Catholic ethos must be a barrier to RSE. Catholic education asks the questions that matter and in its most authentic form holds a mirror up to society. Catholic education will never simply be 'to further the ends of the state, nor simply to meet the needs of the market, but will continue to be an informed examination of the place of the individual within his or her community and society.'[22] Pope Francis urges Catholic schools not to 'isolate themselves from the world' but to 'enter bravely into the Areopagus of current culture and open dialogue, conscious of the gift that they can offer to everyone.'[23]

The observation in a 2007 document from the Crisis Pregnancy Agency still holds: they felt that 'ethos was something of a smoke screen, which, in today's world, had little bearing on the reality of what was now accepted and demanded (by parents, by society at large and perhaps by the church) from school-based relationships and sexuality education.'[24] Catholic schools need to be cautious against the tendency to shut themselves into their own 'self-secured identity' to the point of excluding that which is other as 'illegitimate.'[25] Pope Francis in *Christus Vivit* comments that Catholic schools invite self-criticism if they structure themselves with a view to self-preservation and bunker themselves in to protect themselves and their students from perceived 'errors from without' and the 'dangers, real or imagined, that any change might bring' (n. 221).

Ethos-based barriers, even when erected with every good intention, create a disconnect between what is taught and the reality experienced by students and their parents. Sheltering behind the firewalls of Church doctrine will only risk further widening the gap between the institutional Church and the lived reality of young people. Catholic education, instead, must look to build bridges of compassion, respect and sensitivity through critical dialogue in a manner similar to that of Jesus.[26] Jesus' revolutionary message challenged the prevalent worldview of his time and turned it on its head by demanding a repositioning of the dominant value structure. Catholic education, when framing a factual and objective RSE, needs to bear in mind that

> The culture of dialogue does not in any way contradict the legitimate aspirations of Catholic schools to maintain their own vision of human sexuality, in keeping with the right of families to freely base the education of their children upon an integral anthropology, capable of harmonizing the human person's physical, psychic and spiritual identity.[27]

A FINAL THOUGHT

Catholic education is not about proselytizing or protecting Catholic doctrine. Rather, it seeks to nurture the ability of all students to engage in dialogue with issues of concern. It facilitates a safe space for every student, irrespective of their belief or sexual orientation, to express and develop their view on issues relevant to them with regard to sexuality. In a plural society, Catholic schools have to approach RSE from a perspective of dialogue that does not in any way diminish the Catholic identity or ethos of a school. In fact, it recognises an openness to other positions to provide a meaningful values-framework for RSE that seeks to empower students with the appropriate information and necessary skills to make ongoing decisions about sexuality and relationships.

If Ireland is truly seeking a 'new covenant' between Church and State, it needs to be negotiated through dialogue and not by imposing a secularist agenda that negates the voice of different religious beliefs, particularly in education. Religious belief still offers to many a sense of meaning and direction in life. To undermine religious belief also disregards the rights of many parents who seek education for their children within a values framework in accordance with their constitutional rights and faith tradition.

While Catholic schools have the capacity to engage with cultural changes and challenge prevalent posturing with values rooted in the life and teaching of Jesus, school-based RSE needs to walk the tight rope between religious belief, cultural practice, political thought, and dialogue. This involves attentive listening to identify issues, intelligent reasoning to interpret all of the information available, and considered reflection to choose a path of action to go forward together.

In this time of transition there is a call for courage. Catholic schools, with the capacity to influence transformative change in individuals and society, are well positioned to take up this call in the context of RSE to remain relevant to the lived experience of students and continue integrating the 'knowledge of head, heart and hands.' [28] They have an opportunity to make a choice that ensures a most inclusive and appropriate RSE programme is offered to their students. It is a choice that reflects the basic value of Christian compassion and is open to dialogue with the complexity of the human condition. It is a choice that follows the example of Jesus who bent down and wrote in the dust when faced with the baying crowd calling for the stoning of the woman caught in adultery (John 8:1-11). It is a choice that imitates Jesus who entered into dialogue with the Syrophoenician woman (Matthew 15:21-28). Indeed, when it comes to RSE in a Catholic school,

> It is finding the courage to … say, quietly, unequivocally, 'I think differently about that,' and then explain why. It is stepping up to the issue and claiming the right to think differently about it that turns heads and opens hearts.[29]

6 School Ethos: A Sign of Hope and Uncompromising Love

JOHN McHALE

In a version of Fra Angelico's Early Renaissance painting of the Annunciation, originally commissioned for the altarpiece of the church of San Domenico in Cortona, Italy, the artist manages to capture the momentous significance of the occasion with a number of creative and skilfully employed techniques. The figures of Gabriel and Mary are larger than normal, indicating their importance. The palatial setting with its decorative furnishings, the splendour of the subjects' robes, adorned in rich colours – splendid pink, royal blue, striking red and gold-vermilion – all work to reveal the magnificence of God. Gabriel's historic announcement, 'The Holy Spirit will come upon you and the power of the Most High will overshadow you; therefore the child to be born will be called holy, the Son of God' (Luke 1:35), is communicated through the positioning of his hands. Finally, in the background, there is a faint depiction of the expulsion of Adam and Eve from the Garden of Eden, suggesting that the birth of Christ will bring redemption to humankind, leading us home to our rightful place in the kingdom of God. Working and living in an era on the eve of the beginning of modernity, in a time when people's existence was comprehensively understood in terms of devotion to their religious faith, Fra Angelico was attempting to celebrate in image, colour and texture what he believed to be the unique moment in history when God communicated directly and materially with the world by sending his only Son to engage in the process of salvation.

A little under 600 years later, in a radically different context, where

Christianity no longer maintains the dominant position it once held in the lives of people, the crucial significance of this moment has not diminished and it continues to influence the course of human destiny. Benedict XVI underlines the unending magnitude of the realisation of God in our lives when he writes: 'The kingdom of Jesus, Son of David, knows no end because in him God himself is reigning, in him God's kingdom erupts into this world. The promise that Gabriel spoke to the Virgin Mary is true. It is fulfilled ever anew'.[1] What are the implications of Gabriel's promise for Christian education in contemporary society? How can Jesus Christ be a source of hope and uncompromising love for our students, our teachers and our wider school communities?

Looking at the ways in which Gospel values, as articulated by the life and ministry of Jesus, present us with a model which reveals a dynamic vision of what it is to be human and how this vision carries great hope for humanity in an age consumed by devotion to a culture of materialism. Goan understands that, 'Jesus, as a revealer of God's will, embodies and demonstrates the mind of God when it comes to how human beings should engage with the experience of living'.[2] In his life and teachings, Jesus has revealed the values and the pathways by which we may choose to live lives reflecting the nature of God and what is means to be fully human and fully alive.

Christian educators have a significant responsibility for the wellbeing, care and development of children. In particular, this responsibility needs to be strongly influenced by the model of Jesus as teacher. This entails appreciating and practising his value of unconditional love for all, particularly the marginalised. There is a need to share his understanding of compassion, mercy and the necessity of forgiveness, his desire to heal body, mind and spirit, his core beliefs in people and building community, his reaching out to others through service and discipleship, the cherishing of creation and proclaiming the Kingdom of God on earth. At the core of our belief is the understanding that Christianity is not a philosophy, or an ethical way of being, or an acquired wisdom but essentially a personal relationship with Christ that always opens us to possibility and authenticity.

Certainly an experience of living based on Gospel values such as these would inspire hope of finding ultimate meaning for the entire human family. When one examines and accepts a Christian anthropology, there is much for which to be hopeful. God made creation, but his gesture of profound love in identifying with humankind by making his Son incarnate, and the subsequent experience of the cross followed by resurrection, ensures for us the promise of salvation and human transcendence, not only in the next world but to some extent in this one. Jesus, fully human, fully divine, is God's unselfish gift to us. The realities of creation and incarnation illustrate the depth of God's love and how significant we are in his plan for the universe, 'In creating the world out of love, in order to be its lover, God made a partner not a puppet'.[3] In Jesus the divine and the human become one so that humanity and divinity are not opposed. In the person and ministry of Jesus we see how the infinite God has adapted himself to the ways of finite beings, and has revealed an eternal covenant to us. In Jesus we know that this relationship between God and humankind will develop, and a positive outcome for humanity is assured. In Jesus we find a human life lived in perfect harmony with God and making this a possibility for the rest of humanity. In Jesus, the self-giving of God is realised and, in essence, humanity has become a success. This is our story, this is our goal, this is our source of hope.

In a post-modern world where the promises of consumerism heavily influence human thought and behaviour, where there is an unattainable over-emphasis on the potential of the economy to bring about a transformation of humanity, where society is, according to Eamonn Conway, 'characterised by a suspicion of reason, of naive claims to progress ... by a sense of loneliness and loss of connections,'[4] never before was it as important as now to 'engage the young to experience God',[5] to rekindle, or build from scratch, and then to sustain the faith of our youth so as to give them a sense of hope, a sense of belief in themselves, belief in God, and belief in the future.

We are mindful that there are some significant challenges to faith-formation among adolescents and in society. Young people inhabit a world where there are not as many certainties or cultural staples as were experienced by previous generations. Religious faith is one of the anchors now unmoored. In an editorial in *The Guardian* the question was posed, 'Is the end of western Christianity in sight?' Quoting from the most recent British Social Attitudes Data, the figures would seem to suggest so. '*No Religion* is now by far the largest identification for people. It is very nearly half the adult population, and more than twice the proportion who self-identify as Anglican; it is four times the Catholic population'.[6] It can be argued that Ireland is different from the United Kingdom, and unique in Europe, in terms of maintaining a large section of its population who worship and practise their religion, but it would be foolish to think that Irish people are impervious to such trends, particularly our young.

The pressures and stresses of secular society have had a considerable impact on the choices, decision-making and behaviours of young people. As Fred P. Edie outlines, the weight of cultural factors that influence personal development can be powerful, such as, 'heightened individualism; marketers' efforts to create a youth culture for the purpose of forming youth into consumption rather than agency; familial fragmentation … loss of connections with adults'.[7] Ironically, the revolution in how we communicate has promoted an obsession with the self at the expense of community. The more global our reach becomes, the more insular our regard develops for what can be termed, a virtual self. Time for quiet reflection has been replaced to a large extent by the urgent need for instant commentary. What the young find relevant is fluid, shifting continuously, more related to the immediate rather than long term consideration. Jayne Mondoy notes: 'The current generation of students was born into a world … where hours spent reading deeply into a gorgeous book gave way to skimming through an explosion of unfiltered, unedited information.'[8] The potential to be distracted by social media is all-pervasive while a significant consequence of this behaviour is a harmful emphasis on consumerism, the acquisition of material goods and gadgets. Conway, citing Vincent Miller, argues 'that the real damage done by consumer culture is that it infects our very capacity to perceive what is valuable.' He identifies 'immediate gratification and disposability' as key damaging characteristics of this corrosive way of life, 'When a life choice or a relationship becomes difficult the default position is simply to exit, move on, and try again.' He recognises its contribution to advancing the processes of secularisation, detraditionalisation, and pluralisation. He warns on being complacent when faced with its progress: 'It would be a mistake to underestimate the eroding effect of a consumer-type life style on Christian values,' and, highlighting Miller again, he sees people 'enslaved in a lifestyle and a value system injurious to and diminishing of their true vocation as human beings'.[9]

Lieven Boeve underscores how fragmented organised religion has become in the framework of a detraditionalised Europe. He argues that 'Christianity has not been replaced by a secular culture, but a plurality of life views and religions have moved in to occupy the vacant space it left behind as a result of its diminishing impact.' These include 'nihilism and religious indifference' as 'distinct positions … in their own right'.[10] Michael Paul Gallagher echoes the reality of this breakup of organised religion in an Irish context when he comments on how it seems that as a nation we 'have moved into the complex fragmentation of post-modernity'.[11] He is concerned as to the impact of religious decline on 'people's spiritual imagination' and worries:

> If there has been a rapid loss of cultural roots in religion, especially in the younger generation, this constitutes not only a faith crisis of concern for the church, but an anthropological crisis of concern to anyone who realises how the loss of such anchors can leave people existentially stranded and adrift.[12]

In addition, there are more local influences exerting negative pressures on young people's development. Changes in parental expectations, the obsession with results and gaining access to third level colleges through a points scramble, coupled with trends in national educational policy, emphasising the importance of the economy and, in particular, technological development at the expense of a more holistic growth, have left Catholic school leaders, principals and staff struggling to define what it is they offer uniquely to their existing and prospective communities. What are their priorities when they 'are confronted by a technological-secular-consumerist culture that is universal to those under 35 in every part of the world'.[13] The only response must be to present Jesus as the model and source of hope for our school communities, to give witness to Gospel values, understanding that these values pave the way for the unfolding of the deepest potential in human life – the lived imitation of the divine. This is the rationale for ensuring Gospel values become the lived expression of school ethos. 'To those who believe in him, Jesus reveals who God truly is, who we truly are and what we and our world are finally to become'.[14]

God is our loving creator, and the unconditional love he feels for the world, manifested through the person of Jesus, is his most profound response to our experience as humans. Through our relationships with students, colleagues and parents we must model this love daily – love, not merely expressed in words, but rather in willing acts of care, concern, compassion, passion, tolerance, respect and much more. This is the type of love which is an intrinsic element of one's vocation and can be seen as a vital characteristic of Christian leadership. Prendergast is in no doubt about the source of this love when he writes, 'When a Catholic school is in flow, the love of God is in flow.' He understands that the failures of Catholic schools 'were ultimately failures in love' and when Catholic schools do fail in this manner they miss the essence of what it means to be Christian.

Jesus's love and compassion is for all but in particular for those who struggle with the daily experience of life. His 'justice will always privilege the needs of those without the basics for a dignified life over the wants of those who live in abundant prosperity'.[15] In light of this commitment to serving others, especially when the poor, the least, and the weak are most threatened, schools must be conscious of those in their communities who are most in need of care. Who are the outcasts in schools? Who are the marginalised? The troublesome kid? The non-achiever? The student with SEN? The annoying parent? The tired, past-it teacher? The cynic? The isolated LGTB student or teacher? The non-national struggling with language? The non-Christian? The poor or the Travelling community. Seán Goan reminds us that 'God calls us to a more radical understanding of love' than mere respect or the act of being nice to people. Citing the parables of the Good Samaritan and the Prodigal Son he highlights how most of the time the love exemplified by Jesus is concerned with challenging mind-sets as much as giving succour. 'Behave like the Samaritan — be willing to learn from someone you despise that your world view is too small and that your mind is closed.' Or, as in the case of the Prodigal Son's father, go beyond forgiveness and 'understand that the Father of Jesus whose 'Kingdom' he proclaims can only be understood in terms of unconditional love and compassion'.[16]

John Bollan writes: 'The teacher's business is to love'.[17] The development of positive, meaningful relationships is central to the expression of this love. 'Life is found only in relationships with others. To be alone is to die.' John R. Sachs recognises the significance of reaching out to others. He associates this capacity for the development of loving relationships with freedom and sees it as a process of 'self-transcendence, the power to reach out beyond ourselves' to create 'life-giving relationships of love' with others. He asserts that the original template for this is our freedom and responsibility to choose 'a loving relationship with God.' He believes: 'What we most deeply desire is God. God alone is life and love in unsurpassable fullness'.[18] This freedom contrasts starkly with the freedom of choice described by Vincent Twomey and championed by 'terrorists and the liberal reformers' where 'there is no human act intrinsically wrong, morality is reduced to a calculus of consequences ... relativism rules supreme, the law has no foundation'.[19]

As a source of hope for our youth this uncompromising love must be evident. Despite the often superficial milieu in which young people live, they have a keen sense of what is authentic, particularly when it comes to the development of relationships. Talk of God's love, salvation, self-giving, serving others and spiritual fulfilment rings hollow, if they are treated disrespectfully, if they are not believed. Conversely, if they experience our genuine if imperfect attempts at expressing our love for them and others, as evidenced in our caring attitude and sense of respect, depth of understanding, and readiness to forgive, then the potential to engage them meaningfully in following the person of Christ is greater. As role models, 'We are entrusted to foster and nurture the educational ethos, the culture, and climate of the school. In doing so, we engage and practise the principle of sacramentality – finding Christ in all life, in every person, and in every situation'.[20]

Jesus is a role model and source of hope for Christian educators in faith based schools. In the walk to Emmaus, the evangelist Luke recounts, through the simple sharing of a meal between Jesus and his two disciples, an experience of transformation. A striking aspect of this episode is the very simple yet powerful portrayal of Jesus the teacher, initially a stranger on the road, at first accompanying, sharing, talking, explaining, reassuring, building trust, then, motivating, instilling confidence, inspiring hope, revealing truth and building faith. 'Wasn't it like a fire burning in us when he talked to us on the road and explained the Scriptures to us?' (Luke 24: 32-34).

There is an equally significant episode in John's Gospel. It recounts a moment of intimacy between Jesus and his disciples, when he humbly washes the feet of his friends before his betrayal, subsequent death and resurrection. Again, it is an experience revealing much about the nature of Jesus, the teacher and the leader, inspiring hope. Through Jesus's actions in kneeling down to serve the needs of Peter and his colleagues, Jesus is conveying what is central to his understanding of leadership, and what is at the core of his role is the concept of servanthood. The episode is rich in symbolism too. Jesus, the king, the Son of God, our Lord, is behaving unexpectedly, unconventionally. By washing the feet of his disciples he is exercising humility. He is presenting himself as a lowly and humble servant, and to such an extent that even Peter is taken aback, "Never at any time will you wash my feet!" (John 12: 8). Jesus is acting thus for a specific reason. He is showing what is expected of disciples, as leaders and teachers, if the Kingdom of God is to prosper and people are to flourish in this world. He is being consistent. Throughout the Gospel narratives he teaches and leads by example, whether it is by acting himself, or by making reference to the behaviour of others. He performs miracles to ease the cruelty of life. He makes use of parables to convey understanding. He employs the language and imagery of human interaction and he relies on the symbolism of nature in its various forms to communicate his message, to reveal his vision for humanity. This style of leadership Don Howell refers to as 'taking the initiative to influence people to grow in holiness and to passionately promote the extension of God's kingdom in the world'.[21] Jesus has a profound understanding of this message and his purpose is clear. Jesus is the embodiment of the coming of God's kingdom. He is the model to follow and the source of hope for all.

John Sachs sees us as partners with God but we are also his children. Gerard Manley Hopkins captures the rich quality of his paternal love in the line 'He fathers-forth whose beauty is past change/ Praise him.' He should be praised for he has promised salvation for all humankind, for all creation. In a world where Christian beliefs are under threat and the Christian way of life increasingly considered superfluous this knowledge of redemption brings hope. 'The life of the world is always a life that must be saved … The world has a future because in Jesus Christ it has been chosen intentionally, laboured and sacrificed for by God'.[22]

Ethos Is for Life

7 It's Everyone's Business: A Whole-school Approach to Ethos

KATHERINA BRODERICK

Catholic education is under scrutiny as never before at the present time and our Catholic educational ethos is contested daily. This is a significant change from the unquestioned school culture of times past. Students, teachers and society are undoubtedly more religiously, culturally, and ideologically diverse than ever before. This reflects the changes in Irish society, and challenges Catholic schools to consider more deeply their school values, beliefs and identity.

> There is no such thing as a value neutral education. All schools, whether established by the state or by one or other voluntary group, necessarily and implicitly espouse a vision of the human person and give expression to a particular ethos by their choices, actions and priorities.[1]

Whatever school type we work in, teachers and school management agree that it is a privilege to work with young people who challenge us to help them navigate their world and make sense of their life experiences. Their many gifts and talents can be developed to help them grow to be people of strong values fuelled by an enthusiasm and energy in pursuit of their dreams of a fulfilled and meaningful life. In a Catholic secondary school, the entire community is charged with providing an intellectually stimulating, spiritually nurturing and personally caring environment which gives daily witness to the lived reality of the Gospel. In doing this, our value system influences and guides us towards understanding and expressing the divine-human relationship that exists between God and ourselves and helps us discover and express what it means to be truly human. The boards of management of voluntary secondary schools carry ultimate responsibility for this task as outlined in the Articles of Management for Catholic Secondary Schools. The Education Act (1998) stipulates that the board of management shall

> be accountable to the patron for so upholding, the characteristic spirit of the school as determined by the cultural, educational, moral, religious, social, linguistic and spiritual values and traditions which inform and are characteristic of the objectives and conduct of the school, and at all times act in accordance with any Act of the Oireachtas or instrument made thereunder, deed, charter, articles of management or other such instrument relating to the establishment or operation of the school. (Section 15.2[b])

SCHOOL ETHOS

For a school to acknowledge its ethos, it must ensure that time is spent understanding its characteristic spirit or tradition – because if a school community does not know from where it came, it is difficult to live in the present and plan for the future.

Culture is defined as 'the underground stream of norms, values, beliefs, traditions, and rituals that has built up over time as people work together, solve problems, and confront challenges. This set of informal expectations and values shapes how people think, feel and act in schools. This highly enduring web of influence binds the school together and makes it special.'[2] Therefore, time dedicated to exploring the school ethos, despite the busy school year and demands on time, is necessary if we are to engage in ethos appreciation and development.

Every school has its own ethos or characteristic spirit. In the Education Act, the characteristic spirit of the school is understood as being 'determined by the cultural, educational, moral, religious, social, linguistic and spiritual values and traditions which inform and are characteristic of the objectives and conduct of the school'. (Section 15.2[b])

It's Everyone's Business: A Whole-school Approach to Ethos

In my previous school (Presentation Secondary School, Castleisland) and now in Presentation Secondary School, Listowel, we dedicated time to reflect on the nature and ethos of a Catholic school. This signifies the commitment to being intentional about the Catholic dimension of our school. All our discussions began with a reminder of our founding intention because 'if we lose the reason why our school was set up, we lose our way.'[3] We looked at what exactly distinguished our school, how the Gospel is lived, and how our school meets the needs and challenges of our students as they encounter the many and often perplexing demands of modern society. We did this because we believe the Gospel message is as meaningful and life-giving for us now as it was in the past. The challenge is how to present a fresh interpretation of this life-giving message to counteract the often negative impression people carry with them about Catholicism, sometimes without much awareness of their underlying prejudice. We believe in the truth of the Gospel message but understand that is has to be rediscovered and made real for our times through a committed and conscious search for true humanity. It isn't about writing off the past, or overlooking all that is good in contemporary society; it is, instead, about building on, strengthening, and cultivating a positive Catholic culture in our school.

As a staff, we reflected on our mission statement and spent time developing what we considered to be our underlying beliefs and the deeply held convictions that we, as a school community, agreed are central to our ethos. We discussed where our core beliefs are reflected in the daily life of our school, what values needed to be upheld, and what specific actions and behaviours are needed to implement these beliefs and values. This is a practical and real interpretation of the mission and tradition of our school. It formed the basis of our plan to grow together as a learning community. This process affirmed our ethos and philosophy of education which is to assist the full development of our students as a vibrant community led by Gospel values.

We are aware that not all students attending school have a strong faith. In fact, our students represent a very mixed population of believers, searchers, and non-believers. For many years, our school has welcomed students from all faith traditions and none. We see this as an opportunity for dialogue and overcoming prejudice which is essential in educating our young people for contemporary life.

RELIGIOUS EDUCATION

Religious Education as an examination subject is offered because we believe that the Religious Education syllabus deepens students' appreciation of their own religious tradition and furthers inter-religious dialogue. This ensures that our school is inclusive and that a rich learning environment is available for all students. Teachers in a school with a Catholic ethos are aware that, despite the varying degrees of participation by students, the Catholic faith is given priority and must be honoured, as many parents have consciously chosen a Catholic school in which to educate their child.

RE can justly claim to be an integral part of any curriculum that aims to promote the holistic development of the person since 'RE creates a safe space to test one's own identity, and reflect with others in a respectful manner on the search for meaning and values'.[4]

Recent debate on removing Religious Education from the curriculum overlooks the value the programme offers to students, whatever their faith stance. In line with the Religious Education syllabus:
- Religious Education promotes the holistic development of the student.
- The current RE syllabus invites students to reflect on their own experiences thereby contributing to the spiritual and moral development of the student.
- It aims to identify how understandings of God, and Religious Traditions have contributed to the culture in which we live.
- The syllabus promotes the critical and cultural development of the person in his/her social and personal life.
- It aims to foster an awareness that the human search for meaning is common to all peoples, of all ages and all times.
- The RE programme at Junior and particularly Senior cycle con-

tributes not only to personal reflection and development of young people but is also heightens respect for the beliefs of others and helps build a diverse but cohesive society.[5]

Religious Education teachers are conscious of the value of allowing time for students to experience prayer and reflective opportunities. Students respond very well when afforded these occasions. When the school has a dedicated sacred space it provides a real sense of the value placed on the symbolic and sacramental elements of the Catholic faith and the importance of providing them for our students. Retreats and reflection spaces receive very positive feedback from students who participate in them.

SCHOOL ETHOS IN ACTION: FACILITATING THE GROWTH OF A CHRISTIAN COMMUNITY

As a way of living its Christian ethos, it is important for schools to facilitate and promote faith-in-action programmes which allow students and staff to play a role in identifying forms of injustice in and beyond the school community.

> Catholic schools give expression to the public dimension of Christian faith in their commitment to social solidarity, outreach to those in need and promotion of the common good.[6]

Each academic year, we participate in *Ceiliúradh na nÓg*, a diocese of Kerry project, which challenges students at Senior cycle to develop a project in response to a social need and link it to the school mission and ethos. Similarly, participation in initiatives like Young Social Innovator (YSI), voluntary activities and fundraising can also be linked to school mission and ethos. These Senior cycle initiatives are presented to students so that they are challenged, both cognitively and affectively, to relate the school ethos to their own lives through activity-based approaches to the needs of local communities. Importantly, it is necessary to have discussions about the reasons the school chooses to offer these programmes so that there is a deeper awareness within the whole school community of why such outreach is linked with ethos.

As a Ceist school, we regularly engage in initiatives to strengthen our Catholic ethos. One initiative which has proved very successful in achieving a whole school approach to culture is the ACE programme (Alliance for Catholic Education) developed with the university of Notre Dame, USA.

Mindful of the present-day context and conscious of our strong heritage, the programme facilitated our school to renew our Catholic identity and present our very real ethos in a new way within our diverse society. The programme seeks to identify, motivate and develop leaders that are committed to revitalizing the Catholic character of Irish primary and secondary schools in the twenty-first century.

During the programme, staff engaged in discussions around the customs and practices which permeate the lived experience of all in the school community. We learned how our actions and behaviours express and integrate our core values and beliefs into the daily fabric of school life. We also noted where we believed our school ethos affects the learning, character and behaviour of students. The ACE programme framework helped implement these values and beliefs and thereby strengthened and sustained a culture that is intentional, coherent and consistent. Consequently, our school planning identified and made explicit where ethos was in action in our school. Ethos in action has become a regular agenda item at board of management and staff meetings where all recent school activities that demonstrate ethos in action are presented. The effects of this practice are twofold: firstly, it affirms this initiative is meeting our school's mission, and, secondly, it provides a platform for stakeholders to understand the practical application of ethos in school life.

School Leadership

The school principal is the custodian of its culture; in fact, many believe that the values of the principal become the values of the school. The principal has the duty to develop and shape the school culture to support its characteristic spirit. To achieve this, the principal has to dedicate time to reflecting on the mission and articulating what it means for his/her daily interactions and decisions. It is worth noting that 'Unless the person in a leadership position is reflective enough to discover and respond to a guiding vision, he or she will be constantly overcome by circumstances'.[8] The principal supports the school's mission and moral purpose by demonstrating through curriculum, policies and practices that the school is a values-based school which promotes the holistic development of the student in the Christian tradition. The principal should at all times promote an ethic of care by ensuring that the whole school community knows the principal cares about them and the work in which they are engaged. As Patrick Duignan said, 'one of the distinguishing characteristics of successful educational leaders is their capacity to provide a vision for the future and inspire hope in those with whom they work'.[9]

The principal must also manage change effectively to preserve and enhance the culture. In recent times, all schools have completed a review of the leadership and management needs and priorities in accordance with the Department of Education and Skills Circular Letter 0003/2018 (Leadership and Management in Post-Primary schools) in conjunction with the Quality Framework for Leadership and Management in Irish Schools, *Looking at Our School 2016*. This states:

> The quality framework sees leadership and management as inseparable. The framework defines school leadership by its impact on learning. It sees leadership that is focused on creating and sustaining environments that are conducive to good learning as paramount and acknowledges that effective leadership is essential for schools to be places where successful learning happens. It is a fundamental principle of the framework that, for schools to be led effectively, they must be managed effectively.[10]

It is imperative that this process pays close attention to the school ethos. While the *Looking at Our School 2016* document clearly believes the role of leadership and management is crucial to 'creating and sustaining environments that are conducive to good learning as paramount and acknowledges that effective leadership is essential for schools to be places where successful learning happens',[11] schools with a Catholic ethos believe that middle leadership roles and responsibilities can only be lived with the understanding that all decisions and actions are reflective of the school ethos. All staff, but in particular the leadership and management team, must encourage and support ethos at every opportunity.

As a Catholic Education an Irish School's Trust (CEIST) school, the CEIST Charter clearly identifies characteristics that define our school. The principal has a duty to ensure that this charter is evident in the daily activities of the school, to recall the core values at every opportunity and to allow time for the staff to understand the ethos and re-imagine it for the school each year. The charters of trustees are strong statements of the vision of the schools and it is incumbent on the principal to ensure that this core document informs discussions and decisions on school progression.

All members of the school community are communicating core values through a variety of mediums every day and should be aware of the links between our behaviours and our school ethos. To achieve this, we must begin with staff. Once staff make that connection, they too play a key role in connecting daily school actions and behaviours promoted by the school to the school ethos. Our own actions and words are powerful opportunities to bring the model of Jesus Christ to those we teach and serve. Showing and highlighting for each other the practical examples of how and when this is achieved is a most fruitful exercise. A positive school ethos is based on quality professional relationships between teachers and the way in which teachers and students treat each other. A culture of positive expectation must be built through systems of praise and reward where excellence is understood, written and spoken about not as an absolute measure but as the best that each individual is capable of attaining. Our intercom messages and thoughts for the day are reflecting through the lens of faith our perceptions of life. The school year book and newsletters always convey the core values and beliefs which inform our work.

Classrooms

When teachers develop in the students an appetite for learning and a deep sense of enquiry encouraged by skills in managing oneself and independent learning and critical thinking, our young people are not just preparing for a job but preparing for independent lives with a true understanding and action for the common good.

> The leaders of tomorrow are in the classrooms of today. All pupils are capable of imagining, creating and exploring. Fostering a commitment to critical thinking and creativity is the heartbeat if any living tradition and Catholic schooling is an expression of just such a living tradition.[12]

In the minds of some people, the ethos of a Catholic school is the business of only the principal and the Religious Education team. However, every teacher has the potential to influence a student's experience of school, either positively or negatively. There is more to each class than the content taught in the lesson. Parker Palmer famously wrote that, regardless of the subject they teach, teachers teach who they are, they project who they are, their values and fears.[13] If teachers in the classrooms do not promote and encourage the school's ethos and the value it offers, then they only pay lip service to the school's mission. For this reason, the time and effort that is given to teachers of all subject areas to discuss and tease out what it means to teach in a Catholic school is crucial, even if they are not people of faith. Our vision of Catholic education has to be recreated with the staff.

> The most important step towards evoking the spirit in education is to bring teachers together to talk, not about curriculum, technique, budget or politics, but about the deeper questions of our lives. Only if we can do this with one another – in ways that honour both the importance of our questions and the diversity with which we hold them – will we be able to do it for our students, who need our companionship on their journeys.[14]

While continuous professional development is much more frequent today and linked with the introduction of the Junior cycle, more forums are needed to allow teachers to talk about teaching and what they want for their students. Teachers are doing more than preparing students to get a job; they want to be the influence that makes a difference, be the person who prepared their students for the reality of a world that demands resilience, character and understanding of life. The importance of all staff endorsing the school ethos cannot be overemphasised because 'students will pick up far more by the example of their educators than by masterful pedagogical techniques, especially in the practice of Christian virtues'[15]

Code of Behaviour

The principal and deputy principal demonstrate ethos in their application of the code of behaviour, particularly where difficult situations arise. The code of behaviour is the school's set of practices and procedures that help students behave well and learn well. School ethos is promoted through the code of behaviour by maintaining an effective learning environment and by responding to students whose behaviour presents a challenge to the teaching and learning process.

On some occasions, staff and/or parental pressure may be exerted on the principal to act according to the letter of the law though it may not be in keeping with the spirit of the school's ethos. A teacher's attitude to their most difficult student can often convey a lot about their understanding of ethos. Context and circumstances must be taken into account and the management team must have the courage to apply Gospel values and act as Jesus would towards the student who has breached the code. This is often a very difficult task. The school environment is an emotional one which needs to be navigated with gentle awareness of the importance of Gospel values defining each response. School management must also challenge behaviour of staff which is not in keeping with school ethos and discourage actions and behaviours which do not reflect the school's values. The school principal requires consistent commitment to the demanding work of human relations by inviting people to have a shared sense of purpose. The benefit of having time dedicated to discussions on core beliefs, values and actions is noticeable when challenges to the code of behaviour are presented.

To achieve this, the principal must have the courage to be explicit to parents and other stakeholders about the school ethos and identify for others how the ethos can be reflected in the life of students. Teachers appreciate that explicitly encouraged behaviours, which align with our core beliefs and values, lead to the development of people of spirit and character.

The Timetable

The values of the school are also evident in the timetable. School management face many constraints when timetabling. It is very important to ensure an unbiased timetable which provides opportunities for each subject area to have appropriate time allocated. A hierarchy for subjects should not exist. Religious Education as a subject often suffers where timetabling meets constraints and where the subject (and consequently the school ethos) is not a priority. This is a real indicator of what the management team of the school values. The time of the day allocated to particular subjects can also communicate a message of the priority of a subject for the principal and deputy principal.

The Physical Environment

The physical environment often indicates what the school prioritises: artefacts, and ambiance communicate and reinforce core values and beliefs. While many schools have some outward signs of Catholic

*Ethos Wall,
Presentation Secondary School,
Castleisland, Co. Kerry*

ethos such as crucifixes, there is a need to go much deeper and allow our students the freedom to creatively depict the school ethos and reflect it as part of their own environment. Our 2018 Transition Year students designed and created an Ethos Wall to celebrate the values the school holds and shares as a learning community. (See previous page.) The process, design, consultation, presentation and dedication ceremony expressed the students' experience of ethos in the school. From the initial consultation with the wider student body on the school's purpose and mission to the unveiling of the Ethos Wall in the reception area, the depth of discussion and analysis by the students was invaluable. The Ethos Wall is a visual representation of the connectedness between the spirituality which the school seeks to promote and the daily life of the school. The story of its journey is truly an inspiration and a credit to all involved.

School Self-evaluation

School development planning and school self-evaluation are central to ongoing school improvement. At regular intervals the whole school community checks that key objectives are being met.

> Catholic schools will be more true to their identity when they measure what they value and don't just value what they measure.[16]

> We have found that where an intentional school ethos exists, evaluation is vision driven and clearly communicated to all stakeholders. When staff articulate the school's ethos and directly link it with the aims and objectives for school development, school ethos is at its best. This is an affirmation and empowerment of teachers and students and is directly linked to the realisation of students' full potential and an appreciation of the contribution of the teachers. The outcome for us has been a renewed pride in the school and people motivated to be their best while also building trusting collegial relationships.

Rituals and Practices

The calendar of a Catholic school is punctuated with religious ceremonies, and special occasions are always marked with a celebration among the whole school community. Involvement of students in planning and preparation for the ceremonies enriches their experience and deepens their appreciation of a multi-layered faith. It also deepens their appreciation of the Catholic faith 'that respects the freedom of the individual, indeed freedom as an essential requirement among those who follow the Catholic way as gift and invitation issued to all'.[17]

Parents

Communicating the depth of possibility the specific school ethos offers to parents is a challenging, yet very important, task. When the pressures of examinations are taken away, when a young person meets a difficult time, parents/guardians appreciate the care and respect that is shown them. The support at times of tragedy, the prayer services and Masses that bind the whole school community together provide a great source of strength and support. This is a time when ethos is evident and really appreciated. Parents/guardians expect the school to develop resilience and character in their son/daughter, helping them cope with challenge and able to find a path of contentment in life, regardless of the examination results or points achieved. They often choose a school with a Catholic ethos because deep down they cherish the values and life lessons they learned during their own school experience. While not all parents/guardians value the distinctive ethos of the Catholic school or attribute what they value in the school directly to its ethos, the importance of explaining the ethos to parents at every opportunity cannot be underestimated.

CONCLUSION

Many teachers believe that a deep spiritual hunger is evident among young people today. Catholic schools consciously address this because to avoid it would be to deny a significant part of the development of the whole person. The ethos of the Catholic school is focused on supporting the young person to answer the question: 'Who am I?' The aim of the Catholic school is that the young person will be able to find a meaningful and enriching experience in his/her peer group and learning community, and has had the opportunity to deepen his/her faith and self-understanding. To successfully achieve this task, a whole school approach to ethos is required because ethos is everyone's business. To achieve this in a school today is a challenging but critical task and all members of the school community are responsible and accountable for doing the best job possible to ensure Gospel values are actively communicated and lived in school each day.

8 A Question of Identity: The Contribution of Teachers to Living Ethos

MICHAEL HAYES

I suspect that the relationship between teacher identity and school ethos are viewed uncritically. I believe we often rely on vague assumptions when we speak about them, and we expect these assumptions to be shared by those with whom we converse. Do we all have an identical conception of what it means to be a teacher, or what it means when we say a school is a Catholic school or a Jewish school or a school of any other belief system? Examining what kind of teacher we mean or what kind of school ethos we imply is something that is done all too infrequently. Perhaps we need a common and thorough account of what a teacher's identity might be as we explore the meaning of a school's ethos. I expect we can develop a rich understanding of both by including teachers in the dialogue about teacher identity and ethos.

Research into the development of teacher identity reveals it to be complex, multi-layered, and unique to each teacher, notwithstanding the fact that there are many common traits in the identities ascribed to teachers and in those they create for themselves. I argue that much of what we have learned about teacher identity, and how it develops, can be applied to a discussion of ethos. Teacher identity and school ethos may appear at first glance to be very similar in different schools; but, on closer inspection, are revealed to be unique phenomena, particular to the person and to the school context. Both are never static, but always changing. Ideally, this change is always for the better. Whether it is or not depends both on the overt and covert forces that are encountered and the response to these influences.

To help us uncover the elements that contribute to the unfolding of teacher identity let us consider the insights of Aristotle. In Book Two of the *Nichomachian Ethics,* Aristotle identifies two kinds of virtue: intellectual and moral. According to him, intellectual virtue is developed mainly through teaching, and requires time and experience. Moral virtue 'is the child of habit'. Moral virtues are not given to us by nature, but are formed through habit. Nature provides us with the senses, and we do not learn to see by repeatedly seeing, or to hear by repeatedly hearing. The ability to use the senses is there before we use them. This is not so with the moral virtues: they are developed through use, and their formation is due to habit. Craftsmen, musicians and builders all learn their skills by making, playing and building. Similarly, the manner in which the moral virtues develop depends on the habits that are formed: 'It is as a result of playing the harp that harpers become good or bad in their art'. Performing any activity well or badly habitually results in good or bad performers: good builders will be the result of building well, while bad builders are formed by building badly. This is also true of the virtues. Just as good craftspersons are not born and need to be taught over time, Aristotle says that we become just or unjust in our dealings with others. He says that our early education is so important in the creation of good habits or dispositions of character, that it makes all the difference.

This places the teacher in a role of the greatest importance. If it were not so that builders and harp players developed their crafts under the guidance of instructors, each 'would have been good or bad in their several arts without them'. For Aristotle, moral virtues are developed similarly, requiring teaching and the formation of habits, through which character is formed. Aristotle equates *ethos* and *habit.*

Nobody can develop moral virtues on their own, primarily because of what Jung calls 'the fallibility of all human judgment'.[1] Humans can be victims of their own misjudgment and there are no guarantees that reason will always lead them to make the right judgments. Despite this, we constantly have to make ethical decisions, but as Jung says: 'Nothing can spare us the torment of ethical decision'.[2] Even though it can be difficult, it is through exercising the power of reasoning that we demonstrate our humanity, according to Aristotle.

So, how can this be done in a way that minimises the possibility of making wrong judgments? One way of protecting against the fallibility of our individual judgment is to share our judgments with others in order to test them. In such conversations, we can seek to develop better understanding, or better interpretations, of what constitutes ethical action within a particular ethos. Conversation of this kind is the model of inquiry of hermeneutics, which John Caputo says 'provides our best protection against the threat of tyranny, totalitarianism and terror in politics, and of dogmatism and authoritarianism in ethics and religion'.[3]

Hermeneutics uses the tool of dialogue to lead us to better interpretations of the world in which we live. The radical hermeneutics of Caputo, which couples hermeneutics and deconstruction, brings a layer of scrutiny and critique to the process. Everything is questioned, and assumptions are challenged and examined, so that old interpretations are tested and either renewed, developed, or replaced. I believe that when teachers are encouraged and facilitated to contribute to this conversation on the connection between teacher identity and school ethos, this will result in a better understanding and interpretation of teachers' own identity and the ethos of the school.

A teacher's identity is never developed in isolation from its environment, or as Aristotle would say, the teacher does not live 'the life of a solitary', because each of us is 'a social animal'. The people teachers meet prior to and during their careers, including childhood school friends and teachers, fellow college students, teacher colleagues, their own students and their students' parents, all have the potential to affect teachers' practice. The culture of the school is also sensitive to the influences of people, policy, traditions and events.

The isolation that teachers can experience in their work can be overcome when they follow William Proefriedt's advice and 'systematically and regularly sit down with their colleagues to talk about their daily work ... develop teaching materials together, argue over curriculum matters, exchange classroom visits, and generally provide support and feedback for one another'.[4] For Proefriedt, this activity demonstrates 'a commitment to a lifetime of sustained reflection with other teachers on the work at hand',[5] and keeps the concern for meaning, which is not simply the accumulation of information and skills, central for them.

The routes which people take into primary teaching in Ireland nowadays are more varied than the recent past. Many prospective teachers still follow the traditional route of doing an undergraduate degree in primary education. However, a significant number of teachers have a post-graduate qualification from any of a range of colleges in Ireland or elsewhere in the European Union, most commonly the United Kingdom. These qualifications, obtained in such a variety of contexts, qualify their holders to be appointed to teaching positions in Irish schools. Given the differences in their experience as student teachers, it is problematic to see how anyone might claim that teachers share a common identity. While few, if any, would try to make such a claim, there appears to be a widely held but rarely articulated assumption that teacher identity is largely homogenous. When this assumption is challenged and examined, the research shows that the identity developed by each teacher is highly individual: although it is influenced by contextual factors such as school location and ethos, the availability of supportive colleagues, and each teacher's commitment to continuing professional development, the resulting identity is something that is constructed gradually over time, rather than being something that is prescribed and present in each teacher in identical ways from the beginning of their careers. Even when their theoretical stance on education remains unarticulated, teachers reveal it through their practice, because, as Paulo Freire says, 'all educational practice implies a theoretical stance on the educator's part'.[6]

Allowing, for the moment, that all teachers share a similar theoretical stance towards education, it might appear reasonable to visualise all classrooms at each grade level being broadly identical and interchangeable, with teachers and pupils differing from their counterparts in other similar classrooms only in minor ways. To an extent this is true: the majority of schools teach a prescribed curriculum to cohorts of students organised by age, in buildings that are readily identified as schools, using similar resources, programmes and textbooks. The range of conversation in staffrooms is probably quite close to that in other schools with comparable age, gender and demographic profiles among the teachers. During each school year, many children move from one school to another for a variety of reasons, and most make the transition successfully, slotting with relative ease into their new surroundings. They make new friends quickly, they settle in to new classes with little difficulty in most cases, and get on with their learning, often using similar textbooks and programmes as they did in their previous schools.

However, anyone who has the opportunity to visit a variety of schools will recognise that each is unique, notwithstanding how alike it may be to other schools serving a similar community. The similarity is largely due to elements of the school that are shared with other schools, while what is unique about the school is its ethos, that element of its identity that is shaped by local factors, among the most influential of which are the teachers who work in the school. The identity of each teacher is a particular tapestry, woven from the many threads of background, personality, experience and values.

Conversations with teachers reveal that they are influenced strongly by their own biographies, and by their experiences as students prior to and during their pre-service teacher education. They are sensitive to the perceptions of them by parents and pupils. Their willingness to engage collaboratively with colleagues, including their principals and mentors, affects how their identities are formed. There are certainly many common features discernible in most teachers, including commitment to pupil care and wellbeing, high academic standards, and a desire to continuously enhance their professional practice, but these and other features combine in various ways and intensities, and at different times, to create each teacher's unique identity. So when we speak of 'a primary teacher', a certain image comes to mind, but this image is not a complete or fully accurate likeness of any particular teacher. It is something like a silhouette, recognisable at a glance but lacking in so many details that it is no more than a generic and vague illustration of something that in reality is rich, complex and exclusive to each individual.

Recognising that education involves more than 'relentless and mindless standardized testing', Parker Palmer says teachers 'must live examined lives and try to understand what animates their actions for better and for worse'.[7] His vision of a 'self who teaches' is more authentic than a conception of a teacher as a possessor of knowledge and competences. He illustrates the priority of identity over competence by sharing his students' descriptions of good teachers: a feature of their descriptions was the lack of uniformity in teaching approach, making it 'impossible to claim that all good teachers use similar techniques'.[8] What good teachers had in common was a strong sense of individuality and personal identity:

> The connections made by good teachers are held not in their methods but in their hearts – meaning heart in its ancient sense, as the place where the intellect and emotion and spirit and will converge in the human self.[9]

At its heart, teaching is a moral activity. Aristotle distinguishes between the intellectual virtues of *episteme*, the knowledge of subject matter, and *techne*, the practical skill required to teach this to others, but he shows that even these skills are insufficient. A third virtue, *phronesis*, or practical wisdom, must take precedence over the other two. Shipbuilders, craftsmen and artisans use *techne* to 'produce an object or an artifact', whereas the work of a teacher is 'to realise some morally worthwhile "good"... which cannot be made, it can only be done'.[10]

This fact has important implications when it comes to considering how we should understand and value the work that teachers do. Unfortunately, this practical wisdom is rarely mentioned in discussions on teaching, which generally tend to focus on teacher competence, which is in turn seen as a combination of *episteme* and *techne*. At best, the practical wisdom that comes not only from experience, but from critical reflection on this inner reality of teaching, is mentioned in passing as something that occurs automatically. It appears to me that the drive towards the homogenisation of the teaching profession is challenged so seldom that discourses on teacher identity which do not accord with the dominant competence-based model have been effectively silenced.

Teacher identity, present in embryonic form before entry to teacher education, becomes established in the process of socialisation as teachers construct their actual teacher identities. There are different perspectives from which such development is viewed, including teacher development theories, which identify discrete stages in teachers' professional growth, and teacher socialisation theories, in which the roles played by school culture and by colleagues are emphasised. At one extreme, teacher identity is seen, usually by policy-makers who seek pragmatic solutions to teacher education and development, as unproblematic and as something which spontaneously occurs as teachers progress through predictable and invariant stages. This view has driven the development of competence-based approaches to teacher education and evaluation.

The use of competence-based frameworks for assessment of teachers' work can help create shared understandings of professional practice. However, rigid adherence to frameworks as the sole means for describing professional practice can lead to narrow conceptions of what an accomplished teacher is. Teachers' voices are largely excluded from the discourse on competence. Focusing on teaching as the acquisition and application of a set of competences, while ignoring the character, experience and beliefs of the teacher, results in an impoverished and restricted conception of teacher identity. Fortunately, there is an alternative view which differs radically from the widely-prevailing competence-based approaches. From this other perspective, teacher identity is situated deeply within the person of the teacher and is something which can only be developed through critical reflection on the wide range of influences that teachers experience in their work and in themselves. Such reflection can be done alone, but occurs more usually in the company of knowledgeable others, many of whom have undertaken a similar journey from student to graduate to experienced practitioner.

Teacher socialisation has been described as 'something that happens to people as they move through a series of structured experiences and internalise the subculture of the group'.[11] It is a process in which these structured experiences influence teachers' development since how they respond to these experiences helps to shape the identities they form and the teachers they become. Dan Lortie's view of teacher socialisation has two elements: the need for 'structured experiences' to be provided for teachers to engage constructively with, and the influence of the school culture into which they are socialised. Simply attempting to internalise the school culture is not sufficient for teachers. If teachers fail to establish and maintain a critical and reflective attitude towards the cultures within which they work, they could be 'drawn into seeing things from the perspective and within the culture of the school'.[12] Even when the school's culture is benevolent and supportive, there remains the need for thoughtful dialogue in order to ensure that the culture does not become static or fossilised, rather than something which is alive and growing.

Paulo Freire emphasises 'the fantastic importance of the way people think, speak, act'[13] as they participate in the creation of new knowledge. In conversation with Myles Horton, he speaks of the need to understand the experience and practice of people, because 'without practice there is no knowledge'. To move beyond practice into new knowledge requires that the teacher understands theoretically what is happening in practice. Freire identifies two sources for the information which the teacher will need: reading and conversation. Both allow the teacher to enter into dialogue with others, who are either physically present or whose ideas are available in their writings. It is through this dialogue that new knowledge is constructed. Refusing to allow for the creation of new knowledge binds us to what Freire calls a 'static, neo-liberal ideology ... that converts tomorrow into today by insisting that everything is under control, everything has already been worked out and taken care of'.[14] He rails against a kind of education which is purely technical 'in which the teacher distinguishes himself or herself not by a desire to change the world but to accept it as it is'.[15]

I think Freire would exhort us today to continue the conversation and to welcome teachers as partners in the work of hermeneutics, of interpreting what their identity is and the contribution they can bring to schools of the twenty first century. But there is a word of warning: as Caputo says, 'Some interpretations are better than others'.[16] Giving equal weight to each and every possible interpretation amounts to nothing more than relativism, where we each have our own truths. Of course, the context of the conversation is crucial, and consequently it will look different in a Catholic school to corresponding dialogues in other schools. This is because there are some non-negotiable things. A philosophy of education that claims to be Catholic 'derives from a commitment to truth and is based on a substantial, thick or comprehensive conception of the purpose of human life'.[17]

I believe that teachers' experience with identity, seeing how it changes, develops and reacts with all of the influences and factors they encounter through their careers, offers a template that can be applied productively to the renewal and development of ethos. Inviting them to participate in the dialogue of what ethos means for the continually changing context of their work need not be viewed only as a dangerous or risky act which is best avoided. On the contrary, it can facilitate a continual and positive evolution of ethos. Jacques Derrida claims that affirmative deconstruction 'is not simply positive, not simply conservative, not simply a way of repeating the given institution. I think that the life of an institution implies that we are able to criticize, to transform, to open the institution to its own future'.[18] This opening of the institution to its future is paradoxical, according to Derrida, because as it starts something new, 'it also continues something, is true to the memory of the past, to a heritage, to something we receive from the past, from our predecessors, from the culture'.[19]

So, by opening the question of ethos to critical examination by teachers, among others, we are not, as some might fear, inviting its destruction. On the contrary, and seemingly paradoxically, we are reinvigorating it. Derrida says that this is not altogether without risk or danger, because of 'the tension between memory, fidelity, the preservation of something that has been given to us, and, at the same time, heterogeneity, something absolutely new, and a break'.[20]

The challenge, in my view, is to seek ways of refreshing and enriching our understanding of ethos, while minimising the risk of damaging it. Ironically, I think the bigger risk lies in trying not to take the risk: doing nothing, not questioning what it means for us each day, will only diminish ethos and leave it in danger of becoming fossilised, outdated and losing more of its meaning with each passing day. As teachers' understanding of their developing identity grows through a sustained dialogue with colleagues and with literature, so too can their understanding of the ethos in which they work be enriched through their critical and reflective contribution to the discussion.

I believe that teachers will have much of value to bring to the ongoing renewal of ethos. In turn, their own identities as teachers will be enhanced, not just because their engagement will keep the concern for meaning at the centre of the dialogue, but also that they will see, through the integrity displayed by all partners in the dialogue, that the Catholic school demonstrates its consideration and care for their own development.

9 A Culture of Care:
Ethos and the Quality of Relationships

MARIAN FARRELLY

We live in a time of great social change that has transformed the way in which we participate in the world of family, school, work and community. Despite unprecedented levels of material wealth, society is increasingly focused on the commodification of public goods, the dominance of consumer choice, and economic efficiencies in public services. Globalisation, while offering unlimited possibilities for communication and technical expertise, has placed new and ever increasing demands on schools as they struggle in the quest for higher standards and achievement. Such widespread social change with its emphasis on the individual as a rational and independent being, as an all-encompassing political and moral stance, permeates every aspect of our lives. In the search for standards and targets, the creative and the personal aspects of education have been somewhat marginalised, and this serves to accentuate the inequalities that exist in the system.

Public services, individual rights, and a sense of community wellbeing are increasingly defined in terms of the values of the market. For many, this means that services are only valuable if they are profitable or seen to be successful. Performance indicators are progressively used as a measure of public services and this has been, and continues to be, very evident in education with targets, outcomes and the language of performativity to the fore. This has influenced educational policies and has contributed to the restructuring of the relationship between governments, schools and parents. With market values to the forefront, Henry Giroux believes that we are now governed by three

'fundamentalisms':
- the values of the market place;
- the 'virtue' of self-reliance;
- the idea of 'freedom' as access to consumer goods and commodities.[1]

In contrast, the principle of individuality is one of the pillars on which neo-liberalism and indeed, the ethic of care rests. It is clear that the individual is defined and located as part of a community with its values, practices and culture. In a moral, social and political sense it is the community that constitutes the person, and that a person's aims and values must be considered when trying to understand individual identity. There can be little argument with the view that our human spirit is relational in nature. Charles Taylor[2] contends that it is the caring for the 'other' in society that forms us as moral beings. He argues that human living is dialogical and that our understandings of the good things in life are developed by our shared sense of a common bond with the people we love and those we care about. We need other people and they need us. This mutual dependency is the foundation for an ethic of care. This ethic of care is first focused on family, relations and close friends and then extends to our fellow citizens, students and colleagues, and even the wider world. We are very conscious nowadays of global interconnectedness and that our duty of care extends to all living things.

The effort to maintain and enhance this caring attitude shapes our way of being together. The essential element of compassion in caring, frames the relationship between us and is typically characterised by a commitment to others and a move away from oneself. In genuinely attempting to care we must consider the essence, the needs and desires to understand the reality of the 'other'.

> The commitment to act on behalf of the cared for, a continued interest in his reality throughout an appropriate time span, and the continued renewal of commitment over this span of time are the essential elements of caring from the inner view.[3]

A Culture of Care: Ethos and the Quality of Relationships

The affective nature of care is its most important characteristic in that it requires one to respond to the needs of others as 'unique, irreplaceable individuals rather than as 'generalised' others, regarded as simply representatives of a common humanity'.[4] The ability to focus on the particular needs of individuals and the specificity of distinct circumstances is an essential characteristic of care. Such a focus is important in highlighting the complexities that exist in various social and personal interactions that occur on a daily basis in schools, and the interpretations of individual responsibilities in these situations. Taking experience, status and personal values into account is critical for negotiating the complexity of relationships that constitute the daily interactions in schools. In a school community there are a number of types of relationship to be considered. The main one is, of course, the teacher/student relationship and this is the one that is most focussed on. A number of other interconnected relationships exists. It is obvious that schools are also the workplaces of the adults; and so the type and quality of the relationship between those adults, both personal and professional, frames the fundamental quality of all the interactions throughout the day. This underscores the student/teacher relationship which, in turn, is mirrored in the interactions that students have with each other.

An ethic of care involves an acknowledgement that care, as well as being an activity involving engagement of some kind, is a relational activity. Selma Sevenhuijsen[5] suggests care is both directed at others, at the self and the physical environment as well as at the point of intersection between all of these. Nel Noddings[6] further contributes to this with the belief that there is a difference between ethical caring and natural caring. For her, ethical caring requires an effort and is an activity born out of a sense of duty. Care of the self, care for others and care for the world around us are aims which modern education takes seriously. An ethic of care challenges the supremacy of a rational, intellectual form of learning which has influenced education since the time of Aristotle and has tended to marginalise creative and intuitive education and excluded many from academic success. We now understand that trying to condense teaching and learning to one irreducible method is also to deny the inter-personal nature of teaching. Care, in an educational context, is a way of reclaiming that unique interaction between student and teacher. It can be the framework for the organisation of all school activities and the basis on which academic success can be evaluated.

The constant danger is that the forces of neo-liberalism with its focus on academic targets, public accountability, and performativity pull educators and schools even further away from meaningful personal relationships with students. Continuous messages, both in society and in the school environment, about individual achievement, success and social status can very easily overcome the basic humanitarian principles of the well-being of others, compassion, justice, and the pursuit of the common good.

The affective dimension of teaching carries the implicit notion of well-being or welfare of the individual pupil. Jennifer Nias[7] argues that the process of teaching demands a 'culture of care' and that a child must feel safe and secure in order to learn and develop as an individual. Caring in an educational context involves very highly skilled actions underpinned by a strong ethical commitment which is sometimes at odds with the formal role of teaching. While the technical aspects of teaching are those which are formally valued and rewarded, it is care which makes the difference to the relationships of the school, and it is the tension between care and performativity that individual teachers must deal with on a daily basis. In a world where targets and outputs are used as a means to measure success it is easy to dismiss efforts to establish genuine caring as a waste of valuable teaching and learning time. However, there is sufficient evidence to suggest that schools which make caring the basis for the organisation of curriculum, and have a whole school approach to teaching and learning can also maximise achievement in the traditional sense of the word

The distinctive interpersonal and affective nature of teaching and its involvement with the emotional life of the students is best understood by an examination of Kathleen Lynch's unique taxonomy of 'other centeredness' which maps out and differentiates concepts of

love, care and solidarity in terms of the emotional response and the practice involved. This framework provides an opportunity to evaluate the various school relationships. Three categories are identified:
- love labour / primary care relations;
- general care work / secondary care labour;
- solidarity work / tertiary care relations.[8]

In the first category, there is a sense of intensity and very strong attachment coupled with an all-encompassing engagement. This type of relationship is mirrored most easily in a positive parent/child relationship or in a similar familial relationship. Many studies show that teachers, particularly primary school teachers, develop strong and intimate relationships with their pupils. John Baker, Kathleen Lynch, Sara Cantillon and Judy Walsh[9] contend that good teachers love their pupils, and few would argue with this statement. Students learn best in an atmosphere of mutual trust and respect. It should be pointed out that while this relationship may mirror that of a committed and caring parent, it is fundamentally different. Teachers are not the primary carers of the children and young people in their schools. While they may often carry out actions that are identical to that of a parent, or develop significant supportive relationships with students, their involvement in such caring is for the holistic academic and personal development of the child. In the above model, secondary care relations are normally associated with relatives and friends and represent a less intense engagement in terms of emotion and responsibility. Again, elements of this category are presents in teachers' care. The third category, solidarity work, is similar to statutory obligations, such as paying ones taxes to fund public services or voluntary work in the community. As teachers have a duty of care to their pupils as part of their paid employment, tertiary care relations are also recognisable in teachers' care practices. As we can imagine from an analysis of these three categories of care, it is not easy to locate teachers' care practices accurately in any one specific category.

Each of the three dimensions is inter-connected and each involves varying degrees of emotional engagement, commitment, sensitivity and organisational skills. Kathleen Lynch claims that while each of these three categories involves care responsibilities and attachments, tertiary care relations do not carry the same levels of emotional engagement or personal commitment. Depending on the context, both secondary and tertiary care relations can change to primary relationships in certain circumstances. While acknowledging that they are in paid employment, the care practices of teachers and the emotional labour involved do not carry any formal recognition. However, the presence or absence of such care practices in a school environment is very clear.

A more detailed examination of the types of caring relationships that function in a school show a number of common characteristics. All involve labour of some kind or another and all are premised on the notion that the adults have some understanding of themselves and their personal and professional roles. Andy Hargreaves has indicated:

> Good teachers are not just well oiled machines. They are emotional, passionate beings who connect with their students and fill their work and their classes with pleasure, creativity and challenge.[10]

Although there has been an increase in research on the significance of emotions in shaping teacher identity, emotions are still largely unexplored, and still considered of less significance in the daily tasks of school life. The same may be said to be true of care and care practices. Teacher narratives identify very clearly that care and a caring role in the classroom are fundamental to their sense of professionalism and to the personal and academic well-being of students.

The establishment of deep, personal and professional relationships with pupils involves varying amounts of emotional engagement and is the interface in which care practices are located. Teachers' professional identities are socially and culturally located within the lived experiences of their lives. Teachers can, and do, receive enormous boosts and motivational energy from caring practices. Such practices can be central to easing the natural tension that exists within the competing contexts of meritocratic achievement and the realities of school communities.

The first and most important of these practices is respect. This is particularly important in an organisation such as a school where there is a very clearly defined hierarchy of power and influence. Being able to show respect makes demands on each and every individual. Understanding the nature of the ethic of care can give the adults the necessary support to frame their interactions in a respectful way. When respect is modelled by everyone it is relatively easy to establish it as the basis for all communication and the foundation for all types of relationships.

Empathy is another of the most fundamental constituents of care practices. More importantly, it is a skill that can be taught and nurtured through a supportive educational environment.[11] In schools where there is a particular value placed on interpersonal skills, teachers can frame the boundaries of how students are to interact with their peers. This is because they know that their students learn best when they have positive relationships with those around them. Listening to the other is one of the most important parts of developing positive relationships. It requires an understanding of verbal and non-verbal cues, and learning to understand and appreciate the differences in others.

Teaching is a solitary and individual activity. The organisation of schools and the physical layout of classrooms make it very difficult for teachers to protect themselves from feelings of isolation that such a physical and intellectual environment generates. Care practices thrive in those school environments where the atmosphere is supportive and collegial in a genuine way. We are aware that an absence of positive social relationships between pupils and teachers will have an adverse effect on performance, absenteeism and pupil self-image and will increase the chances of early school leaving. These different relationships are formed in the context of the individual school policies and practices. Thus, the way a school values a child, the way it deals with absenteeism, what its approach to democratic decision-making is, how it develops pupil self-esteem and how it fosters collegial and encouraging relationships among staff are significant in the quality, assessment and effectiveness of a school's ethos.[12]

Care is fundamentally concerned with radical equality where the well-being of the other is to the fore and the response to the needs of the other is of central importance. Equality of outcome, to all intents and purposes, focuses on a similar result for everyone, which realistically is neither achievable nor desirable given the diversity of humankind. Amartya Sen argues: 'Equality in terms of one variable may not coincide with equality in the scale of another'.[13] Those who are wealthy may not enjoy good health. Those who experience disadvantage in one area often experience it in multiple situations. Thus a female member of the Traveller community is very likely to have her life chances mediated by issues of gender, race and socio-economic status. Equality of condition, on the other hand, is concerned with realistically equal choices. Care is a way of maximising those choices.

In the post-modern world, the commodification of knowledge is a feature of globalised society. Consequently, the relationship between knowledge and learners is de-socialised.[14] Care in the educationally disadvantaged context is about re-socialising that relationship and opening up those situations to students, and creating new possibilities to enable them to participate more fully in their own lives. All of this requires commitment on the part of teachers, students and the other stakeholders in the school community. Recognising that we are all receivers as well as givers of care blurs the artificial boundary between the caring purposes of education and the knowledge-creating purposes of education and between pedagogy and curriculum.[15]

Care may also be the mediator for those students who need assistance in negotiating the difficult terrain of school and learning. Care, as a moral stance, is about teachers taking responsibility for their students. Those who are nearest to the problem are those who must act. This requires a strong sense of communal responsibility. As Amitai Etzioni argued, schools are the next line of 'defence' after the family unit: 'If the moral infrastructure of our communities is to be restored, schools will have to step in where the family, neighbourhoods and religious institutions have been failing'.[16]

A Culture of Care: Ethos and the Quality of Relationships

The practice of care as an essential aspect of school ethos remains a hopeful and optimistic sign for the future. Taking steps to value and recognise care as an integral part of teaching and learning will go a long way to making education more meaningful to a sizeable portion of students and will help transform the nature and purpose of education.

10 From the Floorboards up: Ethos and Adolescent Faith Development

ORLA WALSH

> And when we play, we play, we play Mama,
> From the floorboards up.
> And when we dance, we dance, we dance Papa,
> From the floorboards up.
> And when we sway, we sway and sway,
> From the floorboards up.
>
> Paul Weller[1]

What does a 'living ethos' in a Catholic school look like if it is presented in full colour, in Dolby stereo and reverberates from the floorboards up? When seeking to answer this question one might suggest that the answer is rooted in the helter-skelter, vibrant, exciting, stressful, physical, competitive, academic and vivid world of the adolescent. For a Catholic school ethos to be part of the narrative in its teenagers' lives, it ought to have authenticity that radiates from a living, breathing pulse, a pulse that speaks of justice, equity and energy. The job of a Catholic school's leadership team, together with the teaching community, is to find ways of working together to harness their school's specific ethos and empower it to play, dance, sway and come to life. For it is only when we are firmly rooted in our school's founding story that we can confidently soar and carry with us the same creative energy that sparked and flickered into life at the very beginning.

A Catholic school cannot adhere to its ethos if there is a dichotomy between principle and the practice. One might suggest that it is incumbent on all who mobilise the cogs and wheels of a Catholic post-primary school to actively ensure that the faith *does* permeate each and every lived experience in that school. As educators, we know that this can and does happen in implicit as well as explicit ways. The compassionate love of Christ can be wholly evident from the front office to the back laboratories, from the PE hall to the art rooms, from the canteen to the computer suite.

FOWLER

When working to embrace the living ethos in a Catholic school one might find it helpful to draw on the workl of James Fowler. For Fowler, faith is not a specific religion or a set of beliefs; it is interactive and social, embedded in the 'shared visions and values that hold human groups together'[2] and is for all people a 'human universal concern.'[3] Thus it may be suggested that, for Fowler, the faith that one's 'heart is set upon'[4] is the business of the community. A Catholic school is a Christian community and so the alignment of ethos as a living thing is indeed the business of each one of us.

An explicit way of encountering and drawing from a living ethos in a Catholic school is to work directly with students on their faith formation. The faith narrative that abounds in the twenty-first century can create the perception that this is a daunting task but, from experience, it is a most worthy and indeed reciprocal one. The following points can serve to empower and eventually embed a living ethos in a Catholic school.

PRIVATE AND PERSONAL

At the outset, it is necessary to highlight the distinction between private and personal. In contemporary culture, faith is often described as being of a 'private nature'. Many people feel it necessary to defend their religiosity by stating that they are not a 'holy Joe' and add that they 'do their own thing'. In contrast, one suggests that it is necessary to find ways of establishing that Christian faith, by its very essence, is indeed a personal act but is very much within a communal setting, simply stated, one's faith cannot be a private affair.

> A new command I give you: Love one another. As I have loved you, so you must love one another. By this everyone will know that you are my disciples, if you love one another (John 13:34-35).

In order to follow in the footsteps of the Jesus of history and the Christ of faith, it is necessary to recognise that Jesus, at the outset of his public ministry, called together a community of disciples and so began his mission in community. Maria Harris and Gabriel Moran make an important contribution when they suggest that 'to be, is to be with'[5] and that a Christian's being in the world, made in the image and likeness of God, thrusts that person into community with others and God. Any Christian faith development programme must be rooted in the faith dimension that engages with one's belief in self, others and God. This engagement is a foundational tenet of any Catholic school's educational ethos. Faith is much more powerful than a belief system which is presented as a set of doctrines or a creed. Faith is understood as the core value system that is embraced by the heart and illuminates the process of growth graced by God in every human.[6] Fowler gives form and content 'to our imagining of an ultimate environment'[7] which for Christians is nothing other than the Kingdom of God.

RELIGIOUS ADOLESCENTS

To activate a living ethos in a Catholic school through direct engagement with the faith formation of its students – in any era – is not an easy undertaking. One might ask the question: Are adolescents religious by nature? Interestingly, Laurence Steinberg[8] holds that there are a proportion of adolescents who report that religion is very important to them. He clarifies this when he adds that adolescence is a time of re-examining and re-evaluating beliefs and values that have been part of one's story to date. Research has also found that many adolescents state that religion is ultimately very important to them. However, one might suggest from anecdotal evidence that there are many adolescents who describe themselves as religious but may, in fact, be describing an emerging spirituality as opposed to an owned affiliation to an institutional Church. It may also be added that some adolescents join a faith development programme because they are seeking out a sense of belonging, be it of a religious nature or otherwise. In addition, they seek the sense of connectedness that may arise from that belonging as they weave their way toward an emerging identity.

LEARNING AND TEACHING TODAY

In Ireland at present, leaders and the teaching community of many post-primary schools are grappling with the new vision of Junior Cycle education. This involves reframing learning and teaching as well as becoming specialists in a number of new classroom strategies. An interesting point is that these classroom strategies are reworkings of differentiated group work that has operated in classrooms all over the country for many years. Group work activities are designed to enable confidence, peer review and embedded learning in a communal and collaborative setting. This is what educational specialists are calling for.

To that end, one should go about a faith development programme using these same methodologies. In *Youth 2K* David Tuohy and Penny Cairns[9] outline a valid and reliable template for faith development and offer invaluable information to a Catholic school wishing to engage their students in authentic and relevant faith formation that works to inspire a living, breathing ethos. *Youth 2K* notes that anybody who embarks on a faith development programme with adolescents ought to begin first by examining the language employed, the participation called for, the space provided, and the process that will facilitate a holistic experience.

YOUTH 2K

Tuohy and Cairns suggest that those involved in this ministry should develop symbols that speak to the culture and concerns of young people, and adopt language that will illuminate as well as captivate the religious imagination. They found that the language adolescents preferred was that of poetry instead of prose, songs instead of Scripture. Interestingly, the language of faith is often deemed effeminate for young males who are exploring their religious as well as their masculine identity. Words such as 'healing', 'loving', 'meekness', 'forgiveness' are seen as 'soft' and more likely to appeal to males who are more disposed to their femininity.

To add to the confusion, Steinberg holds that from a very early age boys are socialised to refrain from exhibiting any feminine traits and are 'judged deviant if they show any signs of femininity'.[10] Girls, on the other hand, although perhaps pressurised to become more feminine, are not sanctioned for holding on to more masculine traits. It is important to note that the language of religion is in its essence symbolic and it ought to be a quest of any faith development programme to create age- and stage-appropriate language that is true to the tenets of faith while at the same time engaging the adolescent mind and experience in a creative, relevant and authentic way.

PARTICIPATION

Learning and teaching specialists note that strategies which promote participation ought to constitute a very significant aspect of faith development planning today. Adolescents seek to 'lock in', they want to wear the badge, stand for something, and work for a shared goal. We only have to think of the fund-raisers held, from bake sales to lip sync battles, dance-a-thons to sleep-outs, free dress days to 5K fun-run days! Adolescents are always eager to get involved and participate. Joanne Hendrick's 'learning by doing'[11] model is wise advice in any such programme. We know that active participation supports learning and it also provides a progressive path for the emotional journey associated with faith-directed content. In an area such as faith development within a Catholic school, one can only agree that collaborative learning, group work and active methodologies ought to be employed in order to create effective and authentic connections between religious rhetoric and adolescent reality.

SPACE

A third significant factor suggested as supportive for teenagers in faith development is space. In agreement with Patrick Hederman,[12] there is much more to life than the social media and technology. The 'more' he speaks of is an inner garden of the imagination which each of us should be allowed to cultivate.

He also references Martin Buber's I-and-Thou philosophy.[13] Buber held that we are defined by an I-Thou and I-It existence. The 'Thou' references the way we experience the world through good, reciprocal and mutual relationships. The 'It' references the way we experience being objectified, used or controlled in our relationships or by the world. In Buber's view, all of our relationships invite us ultimately into relationship with God, who is the eternal Thou. Hederman proposes Buber's philosophy as an original model of education, and emphasizes that the educational dialogue between leader and learner, between teacher and student takes place in the 'space' between them so that the 'secret of education is transmission from person to person.'[14] In agreement with Michael Hryniuk,[15] who supports a contemplative approach to youth ministry, this creative and dialogical space is where faith development and reflection take place for adolescents.

It might be helpful to add here that the reflective process, often viewed as an exclusive role for the leaders and teachers in a school community, is at the heart of establishing a living ethos within the student body.

PROCESS

The final necessity for any faith development programme in a Catholic school is 'process'. The concept of process acknowledges that one needs to become aware of the different transitions experienced by teenagers. It may be noted that at any stage on the lifespan spectrum, and particularly in adolescence, there is not a progressive set of steps whereby each individual makes headway at the same rate or level as others. Even within similar contexts, developmental milestones are different: urban, rural, race, environment, personal experience and so on impact the process of transition in an adolescent. Thus, to be aware of and allow for differentiation in the process of becoming is an essential criterion for any living ethos that is empowered by a faith development programme.

The transition into post-primary school marks a definitive move away from the local parish. It can be said that while many primary-school pupils participate as altar servers, and that post Confirmation students tend to abandon this role, this loss of role often leads to a loss of the connectedness that they may have shared. It may follow that they also lose their sense of belonging to a faith community. Other life occurrences for the adolescent involve the development of intimate relationships and difficult choices of future study and career. Harris and Moran[16] suggest that the 'age' and 'Age' have a significant impact on one's spirituality and faith development. Thus adolescence (age) is a heightened time of development in their lifespan; and to add one's environment and life choices (Age) involves further impact on development.

Perhaps it is not only called for but is in fact an imperative that each of the above recommendations by Tuohy and Cairns[17] be taken into consideration when working to establish a living ethos that is immersed in the founding story of a Catholic school. A living ethos is only living if it makes sense and is relevant to those who embody it. As stated by William Kay and Leslie Francis,[18] it is necessary to dovetail rhetoric and reality, since the religious and educational policies of a Catholic school must merge with the actual religious and faith development needs of the student body.

BELONGING AS LIFE-AFFIRMING

Taking the aspects of language, participation, space, and process of a faith development programme into consideration will establish a framework for authenticity because it begins with the adolescent learner and how they are in the modern world as opposed to how one might wish them to be. This authenticity encourages a grounding in belonging that in turn can provide a sense of connectedness. In their insightful work on the need to belong, Roy Baumeister and Mark Leary[19] determined that achieving a sense of belonging in a community is both productive and life-affirming at any stage of an individual's life. To experience a sense of connectedness, belonging and relatedness may very well contribute to an adolescent's sense of being at home and at ease in the world and thus reflect and give meaning to his or her Catholic school's living ethos.

THE RITE OF CHRISTIAN INITIATION AND BELONGING

In a helpful discussion of the Rite of Christian Initiation, Michael Drumm and Tom Gunning propose a more lavish and participative celebration of the sacraments of initiation and argue that 'effective initiation guarantees a cohesiveness and security and bequeaths committed members to future generations.'[20] It is equally important to provide support structures that endorse and engage the awakening of a sense of belonging for young members of the Church. Initiation may not remain effective long after receiving the sacraments if the recipients are not afforded the opportunity to reflect critically and to explore the possibilities of integrating faith into their daily lives at school and beyond.

Working within a school setting to embed the Catholic ethos from the floorboards up is an intrinsic and fundamental role that leadership teams and the teaching community are called to undertake. Marian De Souza affirms that leaders and teachers in any school community are invited to address the spiritual dimension of their students. She proposes that 'the levels of connectedness that young people experience are linked to the spiritual expressions of young people which provide them with a sense of self-worth and which help them to find meaning and purpose in their everyday'.[21]

LIGHTHOUSE LEADERS

I have had the privilege to facilitate for many years the Lighthouse leaders programme with both male and female adolescents in a number of post-primary Catholic schools. The Lighthouse Leaders programme is a religious faith development programme that comprises a leadership-training module and a peer-ministry module. It involves senior students (transition year or fifth year) and sixth-class pupils (from a neighbouring national school) who are preparing to celebrate the sacrament of Confirmation. The programme invites senior students to engage in leadership training in preparation for peer ministry, thus becoming more actively involved in catechesis for Confirmation within their community. The programme promotes living the Christian ethos through training senior students in a faith-leadership module and then supporting them in a faith-sharing module. This process happens in two stages: leadership-training over an eight- to ten-week period, (a double class each week) followed by five peer-ministry hourly sessions in the national school.

People learn by doing. It is therefore important that senior students not only learn about leadership but that they also learn *how* to *be* leaders. For a faith-development programme to succeed, it is imperative that the adolescents involved actually become religious faith-leaders. This means that the students spend time exploring and articulating their own understanding and experience of faith. The participants are offered the opportunity to lead the sixth-class pupils in religious faith, *from* a position of religious faith. The process spans two term periods and culminates in the coming together of both groups to celebrate the sacrament of Confirmation with lavish symbolism, vigorous voices and thunderous 'Amens'.

This particular faith-development programme is designed to be open to students of all levels of religious faith. The process depicted in Figure 1 (below) begins with development and moves to development

---

Figure 1: The Lighthouse Leaders Faith Development Process

Development
Development of potential
Development of potential of adolescent
Development of potential of adolescent faith
Development of potential of adolescent owned faith

of potential of adolescent-owned faith. It is an aspirational pathway, a subliminal layering that has the potential to move or pause at any time. The facilitator seeks to allow the senior student participants to explore possibilities and opportunities for growth in keeping with authentic faith development. This means that the founding story of their school can be investigated and incorporated, allowing an ownership of that story to develop which can then become embedded in the narrative of the programme in any school.

For example, the founding story of the Mercy Order lends itself to being part of the narrative of the Lighthouse Leaders programme. Catherine McAuley's life choices as a young woman, her compassion and empathy for others, together with her courage and sense of humour became the blueprint for the ethos in every Mercy school – expressed in care, respect and joy. To harness that same courage and embark on the task of empowering students in a Mercy school to follow in the footsteps of Catherine can only be life-giving and enable the school ethos to live and breathe fully aligned with the first steps of Catherine's ministry and faith journey.

BELONGING

A living ethos can only be authentic if the learning community has a sense of belonging to it. One might suggest that the overarching factor of any adolescent programme, in any context, be it faith development or of a secular nature, is to create a sense of belonging. This is indeed a worthy objective for all schools and particularly appropriate in Catholic schools. Tuohy and Cairns' research asserts that 'when they did find a sense of belonging, it brought with it openness to personal spiritual formation and reflection'.[22] When one thinks of the wonderful school events that take place and how proud we are of our teenagers who represent us in the public arena, surely their courage, motivation and participation stems from their sense of connectedness and a deep desire to express their sense of belonging to a school community. It has been suggested that most young people feel they 'are invisible to many adults and adult systems'[23] and therefore often feel excluded from the faith community that is led and coordinated by adults.

One can add that in the current educational narrative a sense of belonging is indispensable, and is now being proposed as the foundation for motivation and accomplishment among students. When working with adolescents, fulfilling the desire to be needed and respected is paramount and is often the most noticeable effect of participation in the Lighthouse Leaders programme. When one truly encounters the ethos and founding story as an authentic and relevant part of one's heritage, this adds to the holistic development of an adolescent because it promotes adolescent wellbeing, and enhances a school community whose founding ethos is Christian in character and communal by nature. When students feel known and accepted by the school community, as well as having what Cheryl Ellerbrock and Sarah Kiefer call 'academic and emotional support from their peers',[24] it greatly contributes to their sense of belonging.

This in turn feeds into their capacity and will to embrace and express the school ethos. Hryniuk reports that if adolescents are afforded an opportunity to explore their spirituality and faith tradition, together with the chance to engage in social justice, this 'has the potential to respond to the deepest needs of young persons for meaning, belonging, and a sense of religious identity'.[25] Many educators have witnessed this kind of phenomenon within their school communities and see it as an ethos relevant and lived.

CREATING A SPACE FOR GOD

Perhaps a living ethos in a Catholic school can simply be understood as 'creating a space for God'. This is not to suggest that one compartmentalises God and allows the school ethos to be aligned only to the liturgical calendar. Setting out to have a school ethos that is alive is to embrace it as a vital and life sustaining pulse nurturing and nourishing the entire school community. From my work on faith development programmes within Catholic schools I have both hard and soft evidence to suggest that these programmes serve to bring the ethos alive in the entire school. There are the students who participate from a faith perspective, and there are those who participate out of a deep need to belong and feel connected. In addition, such a programme sends out ripples throughout the whole school. Teachers have noted that a faith development and student leadership programme, such as the Lighthouse Leaders programme, does more for bullying and anxiety problems in school than any amount of talks.

INTO THE FUTURE

In a Catholic school environment, the desire to embed a living Catholic ethos into the narrative of each student's journey is a worthy one. To achieve this, it is suggested that a leadership team, together with its teaching community, take cognizance of the holistic dimension of adolescent development. There is a need to create constructs whereby teenagers who search for meaning and values can engage with that search using relevant language, being involved in active participation, generously afforded the space to reflect and always encouraged to freely engage in a process that is driven by the founding Catholic charism of that school. Having the knowledge and conviction to empower a living ethos in a Catholic school promises to secure a long future of cohesiveness, commitment and community and will serve to articulate and transmit the ethos of the school and cause it to be expressed and made manifest in new and powerful ways.

11 Ethos Supports Learning for Life and Lifelong Learning

GENE MEHIGAN

It is now four decades since I completed my Leaving Certificate examination. Despite remembering this experience as a punishing endurance test, what I vividly recall is a ritual that took place in the square of my local town on the afternoon after the final examination. There, much to the delight of a group of newly-freed scholars, a large bonfire raged. Not your typical fire, this blaze was fuelled by books like *Soundings Poetry*, Maupassant, *Macbeth*, and many others including the headline act on the Irish curriculum, *Peig*. All were consigned to the conflagration because of their association with the period of punishment just endured and now finished.

I remember sensing, from those around the rising flames, the relief and joy that our days of studying were over and that, by association, formal education was now finished. I also remember feeling decidedly uncomfortable at this book-burning ritual and its apparent implications. My discomfort was not because of any deeply held affinity for the particular texts but more with the idea that this might signal the end of study and formal learning. The experience I had in school had, in fact, encompassed much more than the narrow utilitarian focus of preparing for examinations. I realised that, along with the prescribed curriculum, the value of ongoing, voluntary, and the self-motivated pursuit of knowledge had also been inculcated in us. A love of learning which was overtly nurtured in our primary school years was maintained in a more subliminal way in secondary school by an ethos which recognised and nourished the quality and values of learning that was personally meaningful.

In retrospect, the bonfire response that afternoon represented a resistance to a prescriptive model of schooling where the emphasis was primarily on knowing and the perceived notion that formal education was to prepare students for employment. The reality is that, notwithstanding the burning ritual, most of the bonfire crew, including myself, continued with formal education thereafter. The reason, I proffer, was the impact of the informal learning that we had experienced through the ethos, climate, ambience and culture of our school.

This non-formal learning, none of which appeared on our weekly timetable, had the effect of fostering and nurturing a lifelong learning orientation to education. This prompts me to examine what it is about the culture or ethos of a school that can promote a love of learning and a more enduring engagement with education.

WHAT IS MEANT BY LIFELONG LEARNING?

The basic premise of lifelong learning in formal education is that it is not feasible to equip learners at primary, secondary or tertiary education with all the knowledge and skills they need to prosper throughout their lifetime. Therefore people need to continually enhance their knowledge and skills in order to address immediate problems and to participate in a process of continuous personal, vocational and professional development. The term 'lifelong learning' may be broadly defined as learning that is pursued throughout life, learning that is flexible, diverse, and available at different times, in different places, for different reasons. It is not just continuing education; it is much more. In education policy documents this has been interpreted in various ways, ranging from 'second chance' education, or linking secondary and tertiary education with industry, through to a much broader interpretation that concerns ways of engaging people with learning throughout all stages of their lives.

Ultimately, fostering a desire for lifelong learning means nurturing a passion for learning, and cultivating an appetite for pursing further knowledge. In order to do this, learning needs to have relevance, purpose, and real-world connection. This continuous pursuit of knowledge is neatly captured by Louise Watson who defines lifelong learning as

> a continuously supportive process which stimulates and empowers individuals to acquire all the knowledge, values, skills and understanding they will require throughout their lifetimes and to apply them with confidence, creativity and enjoyment, in all roles, circumstances, and environments.[1]

The literature also presents a growing body of knowledge about the components and characteristics of effective lifelong learning. Ruth Deakin Crick, Patricia Broadfoot, and Guy Claxton articulate the key human qualities essential for the development of lifelong learning and the creation of learner-centred cultures in schools.[2] They suggest that there are seven dimensions of learning important for lifelong learning.

First, effective learners have a sense of the need for growth and commitment to change as learners over time – this dimension they call the *growth orientation*. Second, effective learners like to ask the question 'why' – this dimension they refer to as *critical curiosity*. Third, effective learners look out for links between what they are learning and what they already know – this they call *meaning making*. Fourth, effective learners like a challenge and are willing to persevere through difficulty and confusion – this dimension can be called *resilience*. Fifth, effective learners are creative in their thinking, using their imagination and taking risks to look at things in different ways – this is the *creative* dimension. Sixth, effective learners have positive learning relationships at home and at school and are not totally dependent on others – they call this the *relational* dimension. And lastly, effective learners are aware of their own learning processes – this dimension is referred to as *strategic self-awareness*.

Together, these seven dimensions of learning are of vital importance for lifelong learning. Deakin Crick, Broadfoot and Claxton argue that significant positive changes in developing the learning power of students are possible where teachers focus on these dimensions.

Furthermore, if teachers introduce practices into their classrooms that stimulate and nourish characteristics like resilience, creativity, curiosity and self-awareness then the gateway to a positive relationship with future learning is opened. These characteristics of learning function like a mirror for the formal curriculum in schools and find a home in what we refer to as the culture or ethos of a school. Two of these learning powers – critical curiosity and strategic self-awareness – have particular resonance with my own experience of school ethos and its influence on lifelong learning.

A school embracing the development of these characteristics or qualities gives teachers the platform to commit to teaching which focuses on learning itself rather than outcomes alone. However, they do not appear on the formal curriculum. Kathleen Lynch suggests that these qualities, fundamental to lifelong learning, are cultivated through what she refers to as the hidden curriculum in schools.[3] The nature of this hidden curriculum can be summarised as those aspects of schooling, other than the intentional curriculum, that appears to produce changes in student values, perceptions, and behaviours. Terence McLaughlin suggests that school ethos determines the content of this hidden curriculum, and hence an interrogation of its influence on lifelong learning is warranted.[4] Such interrogation will lead to an awareness of the educational importance and scope of school ethos.

WHAT IS SCHOOL ETHOS?

Ethos can be a vague and somewhat covert term that is commonly employed in order to describe the range of values and beliefs which define the philosophy and orientation of an organisation. It can be defined as the characteristic spirit of a culture or community as manifested in its values, attitudes and aspirations.

The ethos of a school permeates every aspect of life therein, giving meaning and direction to school activities. It finds expression in shared rituals, in the quality of relationships, in the day-to-day running of a school. Such aspects, ultimately, reflect the characteristic spirit that identifies a school. The concept of school ethos is closely aligned to notions such as atmosphere, ambience, climate and culture. These relatively intangible and elusive concepts can be seen in all facets of school life including faith tradition, symbols, icons, communication systems and relationships with parents.[5] Other factors such as organisation and delivery of the curriculum, timetabling, management styles, decision-making processes, opportunities for staff development, discipline and classroom management also influence and affect school ethos.

School ethos can be both simultaneously high profile and invisible but its impact is vital to the experience of the individual student and the work of teaching. Its dichotomy exists in the aspirational or intended ideals of a school and in the experienced, or lived, ethos of the stakeholders in that school. Caitkin Donnelly referred to aspirational ethos as the declared values of a school, while experienced ethos included the lived experiences of all of the stakeholders in the educational environment.[6] The stakeholders include students, staff, parents, and partners in the wider community.

When I think of the ethos of a school, the feeling of the organisation comes to mind and the character of the school that one experiences on visiting the establishment. Although rarely to the fore in the consciousness of teachers and students, the ethos of a school is often readily perceptible to visitors. Even if the ethos is relatively imperceptible, it is, at the same time, a real element of school life. When much of what we learned at school has been forgotten and texts such as *Macbeth* and the works of Maupassant have become vague memories, a sense of the ethos of the school remains part of us.

Research of the literature brought me to the conclusion that ethos is the product of the culture of the school. Terrence Deal and Kent D. Peterson[7] suggest that although the terms 'ethos' and 'climate' are both commonly and interchangeably used, the term 'culture' provides a more accurate and intuitively appealing way to understand the impact of a school's own unwritten rules, norms and expectations. Culture is the basis on which the day-to-day life at the school is built. It is deeply embedded in the school's beliefs, values, activities and traditions. In this regard, the school ethos can be described as the ambience that is felt at a school as a result of its cultural history and its present experience.

Given the foregoing, it is no surprise that it is challenging to accurately define the ethos of a school. Pamala Munn, Mairi Ann Cullen, Margarete Johnstone and Gwynedd Lloyd describe school ethos as underpinning all practices, touching on all aspects of the school's operation and reflecting a collective understanding of how things are done in a particular school.[8] Similarly, Terence McLaughlin defines school ethos as the prevalent or characteristic tone, spirit or sentiment created from the activities or the behaviour of school members through their social interactions and through matters associated with the school environment.[9] These definitions provide the context for examining how the ethos of a school can nurture a passion and desire for lifelong learning.

IMPORTANCE OF SCHOOL ETHOS IN NURTURING LIFELONG LEARNING

When schools, through the hidden curriculum, put learners and learning at the centre of their activity they begin to move from models of teaching and learning that is based on the transmission of knowledge to ones that focus on developing the learning power in students. This does not mean that the focus of teaching is only on the processes of learning at the expense of the content. On the contrary, the focus ideally is on the integration of the knowledge, skills and understandings of the curriculum with the values, dispositions, attitudes and qualities necessary for lifelong learning.

By developing the power of learning in students, teachers position themselves as creators of learning communities that are ideally primed to nurture a commitment to lifelong learning. They can encourage and cultivate a personal commitment to learning by creating an environment of support that allows students to develop their own ideas, express their feelings, take risks, make choices, and, most of all, grow to be independent and critical thinkers. In schools oriented to lifelong learning, teachers are models for students – they acknowledge that they are still learning, and they are mentors or facilitators rather than detached figures of authority who are experts. Teachers are also models when they work collaboratively with each other and with other members of the local community. As such, teachers can be exemplars of school ethos because in their own learning and practice they function as transformative agents for lifelong learning.

In his autobiography, *The Master,* the poet and playwright Bryan McMahon identified three great hungers in the human being: the hunger of the body, the hunger of the spirit, and the hunger of the mind. He likened this tripartite life to a three-legged stool. The hunger of the body, he contends, is appeased by food and physical activity; while the hunger of the spirit is somewhat appeased by the endeavour to solve the mystery of human existence and to probe what may lie beyond. The hunger of the mind, of the imagination, is so ethereal as to almost defy definition but it does resonate closely with the critical curiosity dimension of learning as identified by Deakin Crick, Broadfoot and Claxton. The nurturing of curiosity has particular resonance with my experience of school and its influence on engendering lifelong learning. The literature, and my own experience, suggest that curiosity generally enhances academic learning. Indeed, some researchers assert that successful teachers often prefer techniques of instruction that excite curiosity; they recognise the stimulation of an inquiring mind as central to education and learning.[10]

When I think back on my school days, the culture of our school was one which promoted an inquisitive and creative stance to learning. It was the teacher who developed a sense of curiosity around learning that motivated me to study. Curiosity was stimulated by receiving regular feedback which identified gaps in our knowledge and reasoning. I still recall the Socratic method of instruction we experienced that cultivated an inclination to inquisitive questioning. We regularly had *fora* for open-ended inquiry, where teachers and students engaged in debate to develop a deeper understanding of a given topic. I particularly remember my history teacher who fed the hunger of our minds and fuelled our imaginations. He was an inspiring man who always left us with the understanding that there was much more to learn on any given topic before moving on to the next. As students we were forced out of our comfort zones through problem-solving and experiential learning activities. We were encouraged to analyse, understand, and think creatively. In doing so, he ignited the imagination, and instilled in us a hunger for what we did not know. In hindsight, this was a representation of our school ethos which promoted an inquisitive stance to learning and unquenchable desire for knowledge.

The second element of learning power stimulating the lifelong quest for learning is self-awareness. Effective learners are aware of their own learning processes, they are conscious of their feelings and understand their capabilities in relation to their learning journey. They use this self-awareness to develop and nurture learning. One important way to achieve this is to invite regular reflection. Reflection is accepted as a practice to facilitate lifelong learning[11] and is crucial in helping students monitor their own learning needs, and set personal goals for further learning. When students are encouraged to acquire reflective independence they build for themselves a richer and broader foundation to assist the development of their sensitivity and judgement. Interaction with both peers and adults helps to develop such independence. However, the space for this to happen is unlikely to feature on the already overcrowded school timetable. The experienced or lived ethos of the school is where this opportunity exists.

FINAL THOUGHTS

The educational importance of ethos in the context of lifelong learning is manifest, and many schools do encourage the development of characteristics now associated with lifelong learning. There are two inter-related impediments to schools focusing on learning beyond their immediate focus. The first is the influence of high stakes summative assessment at the end of secondary school. Prevailing competitive assessment practices in Irish schools may have an unduly strong influence on the school curriculum to the detriment of encouraging learning practices that students may use throughout life. Summative assessment, which is generally used for the certification of achievement, is emphasised for the sake of accountability. Formative assessment, which provides feedback for learning progress, needs equal recognition. To promote a disposition towards lifelong learning, a shift in focus is required to include formative assessment. This shift would reflect the assessment-learning relationship in the phrase 'assessment for lifelong learning'. It is an assessment *for* learning, not only an assessment *of* learning.

The other impediment is the reluctance or possible inability of some teachers to change from a 'transmitting' to a 'facilitating' approach to teaching. This reluctance fosters an emphasis on the content itself and does not attend to the underlying learning processes. It is important to encourage teachers to be transmitters of knowledge as well as facilitators of learning to avoid a superficial approach to learning that only provides the knowledge that is needed to pass an exam. The factor of high stakes assessment poses a significant deterrent to the cultivation of lifelong learning in schools.

To be a school that focuses on lifelong learning is more a matter of changing emphasis than starting afresh. The more difficult changes are attitudinal ones, such as valuing all students as learners, including those who do not have an inclination for study and academic work. The challenge is to encourage students to actively engage in the learning process, develop their own ideas, think more critically, and come to an appreciation of their need for lifelong learning. This cannot happen without teachers and school leaders who see this as an integral aspect of educational aims and values and promote it as part of the ethos of the school. This is what makes an educational institution nurture lifelong learning and inculcate an appreciation of education, not just in order to pass exams but to develop knowledge, skill, attitude and aptitude to their full potential over the course of a life-time.

Returning to the theme of pedagogical pyromania described in the opening paragraph, an idea often attributed to William Butler Yeats is that education is not the filling of a pail, but the lighting of a fire. The fire for learning depends on teachers addressing both the competence of learning and the will or the motivation to keep on learning. Parker Palmer in his book *The Courage to Teach* claims that 'tips, tricks and techniques are not at the heart of education – fire is ... our students want ... not merely the facts, not merely the theories, but a deep knowing of what it means to kindle the gift of life in ourselves, in others, and in the world'.[12] **School ethos can be the context for allowing students to gather kindling**, encouraging them to take risks and hoping that one day the materials amassed will burst into flames and become the impetus for lifelong learning.

12 Creating Good Memories: Ethos and School Gardens

SANDRA AUSTIN

What we call 'place' is to young people a wild compound of dream, spell and substance: place is somewhere they are always 'in', never 'on'.

Robert Macfarlane [1]

In 1984, Edward O. Wilson coined the term *biophilia* to describe the 'rich, natural pleasure that comes from being surrounded by living organisms' [2] and usually defined as the innate affinity of human beings with the natural world. Ask almost anyone what they remember about their school days, and they are sure to mention the rare joy of a day sunny and warm enough for teacher to move lessons out of the classroom to the yard or lawn. Certainly, one of my most vivid memories of school is the scent of wild garlic in the hedgerows as our class went on a 'nature walk' to our local park on one such day. I'd never seen garlic of any kind before, but the aroma was powerful and intoxicating, and I remember the thrill when our teacher told us that the wild garlic leaves were edible, and encouraged us to try them. I still smile whenever I encounter wild garlic today.

My love of plants and my experience of working with both children and adult learners in a garden environment drew me to explore the use and value of school gardens in Ireland for my Master's thesis in 2017.[3] A colourful and detailed picture emerged about the value and role of a school garden in shaping positive and memorable school experiences, drawing both on international literature and my own recent research.

THE SCHOOL GARDEN: CREATING A SENSE OF PLACE

Garden-based learning is a form of experiential learning that can impact children's academic outcomes, health and wellbeing, and social inclusion. The school garden can be a foundation for integrated learning in and across disciplines. Recent research in the UK and US highlights the impact of school gardening programmes on children's social, emotional and academic development, as well as indicating a value for school gardens in connecting schools with the wider community.[4]

How might gardens play a role in the creation of good memories? Memorable learning experiences are hands-on; they involve dialogue and discussion, the opportunity to be creative and to take risks. Research confirms that purposeful fieldwork creates significant and lasting memories and also affective bonds.[5] Students remember fieldwork and outdoor experiences for many years.[6] School gardens provide convenient, practical and accessible opportunities for children and teachers to engage with learning outdoors. They are easily accessible (usually on-site or close to a school), so children can see and use them on a daily basis. They are low-cost, they require no transport and little equipment, and they provide year-round opportunities for learning.

Gardens also foster a strong connection to place. In her recent review of school gardens in the US, Dorothy Blair[7] pointed out that well-designed school gardens can provide the repetitive access, meanings, and associations needed to create a bond with a place. Gardens are 'intensely local', and are a locus for development of children's imaginations, stories, and their sense of the world. In several of his books (*Landmarks* and *The Lost Words* are two examples), Robert Macfarlane warns that many of us are losing our vital connection to nature, including the words to describe nature, and calls for the 'rewilding' of our language, a new natural literacy, to help us to connect with and care for the natural world.

There is a strong affective dimension to a school garden. Positive experiences outdoors in early life are formative, and may be reflected as pro-environmental beliefs and actions in adult life. Exposure to nature and gardening in childhood shapes adult attitudes and values.[8] A school garden can be an educational portal to 'real life', reinforcing understanding of our surroundings, but also contributing to a commitment to manage them more wisely for the next generation.

My own recent research[9] highlights some of the many ways that a school garden can contribute to the life of a school community, fostering connection to place and creating memorable experiences. By probing the experiences, beliefs and values of the primary teachers in six schools around the greater Dublin area ('The Dublin study'), I gained an insight into the value and benefit of school gardens from the teachers' perspective. The teachers' narratives, their stories and anecdotes, emphasized the powerful affective dimension to the school garden and how much it is appreciated. Teachers and children demonstrated a profound emotional connection to the natural world as experienced through the garden. What I found is that the school garden in each of these schools is at the heart of school life. The garden functions as a place of learning, but also as a place of joy, of celebration, of inclusion, of connection, of healing. The garden becomes a space in which to create positive shared memories and experience within the school and wider community.

USING THE SCHOOL GARDEN

International research has identified a multiplicity of functions for a school garden, such as growing food, connecting students to nature and the outdoors, making a variety of disciplines relevant through hands-on learning, developing environmental stewardship, educating for nutrition and health, and bringing balance to students' lives.[10]

This is certainly true of the gardens in the Dublin study. A wide range of imaginative and creative uses of the gardens emerged in the teachers' conversation. The garden provided a space for reading circles, for imaginative play, for growing and harvesting crops, for studying both plant and animal life cycles. From the Aistear Garden Centre at Silverleaf national school, to the Selfish Giant at Goldenbough, from the bird hide at Greenwood to the pond at Wildhaven, school gardens provided spaces for learning across multiple disciplines and all class levels. They also provided spaces for play, whether running through a willow tunnel or jumping in and out of tyres on the ground. There were composting facilities in each of the gardens, linking with the theme of environmental stewardship and responsibility. Each of the gardens provided a harvest of fruit and vegetables that could be prepared and eaten by the children, often as part of a festival or feast. In each of the gardens children were actively involved with growing and harvesting the food crops. The way a school uses a garden is closely entwined with the value it places upon it. Identifying the affordances that school gardens offer for the school community is key to understanding their valued position in the schools that have them.

VALUING THE SCHOOL GARDEN

Several themes emerged over the course of the interviews for the Dublin study. Teachers, either implicitly or explicitly, highlighted the many benefits they felt the garden provided for the entire school community.

Gardens as Places of Joy

> It's a break for the kids, they're on their feet, they're active, they're moving, and they love it, they absolutely love it. (Jim, SN Silverleaf)

The primary feature of the study was the positivity expressed by all of the teachers and principals interviewed. Despite the challenges involved in setting up and maintaining a school garden – finances, time, expertise, and curriculum demands – the garden was invariably seen as a place that brings joy to the school community.

The garden provides a break from the norm, a space to enjoy, where working is a pleasure. Gardens are also spaces that can be enjoyed by everyone – not just the active gardeners – as places to sit, to read or to extend normal classroom activities on a sunny day. Don, at Orchard Educate Together National School, describes the freedom the children have to play in the school garden at break times, and how teachers relax in the garden after school, sitting in a sunny spot with a cup of tea as they gather their thoughts and energies at the end of the day.

Gardens as Places of Connection

Each of the teachers spoke about the school garden as a place for children to connect with nature, to raise their awareness and understanding of their natural environment, and to begin to care for it. There is much discussion in the media about the amount of time children spend on their computers and games consoles, and how that might lead to a disconnection from nature. However, as several of our teachers pointed out, the two are not mutually exclusive.

> They love all their technology, but from what they see … nature to them is still such a source of wonder … never assume that the techiest child is not going to be interested in a bit of earth and a seed, they really, they are, it's amazing to see. (Barbara, Greenwood National School)

All children need is the opportunity to experience the natural world, an opportunity easily afforded in a school garden. Also important to our teachers was the connection between growing food and eating healthily. Each of the schools grew a selection of edible plants, both vegetables and fruits.

> When at the end of the year there was a few of them decided among themselves they wanted to do a little speech at the end, that was one of the things they referenced as their really positive memories and experiences from school, was a chance to grow and prepare their own food. (Jim, Silverleaf SN)

Once again, we see that hands-on, experiential learning indeed creates memorable, positive experiences.

Gardens also give children an opportunity to connect with each other. Many of the teachers emphasised the role of the garden in the social development of the children. The garden naturally promotes social interaction and teamwork.

> I think the fact that they're all equal down there doing their jobs

and they just have to get on with it with whoever they're working with, I think that's very positive for them, that they're relaxed and happy down there and just getting on with it. (Barbara, Greenwood National School)

Gardens also facilitate the connections between school and home. Parents often play a central role in developing and maintaining the school garden. Children bring home fruit and vegetables that they have harvested. Grandparents are invited to participate in growing projects with the children. The learning goes both ways – parents often become interested in growing, or in developing their cookery skills, because their children are bringing home ideas or artefacts from school.

Once [the children have] caught them up, they've got their hands all stained, it's an experience … and all of a sudden you've a piece going home with you to give to mam and dad, and the parents are cooking them at home, making them at home. (Jim, SN Silverleaf)

Gardens as Places of Celebration

A commonality among the schools in the Dublin study is the use of the garden as a place to celebrate with the entire school community, through a school Feast, Harvest Day, Garden Day or Open Day event. This often extends beyond garden activities to include music, drama, and art-related activities. Food and feasting are generally high on the agenda. These are very much social occasions, and often past pupils return to share in the festivities. It's an opportunity to reach beyond the school gates and involve parents and families.

And what they grow, the parents come in and use to make a vegetable, big huge pot of vegetable soup, to give to anybody that comes...It's an absolutely brilliant day. (Mella, Goldenbough Senior National School)

So at the end of the year you have a big kind of feast for the sixth class, where they cook a full meal – dessert and soup and the whole thing, but it's all from stuff grown in the school. (Jim,

SN Silverleaf)

These feasts and festivals are viewed as highlights of the school year. The gardens provide a space, both physically and within the rhythm of the school calendar, to come together and celebrate a common identity, a communion of belonging.

Gardens as Places of Healing

Heather Ohly and her co-authors,[ii] in their recent review of the health and well-being impacts of school gardening, assert that they have particular benefits for children who do not thrive in an academic environment or who may have complex needs. The garden provides a space for calm, for respite from the intensity of the classroom.

One of the most valuable aspects of the garden, as evidenced by the teachers' responses in the Dublin study, is in helping children with special educational needs (SEN). Each of the schools in the study had enrolled children with SEN, either in mainstream classes or in special classes within the school. All of the teachers had similar stories to tell about the importance of the garden for the children in their school who struggled with daily classroom life, of how the children in their school found respite and healing, whether working or just being in the garden. Barbara, a learning support teacher at Greenwood National School, talked about an autistic child with severe behavioural issues who found calm and healing through being in the garden.

> There's a little bird hide in there, with a couple of benches. She was sometimes sent over to cool off, and we'd come down and sit in here and just relax.

Just being in that space helped the child to cope with her stress. It also gave Barbara insight into the power of nature to calm children's anxieties, and encouraged her to take an active role in the school garden. The garden has now become integral to her work supporting children with special educational needs.

> I've another child this year who's autistic ... she adores the garden, you know, she absolutely loves it. Again, I don't know

what it is, the green, the calmness, the birdsong … you can just see how … it just affects her mood, just how much pleasure she gets from it, from her senses. I have to say, that's had an effect on me to see … that it is a healing, a source of healing for them. (Barbara, Greenwood National School)

Mella, quoted below, encapsulates the attitude of many of the teachers interviewed.

I'd put the therapeutic above even the learning, say from seed to plate, how does it come from the ground to the table… Besides all that learning, and cross-curriculum and everything, I think I would put the therapeutic. (Mella, Goldenbough Senior National School)

Gardens as Places of Inclusion and Equality

Diane Reay's[12] study of social class and disadvantage discusses the ability of gardens and natural environments to provide spaces that are unclassified and egalitarian. This is a theme that emerged strongly in the Dublin study, where the garden is described as a space where everyone is equal, a level playing field where everyone can take part. Rowena Passy recognises that gardens have a 'valuable function in helping some children negotiate their way through primary school'.[13] They offer children a chance to feel a sense of pride, to make a valuable contribution to the school.

This is echoed strongly in the narrative of the Dublin teachers. For instance, Mella describes a group of boys that meet with her to garden on Friday mornings. These are children who may exhibit challenging behaviours, and/or struggle with classroom discipline. As Mella describes them, they are the most marginalised ones, the ones who will 'never be best at anything' in their class. Yet in the garden they become 'the head gardeners' for the school, and they feel important; they have a chance to shine. For such reasons gardens are regularly identified as inclusive spaces where children who may otherwise feel marginalised can participate fully. Whether they suffer from autism, behavioural issues or struggle academically, the garden is somewhere that children who might otherwise feel excluded can connect socially, participate fully and feel a sense of achievement.

> I have a special needs child in my class who wouldn't really mix with children, wouldn't be good at sports. You can see, in the garden, this child is amazing, he went around saving all the worms... then the class all brought the worms to him to mind. So there was great interaction there that he wouldn't have had ... before. So, socially I think it's really, really amazing. (Maura, Wildhaven Senior National School)

Gardens build bridges to the wider community, reaching out to local groups and voluntary organisations, encouraging them to come and use the garden. At Goldenbough, the local Men's Shed group helps with weeding the garden. The school, in association with South Dublin County Council, runs cookery classes for parents. There is a cultural garden, where vegetables from all around the world are grown, reflecting the diversity of children and adults in the local community.

Gardens as Places of Learning

Gardens afford experiential learning opportunities that are engaging, relevant and meaningful for children. There is an abundance of evidence from research that academic outcomes are significantly better in schools with active outdoor learning programmes. Children learn better when they are learning outside.

Several teachers in the Dublin study made the link with reading and literacy. At Goldenbough, children read Oscar Wilde's story of the Selfish Giant while sitting around the sleeping giant sculpture in the garden. The fifth classes read *The Boy in the Striped Pyjamas* as their class novel, and each autumn they plant crocus bulbs donated by the Holocaust education trust.

> I think the kind of deep, meaningful learning about the environment and appreciating the environment is best done by practical action, and having to make a bit of effort. Having to be out in the cold, to say 'I grew those, I went out on a wet, cold day and

> I got wet to weed those plants and now I have a plate of pasta. (Don, Orchard Educate Together National School)

> The children learn from being hands-on and active, and then they can bring it back to the class and write about it. (Susan, Berryfield National School)

Teachers see value in the garden beyond the time the children spend in it. 'Bringing the garden back to the classroom' has a lasting and positive impact on classroom and academic activities.

CONCLUSION

Schools use their school gardens in a variety of imaginative ways to encourage children's development across a broad range of areas. Teachers value their school gardens because they provide an arena for learning, space for pastoral care, a focus for school and community involvement, and a source of pleasure for the entire school community. This is labour that both figuratively and literally bears fruit. Results from both the literature and my own research also draw attention to those children who struggle with classroom learning, and the capacity of the school garden to offer respite for these children from the intensity of the classroom. The garden affords children a space to experience feelings of pride, achievement and belonging that may otherwise be lacking in their school experience. It is evident also that learning outside in the garden can be truly inclusive, in a way that is not always achievable indoors.

Ethos is said to be the characteristic spirit that identifies the school. It underpins the policies and practices within the learning community. It is embedded in the fabric of the school and reaches beyond the wider school community. A school garden is both a reflection of the ethos of the school itself, and a force which influences and shapes that ethos. Passy highlights that school culture/ethos plays an important part in decisions related to the garden by providing the framework for the level of integration of the garden into school life. The traditions and choices made by principals and teachers over time help to give schools their own rituals and identities. Having a school garden that is loved, used and valued suggests a school culture that is inclusive, that seeks to encourage all children to develop socially, emotionally and academically and that has a creative approach to fostering this development. Passy also describes the 'ripple effect' that a school garden can have throughout a school community and beyond. The 'sheer pleasure of creating a garden' is shared by those who enjoy the beauty that results.

It is clear too from the Dublin study that school gardens have a profound impact on children, parents, teachers and the wider community. Gardens enrich school life and deepen the bonds between school and community. The positive memories associated with them are lasting and significant. For both children and adults they are places of 'dream, spell and substance', sources of inspiration, of affirmation, of positivity for the entire community. I'll leave the last word to Don, from Orchard Education Together National School). He puts it simply: 'The teachers enjoy it, the children enjoy it. It enhances everything.'

13 Ethos in School Traditions, Symbols and Rituals

JOHN-PAUL SHERIDAN

Some time ago I had an opportunity to introduce a parish to the *Do This in Memory* programme as we prepared the children for their First Holy Communion. Introducing it to a parish that had never been part of it before gave me a keen insight into the gradual initiation of the children into the liturgical assembly. Whether they have been to Sunday Eucharist much before, or if they had just been there as a silent observer, they now began to be involved a little more. The programme has always been a source of joy and encouragement for all involved. Over ten Sundays the children assisted at the liturgy in small ways, and became aware of what 'full, active and conscious participation' might mean. As a form of liturgical socialisation, the children observed the congregation around them, and this was reflected in the way they conducted themselves as time went on. By the time we celebrated First Holy Communion, the children didn't need to be endlessly rehearsed in preparation for the ceremony. This was a positive by-product of their liturgical participation. They became familiar with the place, easy with their readings, bringing up the gifts and, most importantly, very settled into this place of the liturgical assembly, no longer as passive observers, but as contributing members with their parents, grandparents, families, and the community of the parish.

Another recent experience was an invitation to a para-liturgy in a post-primary school to mark and celebrate the events of Holy Week. It consisted of a service of prayer, reflection, readings, accompanied by music and images. It was a beautiful and spiritual occasion and really helped us enter the days of Holy Week in a profound way. Apart from how well it was organised and executed, I was struck by how well behaved the pupils were, how at home they were at this liturgy and how they entered into the spirit of the occasion. It may not have been a profound experience for everyone, but the atmosphere and the silence were never compromised. These two experiences have highlighted for me, again, the powerful role of liturgy in the life-long education and faith formation of children.

Admittedly, there is a big difference in liturgical participation between primary and post-primary schools. We can certainly see the role of the primary school in the sacramental life of the child, but we should not shy away from the opportunities for liturgical formation in the post-primary setting; the principles are fundamentally the same for both learning environments. *The Religious Dimension of Education in a Catholic School* outlines the importance of the liturgical formation of the pupil.[1] It sees Catholic schools as having a complementary part to play in the aims of catechesis within a community. The work done in Catholic schools should be a continuation of what began at Baptism. Baptism is the beginning of the life of faith for the child and as they grow and flourish in their human capacity, they are invited to grow and flourish in their communion with the person of Jesus Christ. 'It is evident … that religious instruction cannot help but strengthen the faith of a believing student, just as catechesis cannot help but increase one's knowledge of the Christian message.'[2]

One of my favourite passages from Scripture, and one that I use at the beginning of many modules on religious education, theology and liturgy, is Acts 2:42-47.[3] It describes the early followers of Jesus and how they lived their lives and their faith. It is something of a Garden of Eden story, before the serpent of ambition, jealousy and rivalry took hold. These early followers were devoted to the person of Jesus as prayerful, generous and, most importantly, joyous people. Their inner life and outer life, their prayer and worship were matched by their witness and service. Followers today are invited to a similar experience of the truth and reality of Jesus today and, in their response, to proclaim and witness the Good News; to build up a caring Christian community based on Gospel values; to celebrate faith in worship, prayer, and liturgical participation; and to serve neighbour, especially the poor and vulnerable. Likewise, we seek to create a living Christian community in the Catholic school, and invite students to mirror and imitate the life and teaching, the human qualities and transforming presence of Jesus by inserting them 'organically into the life of the Church'.[4] How can we celebrate the great events of the school year and laud its successes, except in a celebration of a true thanksgiving that is Eucharist? How can we comfort the troubled and stand in solidarity with the bereaved if not in prayer? Liturgy and prayer are meant to be the expression and language of faith in God and, as such, meant to be the powerhouse of a Catholic school, not simply an occasional activity, but one that pervades everything that the schools is and does.

The *Directory for Masses with Children*, introduced in 1973, is a document replete with a rich theology of liturgy, advocating and promoting the full, active and conscious participation of children at the Sunday Liturgy.[5] Chapter Two discusses Masses in which children participate along with adults. The witness of the adult faithful is mentioned. This is the witness of adults acting in a particular manner in the liturgical assembly. When parents sit in places which maximise the viewing potential for their children it helps them observe the rich and illuminating rituals of the Church. They can also observe the adults around them with their hands joined, with their heads bowed in reverence and respect. They see them standing, sitting or kneeling at various times; they witness the action of a community turning to each other and offering the gift of peace. If children observe adults acting in a manner that is reverent and prayerful, they are likely to imitate this, even before consciously understanding what is happening. Likewise, the presence of the children, taking their first tentative steps into the Sunday assembly, might be an encouragement to adults.

Chapter Three of the *Directory* refers to Masses with children in which only a few adults participate. This is an important chapter for those preparing and celebrating school Masses, class Masses or para-liturgies in a school setting. The term 'children's Mass', often used for this type of Celebration, is not helpful. Liturgy welcomes everyone and so our efforts in liturgical preparation should be to create an atmosphere of community, prayer and worship for all who gather. Jeremy Gallet sees the value of the *Directory* from two perspectives. On the one hand, the guidelines might suggest that much of the *Directory* 'is geared to smaller, intentional liturgies that might be celebrated within a religious education or parochial school setting, however, the solid formative principles in this document may apply to all liturgical celebrations whether with children or with adults, whether celebrated on a Sunday or a weekday, whether the place of celebration is a small school chapel or a large urban church.'[6]

There is something wonderful in assisting children as they prepare the liturgy. As with any group involved in liturgical preparation, they need guidance and assistance to help discern what is appropriate and uplifting in a liturgical celebration. Liturgy prepared for children does not have to be 'all about them'. Liturgy prepared by children is a sure and certain way to avoid this and let their creativity shine through. In children's liturgy there should neither be an excessive creativity nor an oversimplification. In this way, we are not seen to be spoon-feeding the children during liturgy or watering down what is a sacred event. The *Directory* 'does not encourage anything childish, casual, or trivial,'[7] but rather emphasises how children 'can as full members of Christ's Body take part actively with the people of God in the Eucharist, sharing in the Lord's table and the community of their brothers and sisters.'[8] In liturgy where the greater part of the congregation is children we might simplify the language, but we still proclaim the Word of God; while we might temper our preaching for the children's benefit, we still offer something uplifting and encouraging that the whole congregation can understand. While I might address the children during the *Do This in Memory* Masses, the message is just as relevant to their parents and guardians. On the occasion where I preach at Masses to celebrate the beginning or end of the school year, the homily will always be addressed to the children, but with a consciousness of the teachers, parents, staff and other adults present.

It should be noted that the *Directory* norms are meant for children in the 5-11 age-group. This means that liturgical adaptation at post-primary level can and should occur but not to the same extent. Children over the age of 11, even with a limited liturgical exposure, are expected to have enough knowledge and experience of life and the symbolic to be full participants in an adult liturgy and thereby more than capable of entering into the spirit of the liturgy. Having experienced sacramental preparation for both First Holy Communion and Confirmation, children in post-primary education will be familiar with symbol, ritual and word – three aspects that can be focussed on when preparing liturgy for and with older children. They may need some coaxing as to what they remember from primary school, but in a world replete with symbols, it should not be too difficult to begin a discussion.

The *Directory* mentions the link between the liturgy and the human values that are expressed in the Eucharistic Celebration. They are: relationships, community activity, exchange of greetings, capacity to listen and to seek and grant pardon, expression of gratitude, experience of symbolic actions, a meal of friendship and festive celebrations.[9] The parallel between human values and liturgical experiences should not be underestimated. When we gather on a Sunday morning for Mass, or in the school hall for a school celebration, we are. first and foremost, a human community. We act that way. We chat and gossip, we greet neighbours and other people. Then we begin to settle and become a community, a priestly people gathered to tell the story and break the bread. None of the actions and gestures we perform over the course of the next hour are any different, *per se*, to the human actions and gestures we will perform in the remainder of the week; what changes is their significance. We carry our humanity into the Church to be united with the humanity and divinity of Jesus, and we carry it out at the end of Mass healed, nourished, transformed and ready to announce the Gospel and play our part in establishing the Kingdom of God. This is the reason why the presence of children at the Eucharist is so important. When children can create the link between human experience and the sacred then they have made a significant connection for the development of their inner life. Their presence in the liturgical assembly is one of the processes by which children are liturgically educated and prepared to participate in the worshipping community.

Another place for liturgical education is in the classroom and the religious education programme. Educators talk about the spiral curriculum[10] as an aid to the child's learning, and it is as valid and valuable a method of learning in liturgical education as it is in every other part of education. What students are taught is meant to enhance their understanding of what they will experience later in the liturgical assembly. Having been taught about the Eucharist, they will then understand what is being celebrated, how it is being celebrated, and also the underlying values that are being celebrated. Liturgical education cannot just be an intellectual exercise – participation is the key. It is learning by doing or, in this case, learning by celebrating.

It is worthwhile to look a little longer at these human values mentioned by the *Directory*. It mentions fostering a community spirit.[11] Stand in a playground on any day and watch children's ability to have fun, to make up games, to natter about school life or television programmes, to play, to fight, to forgive and make up. While all these moments are occasions of learning, they are also rungs on the ladder of socialisation. The playground and the classroom are places where we learn to act and react with others. It is where we come into contact with adults other than our parents and where we learn to listen; where we learn to take turns, play fairly and put up our hand when we want to speak. We are learning to socialise; to take our place in a community. This is a human value which must be sacramentalised, in that there is a sacredness in learning to be a community. We take moments on the journey of life, *e.g.*, birth, marriage, death and we observe and celebrate them in the context of prayer and sacraments.

Children who are part of the planning stage of liturgy cannot but be invested in its successful celebration. Children who assume different roles and ministries in liturgy should have the opportunity to understand and reflect on that role. This is what builds up their sense of being part of the community, and it is something with which teachers can assist when liturgy is celebrated in the school. These experiences and lessons can have a sustained effect when the children are in the wider sphere of the parish community. Children who take part in liturgy and who also have the opportunity to reflect on what they have been doing will likely lead to a deeper understanding of liturgical action.

Listening is fast becoming a lost art. The social media generation is making it tougher for any of us to really listen. At liturgy, there is a moment when we have to listen. Children are often very engaged when listening to stories in class or at home. They become absorbed with the characters and plots of a story. This is why stories from the Scriptures are so important in the liturgy. Learning to listen is so essential in education and it is the same in liturgical education. The Word of God should never be substituted in any liturgy. It is revelation and it is narrative. It opens up the loving plan of God and invites us first to listen and then to participate in that plan. How much more are children likely to listen when it is one of their own who proclaims that loving plan?

The human value of saying sorry is something that children learn early in their lives. It is a human value that needs to be repeated over and over again. In the school context, prayer services might begin with children reflecting on times when they haven't lived as Jesus asked them to, and asking forgiveness before continuing this occasion of prayer and reflection. This is not in an attempt to burden children with notions of sin or guilt but a means to remind them of the areas in their lives where they need to grow. It is also an opportunity to help them understand that their efforts to change are encouraged and supported by the God who loves completely and forgives as often as necessary. In a time when attendance at the Sacrament of Reconciliation is not what it used to be, perhaps we need more opportunities to forgive and ask forgiveness.

Expressions of gratitude are among our earliest memories as human beings. Like saying sorry, saying thanks is one of the first things we learn from our parents. They constantly remind us of the importance of gratitude. The word *eucharist* means to give thanks, so this expression of gratitude which we celebrate is imbedded in our most sacred action. However, thanks should not be limited to Eucharist. In school we tend to gather for prayer only on special occasions: when there is a tragedy or a catastrophic world event; we gather at the beginning and end of the school year. Perhaps we should gather for happy occasions also when we have something to be thankful for. If the school wins the local camogie league, do we think of gathering in prayer? When the school has done a great fundraiser for a charity, do we think of celebrating the efforts of the staff and students in prayer?

From an early age a child becomes conscious that the world is full of symbols. They recognise brands and logos while often still unable to speak. As they grow, they begin to understand the secular symbols around them. The world of liturgy is also full of symbols and symbolic actions, and teachers have an invaluable role in helping to unpack the world of liturgical symbols. We are very conscious of it during sacramental preparation, but it is not confined to this work alone. The use of a sacred space in the classroom to accompany the *Grow in Love* primary school catechetical programme is a wonderful innovation and assists in the introduction of religious symbols into the classroom. The students have opportunities to complement what they are learning by placing appropriate symbols in the sacred space. This is not only an aid to learning, but also an aid to liturgical formation. In preparing for liturgy, there is an opportunity for the input of children. Asking a group of children what might symbolise the year gone by might elicit different responses and suggestions than the usual globe and copybook. These symbols can then form part of the homily/reflection during the liturgy

No one knows better how to celebrate than children. Ask most children when their next birthday is, and they can tell you months and days. They can tell you the number of sleeps till Christmas. Their excitement and the spirit which surrounds their particular festive celebrations can be contagious. What is it that elicits this excitement?

It is the joy of anticipation and the excitement of what is to come. It is the sense that it will be a special day and there will be rituals and traditions observed. This must not be lost when it comes to liturgy; it should have the sense that it is a celebration. Children's participation in preparing for the liturgy is one way of creating some excitement and enthusiasm. Certainly, liturgy should not be a carnival and there should be sense of the sacred and appropriate reverence. There is a time and place for everything, but liturgy should be joyous. It should be full of life and energy.

The values which children learn in the everyday world, take on a particular significance in Church.

> Liturgy as faith-actions of the Christian community is ... that marvellous meeting point of the whole community both to celebrate its faith and at the same time to have that faith nourished by word and sacrament. In this light the *experience* of liturgy becomes far more significant than merely verbal explanations about the liturgy. Children are not excluded because they so not yet understand; they participate – they experience – and later will develop their rational understanding.[12]

In the past children learned to engage in the liturgical space almost by osmosis (in observing parents, grandparents and other members of the congregation). This may not be the case so much today. However, it is my experience that they are more than willing to learn and are often excited and animated by the variety of new things to be seen, experienced, and learned. With the decline in regular Church attendance, children need particular and specific catechesis when it comes to the liturgy. The school has often become the place of catechesis. It is certainly true that liturgy is education – education through experience and education through participation.[13] The liturgical catechesis of children is not for the purposes of teaching them to behave in Church 'in the sense that the children must keep quiet and not disturb the adults. We are speaking of something far deeper. We are speaking of preparation for worship.'[14]

While not meant to be a substitute for the home, the school acts in a complementary manner. Every magisterial document dealing with Catholic education, religious education and catechesis begins with mention of the parents as the primary educators of their children. The parents should be the primary educators of their children in liturgical catechesis, but often they are not. The *Directory* also mentions the central role of parents,[15] and acknowledges the reality of the present situation:

> Today the circumstances in which children grow up are not favourable to their spiritual progress. In addition, parents sometimes scarcely fulfil the obligations of Christian formation they accepted at the baptism of their children.[16]

In the past, this was often through no fault of the parents. Sacramental preparation became the responsibility of the school and, while there were limited opportunities for parental involvement, dedicated teachers find new and exciting ways in which to engage the minds and hearts of children as they learn about the liturgy and begin to express their faith. This is beginning to change. Many parents have been enthusiastic about the *Do This in Memory* programme. They have entered into the spirit of the programme and it has been a good experience for them as well as for their children. The *Directory* recognizes that even if the faith of parents is weak and they still 'wish their children to receive Christian formation, they should be urged at least to communicate to their children the human values mentioned already and, when the occasion arises, to participate in meetings of parents and in non-Eucharistic celebrations held with children.'[17] Perhaps this is the key: the parents teach the human values to their children and it is the school and the parish that teach the children how these human values find their highest expression in the liturgy.

The same documents mentioned above emphasise time and again the place and importance of the school community. It is one of the many communities that children inhabit in the course of their childhood – Church, home, sports and other clubs or associations, the village, town or housing estate. Each is governed by its own *mores* and traditions and by its own rules and norms. The school is probably the most influential after the home, by virtue of the amount of time children spend there. School can be many things to students, especially in difficult situations. The school is a community where there is support and encouragement, security and routine. In as much as we seek to create a community of learning for our students, we also seek to create a community of faith, which must 'continually be fed and stimulated by its Source of life, the Saving Word of Christ as it is expressed in Sacred Scripture, in Tradition, especially liturgical and sacramental tradition, and in the lives of people, past and present, who bear witness to that Word.' [18] The *Directory* mentions that this community assists the children through witness, charity and celebration.[19] This is done in times of prayer and sacraments and celebrations in the life of the school. Edward Matthews sees these qualities as equally applicable to teachers as part of the whole community. Teachers understand this and seek to impart this knowledge to those in their charge. This makes for what was mentioned earlier, 'that marvellous meeting point of the whole community both to celebrate its faith and at the same time to have that faith nourished by word and sacrament.' [20] Regardless of its academic prowess or its sporting achievements, the Catholic school must take recourse constantly to the life-blood of its faith, ethos and identity, thereby manifesting the highest expression of what is at the core of its life and work.

14 Creating a Sacred Space: Reflective Practice

GERRY O'CONNELL

Almost every teacher I know came to teaching with some sort of vision of the kind of teacher they would be and what kind of care they would bring to those they teach. They came filled with inspiration and enthusiasm, wanting of make a difference in the lives of children. They wanted to live the dream the poet David Whyte calls 'that astonishing magic that you create when you say the right thing at the right time in a child's life – and they remember it for the rest of their life'.[1]

What happens to such a vision in the busy world of teaching and learning? Why is it that teachers settle for something less? Does their dream get choked by the 'system' and stifled by the ways in which education is evolving these days? Or, does the culture of the school decide what kind of teacher each one becomes? Knowing that the ethos of the school plays a critical role in nurturing that vision, it is important to ask the question: Can a school provide reflective space for the original vision of the teacher to take shape and continue to develop so that they thrive and grow in themselves, in their teaching, and in the quality of their presence to their pupils? As educators engaged in teaching and teacher preparation, McClain, Ylimaki and Ford ask an important question for which ethos may provide the answer.

> How is it possible for those of us involved in education to bring to life, the language and ways of being together in schools that sustain the heart of education, cultivating wisdom and compassion in ourselves and those in our midst, while tending to our educational responsibilities associated with standards and assessment?[2]

Creating a Sacred Space: Reflective Practice

A school ethos cannot live and breathe unless the teachers embody it. The mission statement and ethos of every Catholic school in Ireland wants the children in the school to be the best they can be – for themselves and for others. In this way, the ethos of the school is uncompromising in its commitment to help all students flourish in themselves and learn to become all they can be in community with others. The mission of the school also includes following in the compassionate footsteps of Jesus, to reflect the love of God, and introducing children how to do this in practice. My belief is that such love and compassion can only be developed in children if space is made that will speak of the greatness of that love and the real need for compassion. This does not happen in the busy-ness of school life but in the hallowed spaces we find in-between the everyday activity of school life. Fire doesn't burn in coal. It burns in the space between the coals. Perhaps an ethos advocating love, compassion and the need for community, like fire that needs space in which to burn, requires reflective space for it to grow and develop. Judy Brown puts it well in her poem 'Fire'.

> A fire
> grows
> simply because the space is there,
> with openings
> in which the flame
> that knows just how it wants to burn
> can find its way.[3]

Ethos can be the life-giving fire that burns in a school, not in a 'burns down the building' kind of way but rather an Emmaus 'burns in our hearts' inspirational, energising and captivating way that the world really needs.

Perhaps that fire gets smothered by the fire blankets of our current dominant narratives so that everything becomes bland and safe and, like central heating, the ethos of the school can stay lukewarm as a result. The dominant narrative that seems to be present in the media and seems to be guiding the DES approach to school inspection, for example, would see schools as places where children are formed and conformed into useful and productive members of society who will be helped to achieve better test scores, by teachers who see this as their job. Such an approach to a teacher's work is so limiting. It is a lukewarm approach. I have always been struck by what The Book of Revelation says about being 'lukewarm'.

I know your deeds, that you are neither cold nor hot. I wish you were either one or the other! So, because you are lukewarm – neither hot nor cold – I am about to spit you out of my mouth! (Revelation 3:15-16)

'Lukewarm' is not a good choice for a Catholic school, centred as it is on the vision and ministry of Jesus, who reflected the mind and heart of God, who looked for the outcast, whose message of compassion for all was expressed in companionship, healing, table fellowship, story, prayer, inclusion and service of all. The ethos of the Catholic school requires space to foster that vision, or recover it if it is lost, and find ways of living ethos in teaching and in the everyday life of a school.

The approach that I advocate for primary school religious education ensures that each RE lesson has contemplative space, space for wonder or conversation, space for symbol or story. Contemplative space might include prayer time or silence, mindfulness or meditation. It might also include music or song or ritual. Space for depth might include conversation or wondering or searching for new meaning in creative ways. The RE lesson can afford teachers an opportunity to engage children in deep conversations about things that matter. Space for symbol or story narrative might include a story or poem or some form of meaning-filled subject matter, such as a video piece, photograph, illustration, image, melody, work of art, or children's activity. The aim of the approach is to enshrine reflective space for the child (and the teacher). Incorporating such space attempts to ensure that an RE lesson does not just pay lip service to the patron's half hour per day but rather seeks to provide the space that children require to learn and grow.

Making room for ethos by putting reflective space in place is not rocket science. Such space is found, not only in one particular lesson every day, although the religious education lesson has a particular role in that regard, but across the curriculum. We have prioritised literacy and numeracy in Irish primary schools, for example, where small groups of children are worked with intensively in small groups via in-class support. Might it not be worthwhile, even once in the day, to have children in small groups being worked with socially, morally, spiritually and contemplatively, where the teacher would have an opportunity to make real connections with the children and where the children would have an opportunity to make connections with one another? Perhaps making a connection with even one child or student is the single most important thing that any teacher can do. It is probably the one thing that lives on after the class, after school is finished and perhaps even after the teacher's lifetime. More than a decade ago Daniel Goleman was writing about social intelligence and its importance for teachers.

> Mounting research shows that students who feel connected to school – to teachers, to other students, to the school itself – do better academically. They also fare better in resisting the perils of modern adolescence: emotionally connected students have lower rates of violence, bullying, and vandalism; anxiety and depression, drug use and suicide; truancy and dropping out … 'Feeling connected' here refers not to some vague niceness but to concrete emotional links between students and the people in their schools: other kids, teachers, staff … even one supportive adult at school can make a difference to a student.[4]

Teachers also need to find reflective space to keep in touch with their vision and find the time and space to maintain their passion for teaching and nurture a quality of presence to their pupils. Nourishing the teacher spiritually is not a difficult task but it does require space. My work with practising teachers on summer courses in reflective practice has been hugely formative for me in relation to the importance of the reflective space provided to them. One of the teachers on the summer course sent me an email a couple of months afterwards to say how much the course meant to her. She wrote: 'I was talking to someone the Saturday after the course ended and they asked was I going to be able to use the course when I went back into the classroom in September and I heard myself say: "Put it this way … I wouldn't be going back into the classroom in September if I hadn't done this course!"'

My work with teacher education students has also informed me in this regard. I have found that student teachers value reflective space as a key element of their own professional development. The participants (former Marino Institute students) in my doctoral research into my own teaching practice in Marino spoke of the value of the reflective space created for them on the course as being critical in forming them in their own professional identity, and that the focus on their inner lives was seen as a critical part of their own professional development. They also signalled that it met a deep need in their lives as students. They spoke of RE sessions in college teaching them to be present in the moment and how to be present to the children. They gave them space to develop their own spirituality and made them intent on providing the same opportunity to the children they would teach, forming them as a group by creating community and affording them the space to make connections. They also spoke of RE sessions bringing them to the kind of reflection levels that didn't finish with the end of the session, or the end of the semester. They spoke of RE sessions teaching them what it means to be a teacher. If student teachers do not experience such professional development in college, they will most likely not bring it with them into their classrooms as teachers.

My practice in religious education with teacher education students in Marino has seven elements, designed to create reflective space and facilitate reflective practice. My doctoral research participants, all past students of mine in Marino, have spoken not only of the importance of these elements for their own religious education in college, but also of incorporating aspects of those elements into their teaching in primary classrooms. These elements are not fixed. They do not always appear in a particular order nor do they all necessarily need to appear within the one session. However, each element contributes to the process.

WAITING AND WONDERING

This is an important stage for the students who are welcomed into silence and the sense of never quite knowing what will unfold. I insist on welcoming latecomers to class, knowing that they take a risk to arrive late. I also take a risk in waiting for silence at the beginning even though it sometimes takes time, because this results in real engagement with the session, not a forced engagement. I sometimes wonder aloud about the centrepiece, which always contains a symbol related to the day's subject, as well as candles and incense. I have always considered it important to have a rich centrepiece as part of every session as it helps focus attention in some way on the work at hand that day. Past students have spoken of 'welcoming the latecomers', of using centrepieces including a focusing symbol and of holding the space and being 'really present' to the children.

THRESHOLD EXPERIENCE

Since the students may be coming to RE from another subject, such as maths or PE, I deliberately set out to make this space different, to change the context in a meaningful way, to enable the students to move, as it were, across the threshold into this different space. This may be done by going outside to change the context physically, or by changing the context metaphorically, using a transition exercise such as mindfulness or meditation, verse, song, music, a YouTube clip, story or other. While past students have always used transition activities between their lessons on school placement, RE showed them the value of contemplative space as a transition.

ASKING THE QUESTION

We bring who we are into the classroom. This stage tries to honour that, acknowledging that how the students are affects how the day's work will be for them. It also acknowledges that their presence, and their contribution, is not only welcome, but life-giving and vital to the group. It is often enfleshed by simply asking the group how they are. Recognising the importance of a question, even one as simple and mundane as 'How are you?' is recognition of the importance of each learner to the group as a whole. I frequently ask students if there are any questions, not with the intention of answering them but just wondering what's happening in the group at that moment. I also frequently ask, following Rilke, what question students are 'living' at this moment in time. I sometimes wonder about questions that have arisen from the previous week, not providing answers but, as Rilke says, just 'loving the questions'.[5] Some past students spoke of finding my non-answering of questions annoying but professed to doing likewise in their own classrooms. They understood that the really good questions don't need to be always answered but to be treasured. Some have even spoken of having a 'treasure box of questions' in the sacred space of their classroom, containing deep questions that children have asked and that can be dipped into occasionally for a time of wonder.

GATHERING ROUND THE SUBJECT

The session continues by working with the students' experience of the subject – whether in pairs, small groups, whole group, via journal work, or by using insights from past students' reflections or my own experience. This element has taught the students what an experiential approach really looks like; and they have again adapted it for their classroom teaching.

JOURNALING

Journaling is rooted in the student's own experience of that day's work, often by engaging with these three questions:
    What did I learn?
    What does it say to where I am?
    What am I going to do about it?
 The students are reminded that these questions are directed at their experience of what has been happening for them in the group emotionally. The journal has long been part of RE lessons, but the

students develop an understanding of depth of reflection, which again they have brought into their classrooms as teachers. One past student spoke to me of individual children coming to him to allow him to read what they were writing about. He said it felt like they were giving him a glimpse of a treasure that they had found.

PUSHING BACK THE HORIZON

In working with a particular subject I try to connect the content to the experience of the students and/or the primary school classroom, while aiming to push back the horizon, opening up new territories to left and right. Religious education should always be exploring new boundaries of knowledge, and past students have spoken of being on a journey of exploration with the children in their classrooms.

CONCLUDING RITUAL

The small group session generally ends with a ritual. This gives the students an opportunity to reflect, while also helping create that sense of 'unfinishedness' where students leave knowing that they have more to learn. Students comment that the ritual is often the most meaningful and memorable part of the session. Ritual can happen inside or outside; it can involve movement or dance; it can include song or verse; it can be meditative or contemplative; but always it seeks to arise out of, and give expression to, the work of that day. Past students have spoken of bringing ritual from RE sessions in Marino not only into their classrooms, but into other arenas also. I have been told that the 'Neighbour Dance' has been seen in 'Copper's' night club!

The process of RE in teacher education in the Marino Institute, as outlined above, attempts to honour the need for reflective space in the lives of the students, to find truth and meaning in the message of Jesus, to make connections with and between them, and to enable them to form community.

If we can learn one thing from the Gospels, it is that Jesus' ministry is primarily about creating good relationships, it is about the practice of care and compassion; it is about giving life in whatever way we can to whomever we meet. For instance, you make space for this in welcoming the 'stranger'. For primary school teachers, the stranger may be the child who constantly comes to school late and the teacher is persistently challenged to make space for the child, in spite of the daily disruption. In a Catholic school, the teacher is particularly called to make space for that child, a welcoming, loving, compassionate space. That child really needs to be welcomed, and that may not be easy. The space that needs to be created is counter-cultural. It is counter-cultural in the same way as the practice of table-fellowship for all was counter-cultural in the society of honour and shame in which Jesus lived. It was just not the 'done' thing to sit at table with tax-collectors and sinners. In the same way, perhaps setting aside middle-class values that see punctuality as the essence of efficiency may be as counter-cultural as leaving the 99 in the wilderness to go after the one that is lost.

Finding the courage to teach in ways that are counter-cultural will not happen in a school unless the teachers are nourished spiritually. There is an old story of the teacher who was spiritually exhausted to the point where she couldn't function in the classroom at all. Then she heard about an old wise woman who lived in a cave up in a remote mountain range who was reputed to have the gift of asking the most searching spiritual question that could utterly change one's life. When holiday time came she packed a rucksack and went in search of the wise woman. For three days she trekked in the wilderness until she came to the wise woman's cave and, not wanting to waste a moment, called out to her in her need. The old woman came out of the cave and looked at the teacher for a long time. Then she said to her: 'Your question is "What do they need?"' Then she hobbled back into her cave. The teacher repeated 'What do they need?' again and again as the anger rose up in her. Then she stormed off down the mountain. After a day's angry march, with anger unabated, she decided to go back up to give the old woman a piece of her mind. However, when she got to the cave the old woman was standing there crying and waiting for her. She said that she was so sorry, that she had given her the wrong question. 'Your question,' she said, is "What do they really need?"' The ethos of a school should always be focused on what they – the pupils – really need. Reflective space for the child is essential but is utterly dependent on the teacher's willingness and ability to create a space for a holistic approach in their classroom, in spite of the pressures of conforming to the transmission of a packed primary curriculum.

Some years ago Parker Palmer was writing about the importance of creating a space in order to remove impediments to learning. He wrote of such space bringing openness, holding boundaries that make the space safe, and offering hospitality to all. For those who work with children, such qualities are essential to a holistic approach.

> To sit in a class where the teacher stuffs our mind with information, organizes it with finality, insists on having the answers while being utterly uninterested in our views, and forces us into a grim competition for grades – to sit in such a class is to experience a lack of space for learning. But to study with a teacher who not only speaks but listens, who not only gives answers but asks questions and welcomes our insights, who provides information and theories that do not close doors but open new ones, who encourages students to help each other learn – to study with such a teacher is to know the power of a learning space.[6]

We have looked at the question of reflective space for the child and for the student and teacher. A third element is also worth exploring, the question of institutional space. A 'pause hour' or time of reflection called *Suaimhneas* (a Gaelic word meaning 'tranquillity') was, for some time, provided every Wednesday at noon in Marino, when no lectures, seminars or meetings take place; instead, students and staff are offered spaces for reflection. In this way, the inner life of students and staff was valued and nurtured institutionally. Such a practice would be a unique development for teacher education whereby for one hour each week, opportunities, in keeping with a college's ethos or guiding principles, are provided to facilitate lecturers' and students' own spiritual and holistic development. Many educational establishments aspire to nourish well-being in the midst of a busy academic programme, and such a practice would reflect a serious commitment to the needs of students and staff.

In a chapter such as this, it would be remiss to omit writing something about the mindfulness movement. Mindful space for contemplation has been part of the RE programme in Catholic schools since 1995. It wasn't valued until it became a fad but, interestingly, its existence in the RE programme is now being recognised in the mainstream media. The experts see mindfulness as very simple. Thich Nhat Hanh tells us to look at the blue sky, smile and breathe. Jesus asks why you would worry when all you have to do is look at the birds of the air, who do not sow or reap. Pope Francis has put a huge focus on care for our common home, our common home where we live together mindfully, and with compassion. At the beginning of the current decade, Aostre Johnson rang a warning bell that should perhaps begin to be heeded.

> There is a dawning realization around the globe that many people and cultures are losing touch with their inner lives in this era of increasingly high-speed, multitasking, high-stress, acquisition-oriented ways of living – and that this is taking an enormous toll on all forms of life on earth. A restoration of these inner human capacities is critical not only for the well-being of youth but also for the survival of the human species and the planet.[7]

In relation to reflective space, three elements have been explored in this chapter – space for the student and teacher, space for the child, and institutional space. We need to take the nourishment of people's inner lives seriously and provide space for that to happen as part of an ethos that sees people as important. We need to take reflective space seriously, as a space where the ethos of the school lives and breathes, where the inner life of teachers, students and staff is nourished, where the children breathe and live and work and play together, where the way to live together with love and compassion in community is worked out, where the future is approached with hope, where God is invited to reign.

Ethos and the Wider Community

15 Parents as Partners: Ethos at Home

ROSALEEN DOHERTY

Parental involvement is a key issue in all schools. The move towards parents being in partnership is a crucial and clear target within the policy document *Delivering Equality of Opportunity in Schools* (DEIS). This is important because, in many instances, parents are still on the periphery of school communities, engaging when asked, leaving their child at the school gate, and then taking over again in the afternoon when school is finished. The school and the parent may only engage at a rudimentary level with little discussion on what is happening from the perspective of their roles as teachers and parents. There are some parents involved to a greater degree such as when participating in parent associations or on boards of management, but it is often the case that the issues that connect school and family life are not fully discussed or considered. Parental involvement has now become a crucial topic because studies have shown that when parents are involved in the school community, at any level, students benefit. The role of parents in the home environment is essential to a student's academic and holistic progression. This is a critical element in the ethos of every school.

Parents are the first educators of their children and it is important that this is emphasised and supported. Parents continue and complement the work that is done in school. If parents are not really involved in the life of the school, it does not mean that they are not involved with their children's education, nor does it mean that parents need to be experts in all subjects. They can supervise homework, make sure journals are done, and check the school website for events. These are all integral parts of the school and parents working together as a community.

We want all students to grow and flourish in their school environment; this is more likely to happen when parents participate as part of the school community. The benefits are obvious for everyone, yet organizing and achieving this can be a struggle in certain school communities. There is also the fact that parents have busy lives; there are some who have negative images of school so that the school may seem like a hostile environment for them; there are many who are in full-time employment and, with their many commitments to family life, engagement with school can be low on their list of priorities. To support and encourage more direct participation, they need to feel their contribution is valued and welcomed, not only because it is the right thing to do but because their role and contribution is vital to the school community.

It has been long established that an essential element of school life, and towards the progression of students in the education system, is parental involvement. For this reason, schools need to move towards parental partnership, where parents are involved at ground level, and in planning and policy development. Their involvement is essential to a co-ordinated approach to education because they are invaluable resources and their unique contribution needs to be encouraged and welcomed. This may not be easy for some and it may take time and patience for all parents to see the benefits of being actively involved in their child's education. We see the consequences of parental involvement when a student is beaming with delight because her mum has volunteered to do a reading at the school Mass, or when a student has encountered a problem in school and is comfortable to sit down with parent and teacher to discuss how they are going to overcome this. These are clear indicators that barriers are being removed and relationships of trust and support established. For instance, when a parent is engaged in a cookery class within the school and her daughter waves through the window, both are delighted and can feel connected within the school environment. The meeting of home and school is where relationships are built and progress in partnership becomes possible. The next step can be to encourage parents to become involved in a more formal way in the school; the award ceremony, the parents association committee, the parent-teacher meetings, and the board of management. These are the occasions where informal and the formal parental involvement takes place.

If parental involvement is such a defining factor and at the heart of successful, holistic education, why is it a struggle for many school communities to involve and incorporate parents? As we have seen, building relationships toward partnerships can often begin through the informal, nurturing and fun events of school life: for example, the parents helping out at graduation, the hot chocolate morning just before exam time, the casual conversations between teachers and parents at the end of the school day, and especially during parent-teacher meetings. These are the times when parents, students, teachers and management can engage, share information and get to know each other. Research shows that the crucial ingredient at this stage is not making any judgement on the parents. Judgement can emerge on the basis of background, race, religion, their engagement with the school, the language they use, their point of view, or their education. I have never come across a parent who did not want the best for their child. What parent and teacher have in common and what unites them in their different roles is their mutual concern about the education and holistic development of the children. This is where the relationships develops and the possibility of involvement begins. This is supported by Joyce Epstein and her fellow authors who describe parental involvement as communication with educators, volunteering at schools, fostering learning at home, engaging in the decision-making process, and participating in school and community partnerships.[1]

Parental involvement does not happen overnight, it's a process that takes time and effort. The most important starting point to building relationships is having an open door policy for parents so that they feel the school is interested in their participation and welcomes their involvement. It is only when this happens that we can then move to the next stage of parental partnership.

All schools are at different stages in their progression towards the goal of having parents as partners. From my own experience it is apparent that if we are invested in the education of the whole child, and not just academic progress, we have to build a sense of partnership and break down the barriers that discourage parental involvement. One of the main obstacles to parental involvement is fear. Fear because their roles are ambiguous and that the relationship between parent and teacher is often not clearly defined. Parents may also fear that teachers will know too much about their family life, and teachers may be afraid that parents will interfere in their classroom. These fears need to be acknowledged and overcome. The most important element is building a trusting and mutual relationship which recognises the need for a four-pronged approach involving parents, students, teachers, and management working together to support the work of the entire school community.

Students in a DEIS school may be presenting every day with a range of issues. Some families are barely surviving. The issues of poverty, homelessness, mental health and addiction are part of our students' lives. This has to be taken into account in the classroom. The students that come from challenging situations still have loving parents who want the best for them and need the school's help and support in this. These parents want to see their children progress through school and into third level. They want to break the cycle that they themselves have been brought up in, essentially the cycle of failure in education. If schools want students to break this cycle they have to involve parents; it is impossible unless school and home work together. Why? Parents are the prime educators of their children and if this is not supported at home there is a reduced chance that these students will be successful at school. The simple things like a good breakfast before school, a place to study at home, a supportive environment at home: whether this is provided by school or parents has to be decided and provided in consultation with both. If parents cannot provide what their children require then they need to know the school will provide what they can without judgement on them.

According to Garry Hornby and Raylene Lafaele,[2] the unquestionable, tangible benefits of the connection between home and school includes: better parent/teacher relationships, improved teacher morale, better attendance, improved attitudes, increased well-being and mental health of the children, growth of parental confidence, and, not least, an improved interest from the child in their own education. These benefits are clearly integral to promoting a child's overall education, academic progression, attainment in school, and personal development. It is important that parents, teachers and management are aware of these benefits and gain an understanding of the impact they can have on each individual child and the wider school community.

It sometimes happens that teachers dictate the role of the parent in the education of their child so that the parent-teacher meeting can be more about the teacher giving information and the parent merely listening as a passive participant. There is much capacity for change in this area. We need to recognise that the parents have speciality skills. They know their child; they know what is going on in their lives, they know them better than anyone. Teachers can gain information on what type of learners their students are, what difficulties they might be encountering. Parents have ideas about what will work for their child. In such conversations teachers can gain insight into a student's life outside of school and the dynamics of the home environment. Teachers have a lot to learn from parents. That is why the parental voice needs to be heard so that parent-teacher meetings become opportunities to share information, to have a conversation about the student, and a discussion of the strategies to further the child's progression. Such sharing and caring is a collaborative enterprise and a unique opportunity to concretely express and positively implement parental partnership in the education of their child.

Those who take on roles in parent associations and on boards of management need to be supported and commended for the gift of their effort and time, and assured that their contribution is valued.

These are the parents who will bring other parents with them on the partnership journey to build up, advocate and promote the bond between home and school. School management have a responsibility to take the parental voice and use it, to reflect and implement their voice appropriately in school policy. This can often be difficult since it might differ from the school perspective or plan at the time. This is where the relationships that have been developed can help forge a perspective and through negotiation and compromise work toward a unified view of the future of the school.

This type of parental partnership articulates clearly the role of equality between school and home:

> It implies that relationship has been formed on a basis that recognises that each has an equally important contribution to make to the whole, contributions which will vary in nature are compatible and each of which is unique.[3]

Inviting a parent for the odd coffee morning and parent-teacher-meeting is not a partnership. A partnership materialises when there is a meeting of minds for the benefit and interest of both parties.

There can be barriers to initiating and implementing parental partnership. Parents might feel inadequate to the task, or lack confidence and feel overwhelmed in the formal environment of the school. They may feel their voice will not be valued or welcomed; or that they are merely token representatives of the parents with little power to influence school life and policy. To pre-empt such difficulties small steps can be taken to introduce parents into the school environment. Events where they are invited to an informal coffee morning where the main aim is for them to meet other parents, when the school hosts a positive evening where their child gets to show some of their work, or a parents/grandparents day, can broaden the school community as many grandparents are responsible to some extent for the care of their grandchildren. These are positive measures that entail no pressure or long-term commitment but can lead to more meaningful and prolonged involvement in the school and allow partnership to evolve.

By such means parents will know that their role in their child's education goes beyond the front door of the school and that the relationships that have been built will make parental partnership a reality rather than an aspiration

We live in changing times, times of diversity and pluralism when many families live quite secular lives yet choose to enrol their children in a Christian school. This adds another dimension to the understanding of parental involvement and partnership. In my research I discussed with parents how they felt about Catholic education. 60% agreed that the religious / spiritual life of the school was important to them. When parents were asked would they like to be involved in religious events 23% replied in the affirmative.[4] The responses ranged from the Christian faith being very important, to the emphasis on spirituality, respect for other religions, or admiration for the values of the school. For them is was important that good values are evident and practiced in the school community, values such as respect, love, forgiveness, and non-judgement. These are the values that forge the ethos of the school and these parents wanted to actively participate in the school community to see that this happens.

The Vatican II Declaration on Christian Education, *Gravissimum Educationis*,[5] stated that parents are the primary and principal educators in the faith formation of their children and that the role of a Christian school is to help and assist parents in this role. Consequently, fostering a partnership with parents is seen as imperative. If the school and teachers are to carry out parents' wishes for the faith formation of their children, then there needs to be consultation and collaboration. While students first engage in faith formation in their family environment at home, this is expected to continue in the school where Christian values and rituals link home and school. Active involvement and partnership with parents are essential elements in this process.

In the context of DEIS schools, we are striving, and struggling in some cases, to ensure that parents are involved in the school. It is one of the principal targets of such schools. It is essential that the voice of the disadvantaged parent is heard and that they know their voice is just as important as any other. We find that parents are usually fully engaged at the time of enrolment; yet this tends to decrease as the years progress. The aim within a DEIS school is that parental involvement/partnership increases and parents be engaged at every step of their child's progression within the school. This does not mean that parents have to be on site every day but that they are aware of what is happening within the school and feel they can engage when they want to and is needed.

The Home School Community Liaison Scheme is an integral part of every DEIS School. Some of the main principles of the scheme are:
- Partnership: This implies a co-operation for mutual interests. One does not dictate to the other.
- Respect for the individual as a parent: without respect for each other, there is very little possibility for anything positive to emerge or grow.
- Pupil and teacher interdependence: this is the key to parental partnership. We can perform our distinct roles but we can also be a resource for each other to make our responsibilities more successful and to ensure the best for the students.
- Analysis of needs: at different stages in family and school life we can struggle. Schools can help provide certain things that cannot be provided at home. If this works parents can feel comfortable asking for help and secure that the school will always endeavour to do the best for their family.

A school ethos has the education and well-being of each student central to its mission. This means engaging in collaboration and partnership with parents to unite home and school in providing all the resources necessary to help students achieve their personal and academic potential. These are partnerships based on mutual trust, respect and shared responsibility for the education of young people. Such an ethos welcomes the unique contribution of parents to shared decision-making as essential, effective partners. Without them a constituent element is missing in the education of children.

16 Ethos at Play: Extra-curricular Activities

AODÁN MAC SUIBHNE

Past pupils of schools often develop an affinity with the building which was their '*alma mater*'. When they visit their former schools the smell of the polish brings memories rushing back, they seek out the desk in which they sat during Leaving Certificate year, the bed in the dormitory in which they slept, the tree in which they carved their initials, the twisted rusty nail in the wall in the school yard. When school buildings are demolished to make way for new ones, when the playground is bulldozed and laid over by a synthetic 3G surface, they lament nostalgically the passing of the old. But if you were to say to those past pupils that they could place a preservation order on one particular thing from their former school, I would think that many of them would nominate the preservation of their school ethos. School ethos is always deemed to be an abiding good.

I have never come across two schools which are exactly alike. The ethos of a school is particular to it. It is what makes each school unique and different. A school's ethos may defy exact definition in a mission statement; yet, ironically, it is the clearest and most powerful statement a school makes about what it values. It has less to do with national curricula, official syllabi, formal timetables, nationally used textbooks, school rules and state examinations, and more to do with 'the hidden curriculum' and the extracurricular. In reality ethos is caught rather than taught, it is intuited rather than studied; it has the power to permeate a place with ether-like quality.

Ethos becomes tangible in the choices we make, it is forged out of tradition and expressed in handed-down values, values which are cherished and adhered to by successive generations. It is found in deeds and words held in shared memories. It is commemorated in photographs on school walls, it is preserved in school lore, it is celebrated when past pupils and former teachers come together, it is deemed to be worth preserving when everything else has changed.

The ethos of a school can be most visibly expressed and clearly communicated on the sports field. Ethos can be defined by the particular sport which takes pride of place. How the school engages in sports can become the badge by which the characteristic spirit of the school is made manifest. Ethos is found in the emphasis or lack of emphasis which is placed on participation, on fun and enjoyment, on inclusion, on success, or on a 'win at all costs' mentality. Ethos can be expressed in terms of sportsmanship. A good sportsperson prizes honesty and fairness, and how to react well to circumstances on the field, and how to conduct oneself off the field. Respect is of upmost importance, respect for opponents, the referee, and the spectators. It honours co-operation, advocates control of the individual ego, promotes humility, inspires forgiveness, and teaches team spirit, and, most importantly, how to win and how to lose. These values lay the foundation, not only for sportsman-like conduct, but form the basis of the life skills needed to live an ethical, caring and compassionate life.

From where does the sporting ethos of a school come? The principal of a school or those in charge of sport have a vision of what they would like the school to stand for and how its ethos is expressed in sport. That vision crystallises, emerges and evolves over a period of time, laid down by the words and deeds of those in charge, by the example set on the field of play and on the sideline, by what is celebrated and highlighted in moments of victory and defeat, by what is recalled with pride, by what is referred to as being important before going into big games, by what is highlighted as to what really matters, by the good name and reputation which is established and subsequently cherished and strengthened.

The sporting ethos of a school can also be shaped by the value which is placed in informal conversations with students on incidents in or surrounding games, whether those games are All-Ireland finals, games that seal Grand Slam victories, international play-offs, school games or in-house league games. I remember in particular the All-Ireland Hurling Final of 2017 between Galway and Waterford. For me, it was a momentous ocassion, rich in history, emotion and significance. There were so many poignant moments which could be alluded to, to point out acts of sportsmanship and generosity. Long cherished dreams were going to be realised by one of the participating teams – one hadn't won for 29 years, the other hadn't won for 56 years. Years of yearning would come to an end. The Galway team was mourning the recent passing at a relatively early age of one of their all-time heroes, Tony Keady. In the immediate aftermath of the All-Ireland Hurling Final, Galway's greatest hurler at the time, Joe Canning, having eventually realised his dream, chose to remain pitchside alongside the widow of the former hero rather than climb the steps of the Hogan Stand to lift the McCarthy Cup along with his team mates. There was more to life than sport. The same player made it his business to go around to each of his opponents to commiserate with them and to wish them better days. The private words of consolation whispered by the winning manager into the losing manager's ear do not go unnoticed nor the winning manager's unbridled joy embracing his wife and parents in the moments after the final whistle. Sport is meant to be enjoyed. The losing players, as is customary, chose to stay on the field to show their respect to the winning team. The Galway captain, David Burke, in his speech remembered those who played for years for their county and never tasted victory like this, he remembered the sacrifices made by family members, the Trojan work done by club mentors, the personal losses and trajedies experienced by panel members, the people who worked behind the scenes, the vanquished and how they must feel now.

> To be present at any All-Ireland hurling final is a truly spiritual occasion – players pushing themselves to their limits, sublime skill, bravery, agony and the ecstacy. Oh, that everything was rosy in the garden! I regret to say, however, that I agree that 'Most major

sporting events carry shadows of the human stain.' [1]

Teams have won All-Ireand Finals by deliberately cheating on the field of play and those incidents too can be referred to and condemned. I'm not talking about one player fouling another player and a free being given; or about a player striking another player in the heat of the moment and being sent off. In fact there is something wonderfully flawed and human about such an honest reaction. What I'm talking about instead are 'the dark arts', deliberate underhand cheating, stealing, the end justifying the means. 'The dark arts' obviously, have become part and parcel of modern day sport as have 'borderline tactics, such as gamesmanship, trash talking, strategic fouling.' [2]

Individual players and pundits acknowledge that this is what is required in order to win at the highest level. There is no shame involved any more. That contrasts with the reluctance of Michael O'Hehir – the legendary Gaelic games radio commentator of days gone by – to name in his commentary the player who had been sent off, not wishing to bring any shame to the player's family.

Sport can be very revealing. Ethos at play, like gold, can be tested in the furnace of competitive sport. True colours emerge. The 'Colours Match' is an annual rugby fixture between UCD and Trinity. Players speak with pride of the times they first received their 'colours' or wore their college jersey. Their true colours, however, they show in the heat of the game and in how they respond to different situations and challenges. How players react is often commented upon against how well that reaction is in keeping with the school / college ethos or indeed how out of line it is with it.

Children often declare who their sporting heroes are by the jerseys they wear at training, the number on the jersey and the name they get printed on the back. Younger children tend to go for the top goal scorers, the most flamboyant, the ones that grab the headlines for the salaries they earn, how much they were sold for and the number of cars they own. When writing their essays, 'What I Want to Be when I Go Grow up', they often declare that they want to be professional footballers. As they grow older, they tend to be more circumspect.

They refer to a lot of hidden work done by players, to dedication, to lack of selfishness, to leadership skills, to sportsmanship, to loyalty, to team play, to humility. As a teacher, I was asked once who my own favourite sporting hero was. I suspect that the questioner expected me to name a Gaelic footballer or hurler first. So, for that reason, the first one I named was Neil Jenkins, the Welsh rugby full back at the time, a sportsman who has always been one of my true sporting heroes. Neil Jenkins? A rugby player and a Welsh man? Neil Jenkins was a sporting hero of mine, I said, because he was a work horse. He rose from being a working class boy in the Welsh valleys to the pinnacle of rugby. At first, he was not deemed to be good enough to wear the Welsh jersey. He worked hard at his game, however, and went on become Wales' record points scorer and to play for the British and Irish Lions. After picking up an MBE for his services to sport from Buckingham Palace in October, 2000, he went straight back to the Welsh capital for a match in which he scored all 24 points for Cardiff in their 24–10 win over Saracens. In my own way, I was conveying the importance I placed upon dedication, hard work, sincerity and loyalty.

On another occasion, I raised the ire of a Kilkenny man in my class when I said that the great Kilkenny hurler D.J. Carey – one of the greatest hurlers in the history of the game and the winner of five All-Ireland medals – should not have been allowed to play for Kilkenny in the last All-Ireland Hurling Final in which he was victorious. My point of view was challenged, as I expected it would be. My answer was that D.J. Carey used magic in his hurling and that magic shouldn't be allowed. In my own way I was complimenting D. J. Carey on his peerless skill, something which was realised straightaway by my challenger to his great satisfaction.

My mischievous declaration that D. J. Carey used magic in his hurling had its origins in a folktale I had heard many years previously and it provided me with a precedent for objecting to use of 'magic' in sport. In the folktale, the fairies of Munster challenged the fairies of Connacht to a hurling match. The match took place on the summit of Nephin Mountain overlooking Lough Mask in Mayo. The fairies of

Connacht routed the fairies of Munster and chased them down the side of the mountain. The fairies of Munster, however, turned around and shook their fists at the fairies of Connacht, accusing the fairies of Connacht of using magic in their hurling and vowing that they would be back the following year. Equating D.J. Carey's skill to magic was indeed complimentary. I have always felt that such levels of skill were a gift from above and that credit should always be given to a player who reaches a level of excellence through years of practice and dedication.

When pushed as to who would be my all time greatest sporting hero, my answer is Ronnie Delany, arguably Ireland's greatest ever sportsperson, winner of the gold medal in the mile in the Melbourne Olympics of 1956, arguably the blue riband of Olympic achievement. It is not because of his prowess on the running track that he is my greatest sporting hero, but because of the use he made of the talent which was bestowed upon him, his singlemindedness, his determination, his dedication, his sense of gratitude, the genuine love he had for his sport and the joy he got not only from winning but from competing also. In the Preface to his autobiography, *Staying the Distance*, he states:

> I ... began to realise that I had been gifted with a special talent for running. I knew then that I wanted to be a great athlete and no one, and no circumstance was going to deter me. With determination that surprised even me, I took control of my own life and made decisions with the foremost goal of furthering my athletics career. [3]

Ronnie Delany had the potential to have a great impact on the children whom I taught, having grown up in the same area himself. He was somebody with whom the children could identify. He lived on the same road as some of the pupils in my class, he trained in the sports ground where we held our annual school sports, he won a two-pound pot of raspberry jam for coming in first place in the wheelbarrow race in his own school sports, he competed in the primary school sports then held in Croke Park, and in his quest for Olympic glory he prayed for victory in the church next to the school. In his local Crusaders

Ethos at Play: Extra-curricular Activities

Athletics Club he learned 'to see running as fun and as something to be enjoyed, above everything else. I was to carry this message with me all my competitive life.' [4]

In the pursuit of his dream and in order to free up more time for training, he gave up his cadetship in the Irish Army, going respectfully against his father's wishes to take up a position as door-to-door Elecrolux vacuum-cleaner salesman in Kilkenny.

> I was not to be deterred. I was pursuing a personal goal with missionary zeal; I was determined to discover the unknown – how good an athlete I could become. It was lonely, too, for I could not share my mission with anyone else in case they thought I was mad. [5]

Leaving Ireland to take up a sports scholarship in Villanova University under the tutelage of Jumbo Elliott or training on the sand dunes on the Pacific Coast all bear testament to Ronnie's determination to take whatever steps were necessary to realise his ambition which others might seem so unlikely. While in Villanova he applied himself in an equally dedicated manner to his studies and his nightly visits to the library were a feature of his time there.

Ronnie Delany's thoughts on the morning of the mile final are worth recounting:

> The day I had lived for dawned bright and warm. It was difficult to remain calm but I tried as best I could, for I knew every moment of anxiety used up valuable energy. I resigned myself quietly to the will of God and prayed not so much for victory but the grace to run up to my capabilities. [6]

What has forever drawn me to Ronnie Delany, however, have been two black-and-white photographs – so familiar to many people - taken of him in the immediate aftermath of the mile final in Melbourne. The first one shows him on both knees, stooped in prayer, head resting on tightly clasped hands, thanking God for victory (printed in his book, *Staying the Distance*). He knew that his talent for running was a God-given gift. The second one shows him on one knee, hands still tightly clasped, head raised, sheer joy on his face and being embraced from behind by his great rival and lifelongfriend, John Landy of Australia. That photograph, for me, shows how one should win and how one should lose, how to enjoy the realisation of a sporting dream and how to equally joyously feel part of a great sporting occasion having been a runner up – such generosity and nobility.

> Now when I run against a man I enjoy it. But if I were to set up a timepiece there and try to beat it, I wouldn't get enjoyment out of it at all. The thrill of running, the pleasure of running to me is not in making records and getting your name flashed around the paper, but winning races and winning them by beating another man in a fair run. [7]

Is fair play simply oldfashioned? 'The very thought of fair play conjures up sepia photographs of moustachioed gentlemen in long shorts and striped blazers, characteristic of the Victorian era, adhering to high moral codes.' [8] Ronnie Delany realised the responsibility that comes with being an Olympic champion and the influence that people like him have as role models, something worth reminding young sports stars in schools who are placed on pedestals by their peers and teachers:

> I have long since retired from active participation but I find that every sports fraternity I encounter renders me respect because I am an Olympic champion. It is as if you are a living part of history ... But when you win an Olympic title you live on as part of the sport after you retire from active competition. There are responsibilities to live up to also. I am always conscious of the need to give youth good example by word and action. [9]

Great successful players of the past often declare that what they cherish most of all are not the victories or the medals but the friendships, the memories, the shared never to be forgotten moments in those few minutes on the field after the final whistle.

Where people gather and community forms, where team spirit and loyalty endure, where relationships are more important than achievement, where challenge is seen as eliciting the best in us there you will find the essence of a genuine ethos at work fostering and promoting human flourishing in all its possibilities. Ethos becomes embedded in our minds and hearts by osmosis, through role models, and the positive experiences we have of sharing part of our selves with others in the classroom, on the playing field, in friendships. We may be unconscious of the fact that a school ethos permeates one's life with values and attitudes, that, perhaps unknown to us, it helps us develop a set of life-skills, and engaging with reality that encourages us to be the best we can be. Ethos at play, for better or worse, encapsulates the essential features of what is important to us, it reflects what we value and what we want from life.

17 Going the Extra Mile: After-school Support

SIOBHÁN SHOVLIN AND MAIREAD MINNOCK

In 2005 primary and secondary schools designated as disadvantaged became part of the Department of Education and Skill's Action Plan for Delivering Equality of Education in Schools, referred to as DEIS. The DEIS Action Plan focused on addressing and prioritising the educational needs of children from disadvantaged communities. One of the needs identified in the Action Plan was school attendance. Historically, schools designated with disadvantage status, have had higher levels of absenteeism and truancy.

Analysis carried out by the National Education Welfare Board (NEWB) in 2004 show that schools serving disadvantaged communities have significantly higher levels of school absenteeism. On accepting entry into the DEIS scheme in 2005, all schools were asked to explore four areas for particular focus in order to address issues of educational priority, these included: literacy, numeracy, parental involvement, and school attendance. Both primary and secondary schools included in the DEIS scheme focused on these four areas and set targets for improvement. As school attendance and promoting school attendance were incorporated into the plan, they became central to the school communities who tried to achieve improvement in this area. Research informs us that improving school attendance has a clear domino effect because it supports students in their academic achievements and in their social and personal development. On a day-to-day basis teachers know this to be true and understand and value the importance of attendance in school and, particularly, participation by students when they are in school. Research has also shown that linking positive school experiences to their lives is pivotal in ensuring a student can reach their full potential. Therefore, we focus on how exactly schools encourage and promote children to come to school with a willingness and readiness to learn.

'The vast majority (92%) of primary schools in Ireland are owned and under the patronage of religious denominations and approximately 88.6% of these schools are owned and under the patronage of the Catholic Church'.[1] In planning and moving forward for the betterment of pupils, schools must reconnect with their ethos and mission statement as a starting point for future success. In these mission statements, schools describe what they endeavour to do for those within its learning community and base its ethos on Gospel values that are central and important to the school community. Catholic primary schools are caring schools committed to Christian values; they are communities where Christ is presented as a model for educators and where opportunities for inclusion are created in an attempt to reach out to all members of the school community. Inclusion and the opportunity to achieve one's full potential are at the core of what it means to be a Catholic school.

In an ever-changing society it is imperative for educational leaders to express the values and vision of the school by helping each child to flourish in education and be prepared to participate fully in life. One of the ways of achieving this is through the provision of extra before or after school activities or initiatives. These are obvious ways to enable students to learn, to form new and improved relationships, and develop a sense of belonging to the educational community. Creating an inclusive environment, by providing positive school experiences and equal opportunities on the pathway to educational success, can be lived out in the school on a daily basis through many practical measures. These practical measures are often not directly related to the curriculum. It is through, for instance, the provision of support programmes, extra-curricular activities, a variety of initiatives, and by going the extra mile, that schools can ensure there is something on offer which appeals to all learners and helps to provide a positive school experience. We know that for children to succeed educationally and socially requires attendance and punctuality on a daily basis. While showing up to school is a step on the learning journey, it can be a difficult step for some children. It is in such challenging situations that opportunity arises to reach out and encourage all children to attend school regularly.

Long before the initiation of DEIS, Catholic schools serving in communities of socio-economic disadvantage have endeavoured to reach out to the marginalised. Care and compassion for those who are vulnerable or disconnected in any way is a characteristic feature of Christian values. Schools with a Christian ethos follow the example of Jesus who unambiguously reached out to those on the margins of society and showed not only his love, respect, and desire for their well-being but did what he could that they might flourish as human beings, as God intended. This is the intention of those who make available interesting and engaging learning opportunities such as planting seeds in the school garden, cooking a traditional dish to celebrate learning about another culture, or building boats which float to mark Engineers' Week. Activities such as these may appear simple and familiar to those working in school communities but they do require conviction, extra initiative, and effort on the teacher's part to ensure their smooth running and success. This is what 'going the extra mile' looks like in practice. When we think of the role of the teacher in encouraging children to come to school, it is active learning experiences like these which spring to mind, activities that are stimulating, motivating and a real incentive for children to come to school and enjoy learning.

In recent years, strategic approaches by government bodies such as TUSLA[2] have asked schools to look at the factors which influence school attendance, in order to reach out to children who are at risk of absenteeism and of potential early school-leaving. One factor is the availability of support programmes and group events for children. The provision of such activities can prove particularly beneficial and positive for children to improve attendance and motivation. TUSLA recognises that both 'enrichment activities and sporting activities can support students in their school attendance.'[3] This is particularly relevant when the enrichment and sporting activities cater to the particular interests of the students who are experiencing attendance related difficulties. Activities and support programmes in DEIS Band 1 Primary Schools, are wide-ranging, such as: breakfast clubs, dancing, football training, athletics, social clubs, swimming, cycling, and cooking. School personnel are the ones providing these opportunities to ensure the support programmes are available for children on a daily or weekly basis. These programmes help to provide children with a new, positive outlook on school and the learning environment. Teachers and school staff, who care for the children they work with, are giving generously of their time and talents on a regular basis before, during, and after school.

It has been found that through developing positive relationships with the school and school personnel many at-risk children find a point of connection and a sense of belonging. The formation of positive child/teacher relationships is made possible in the provision of non-curricular support programmes and active learning experiences. Positive relationships are known to have a number of benefits for children, including better engagement levels, overall positive personal school experiences and improved academic performance. Undoubtedly, the combination of positive school experiences and performance are associated with higher levels of school attendance. Credit must be given to teachers who promote such positive personal school experiences and help ensure children feel included and part of the learning environment.

TUSLA recommend that working with the broader school community to prepare a school attendance strategy, schools have the chance to 'give all the partners in the school community a sense of responsibility for school attendance'.[4] This highlights the fact that full responsibility for attendance does not lie with any particular person. Attendance should be a high priority for all members in the school community; setting high expectations and raising awareness must form part of a school's characteristic spirit. Schools are encouraged to provide opportunities for parents to be part of the formation of the high expectations for their children.

Celebrating attendance is part of the school attendance strategy. Such celebrations can happen at an individual level, class level, or a whole school level, all of which helps to reinforce the value of attending school. Attendance celebrations are recognised internationally as a positive way of rewarding students for good attendance. It has been found that the wide variety of reward systems in place in DEIS Band 1 schools is one of the most effective ways to encourage good attendance. Principals speak enthusiastically about the use of reward systems to encourage good attendance.[5] The rewards in place vary to suit the dynamic of the school, and try to meet TUSLA's recommendation that they are 'meaningful' and are 'adapted to the school's own cohort'.[6] Among some of the rewards are: homework passes, extra Golden Time, Attendance Trees, Attendance displays, trophies, and cinema outings. Prizes are distributed either at the end of each week, month or term. As evidence of the high regard some schools hold for attendance reward ceremonies, family members are invited to take part.

These occasions enable schools to reach out to the rest of the family and the wider community by including them and creating positive feedback with all stakeholders in the child's education. This encourages a united approach in promoting and improving attendance. While these rewarding strategies sound appealing and are valuable structures to have in place, we must be mindful of the school staff who are responsible for ensuring the success of these incentives and reward systems. It is school staff who are willing to implement the reward systems to ensure a positive experience within the school. Undeniably, reward systems have an important part to play, especially in schools where attendance and punctuality is already an area of concern.

The importance for school leaders, such as principals, teachers and the wider school staff, in building solid, close relationships with the children is very important and must be considered when encouraging, promoting and celebrating attendance and participation in schools.

Seán Ruth highlights the insight that 'all effective leadership rests in building solid one-to-one connections with people'.[7] The role a teacher can play in promoting attendance within his/her own classroom can vary from keeping up-to-date records so that children at risk of poor attendance can be monitored and encouraged to attend school regularly. Teachers are also in a position to deal with attendance issues by providing a relevant and appealing curriculum, by acknowledging good attendance, and, when children return to school after an absence, the teachers showing they care and that the child was missed in the class. Most importantly, a class teacher can help by ensuring that children establish positive, strong relationships within the classroom with fellow students, and with the staff. It is important for teachers and other school staff to reiterate the vital message that a child's presence in class matters to them.

DEIS schools are endeavouring to counteract inequalities in the education system. It is encouraging to see so many schools providing engaging and exciting opportunities to make school the most pleasant and rewarding experience it can be for their students. Schools have a wide range of supports in place, which are designed to influence various aspects of school life and are proving to have a significant impact on school attendance. One principal highlighted the role such support programmes and activities play by stating in conversation that if there are persistent truants and they know certain activities are taking place 'the child will get up and get out' because they know they have G.A.A. or cooking or whatever may be on offer that particular day. Another principal stated: 'You're hoping it will also gently encourage the children to come in for the activity and therefore make the day in school as well'.

Among the range of support programmes and activities helping to promote school attendance and punctuality are the provision of breakfast clubs. One of the benefits of breakfast clubs, highlighted in *A Good Practice Guide for Breakfast Clubs*, is that they have 'a positive impact on school attendance and punctuality'.[8] Noreen Flynn states that in trying to create equality of educational opportunity 'children who experience deprivation in early childhood need intensive holistic early intervention, in the community, in school, and the home, to support the education process as they develop'.[9] Breakfast clubs provide part of the intervention required for children who experience deprivation. They are proving a prominent support structure in improving punctuality and attendance. Such clubs are among the early intervention strategies because schools are aware that a 'lack of a nutritionally adequate diet can have a negative impact on a child's capacity to learn'.[10] Breakfast clubs have been cited as the 'fourth most effective intervention of the School Completion Programme which aims to support those at risk of early school leaving'.[11] It is through practical supports like this that schools can help to ensure that children arrive in the classroom ready to learn, ready to discover their potential, and cut the risk of poor school performance, and reduce the incidence of early school leaving.

These are some of the reasons why breakfast clubs are a prominent part of the DEIS school support structure. Schools receive funding through the Department of Social Protection's school meals programme to provide food for these clubs. The Child and Family Agency's school completion programme provides funding to pay two assistants to run the club each morning. Other schools run breakfast clubs with the help of volunteers and school personnel. While these clubs have many benefits for the children availing of the service, there is a reliance on school staff and volunteers to ensure that the provision of such services continues so that children can really reap all the benefits they provide. This involves a willingness on the part of school staff and volunteers to go the extra mile in order to guarantee their successful organisation and implementation.

It is evident that schools can really assist children to flourish and achieve their full potential by providing extra-curricular activities and reaching out through the provision of exciting and engaging learning opportunities and reward structures. Research finds that principals are concerned that current structures should be maintained and a combination of initiatives including rewards, support programmes, activities and breakfast clubs be recognised and supported as vital in promoting good attendance. Schools serving areas of social disadvantage rely on the additional supports to tackle issues such as absenteeism and DEIS Band 1 Primary Schools must maintain such structures 'for education to more fully become a proven pathway to better opportunities for those in communities at risk of disadvantage and social exclusion'.[12]

18 Ethos in the Wider Community: Community Service

TOM RYAN

'In so far as you did it to the least of these brothers and sisters of mine, you did it to me.' (Matthew 25:40)

In May 2014, at a conference organised by Italian bishops to support Catholic education, Pope Francis noted that the most important thing that school will teach its young people is 'the language of the mind, the language of the heart, and the language of the hands. All in harmony. In other words, think of what you feel and do; listen to what you think and what you do; and do well what you think and do. The three languages, in harmony and together.'[1]

Today when schools speak of offering students a 'holistic' or rounded education, and this is an ambition that lies at the heart of school mission statements throughout the country, what they are hoping to do is to teach the 'three languages', to engage the Head, Heart and Hands of the students in their care, and the way in which schools go about achieving this will reflect the understanding and expression of their ethos.

I am a teacher in a Catholic voluntary secondary school and our particular school ethos is modelled on the public ministry of Jesus and formed in a missionary tradition which emphasises reaching out to those outside the school community and building relationships with those in need. One particular approach in which our ethos is lived in the wider community and engages the 'mind, heart and hands' of our students in a very specific way, is through a service-learning programme in Transition Year called the Matthew 25 Programme. After a period of in-school preparation, our Transition Year students, aged between 15 and 16, spend two consecutive school weeks in a pastoral centre that provides expert services in the field of disability, located within the vicinity of our school.

In August 2014, I was appointed director of this programme and from the beginning I noticed a joy, a depth of response and an animation within and among the students who had completed the programme that was really eye opening. In 26 years of working in religious education, I had seldom encountered such a powerful response and it highlighted for me the value and importance of engaging not only the heads of our students, as we spend most of our times in classrooms 'doing', but also their hearts and their hands. It has convinced me of the value of helping our students to live the Christian ethos outside of the classroom in the wider community.

SERVICE LEARNING

At the heart of service learning is action, doing, or experiencing, where students come to a deeper understanding of a concept though their participation in service. This process reflects the 'experiential education' theory first espoused by John Dewey (1859-1952). Dewey's involvement with the work of Jane Addams in a settlement house in Chicago in the 1890s led him to see education as linking action and doing on the one hand, and knowledge and understanding on the other. Myles Horton, the co-founder of the Highlander Research and Education Centre in Tennessee in 1932, an educational establishment credited with the formation of many of the civil rights leaders in the southern United States and Paulo Friere, whose educational theory led many oppressed people in Latin America to take a more active role in shaping their destiny, were supporters of experiential education. Both agreed that 'Without practice there's no knowledge'.[2]

Studies of the impact of service learning on young participants have also highlighted a strong sense of civic and social responsibility as one of the recurring learning outcomes for students. Shelly Billig found that 'students who engage in service learning feel they can "make a difference" and become active, positive contributors to society.'³ While studying the effects of 62 service learning programmes on participants, Richards et al. discovered that students benefitted 'personally, civically, socially and academically' through their participation'.⁴ These findings point to the huge potential that encouraging and facilitating students to live school ethos within the wider community holds. So, in September 2014, I decided to examine the impact of our own Matthew 25 programme on a class group of 22 Transition Year students to see if such claims could be supported. All participants completed a qualitative and quantitative questionnaire on their experience of service in the community under three headings: Preparation, Service, and Impact.

PREPARATION

We need to take students at their starting point and intentionally design curricula, experiences and reflection activities that respectfully point them on their journey of self-discovery, discovery of others and appreciation of the world.⁵

Over the years, the ethos of our school has become summarised in four key phrases that all partners in our education process are familiarised with. The first is to 'Be There', to be in the right place at the right time and to be there for others at all times. This availability to others is reflected in the second key term that challenges our school community to 'Be Caring' to all. 'Be Truthful' is our third phrase and this calls for honesty in word and deed and recently we have added the challenge to 'Be Grateful' for the talents, gifts and opportunities that we have been given and to use them for the benefits of others. These four terms reflect the spirit of our school (*'la philosophie de l'ecole'*) and they influence everything we plan and do.

As a Catholic school, our ethos is very closely linked to the mission and ministry of Jesus of Nazareth, so the guiding orientation behind our service learning programme is that of Christian service. Parables and teachings of Jesus such as the Parable of the Good Samaritan (Luke 10:25-37), the greatest commandment of all (Mark 12:28-31), the Last Judgement (Matthew 25:31-40) and the leadership of Jesus displayed in the Washing of the Feet (John 13:1-15) are interwoven throughout the preparation process.

The period of preparation challenges the students to undergo a personal 'Copernican Revolution' and instead of having 'Self' at the centre of their universe, they are asked to give priority to the 'Other' for the duration of their placement. For their two weeks of placement they are asked to do all they can to befriend the clients and to support the staff at all times. 'Client' is an umbrella term used during preparation to refer to the people the students may encounter; clients may be patients, long-term residents, day-care attendees or primary or secondary school students. I found it interesting to note that in our modern world where more and more communication takes place in group mode via social media, the students identified the time spent in class on improving one-to-one conversation skills as being of particular value. One student observed: 'I found the classes where we were taught to talk to patients the most useful. It enabled me to keep a conversation going and helped me engage more'.

At the end of the period of preparation, just as Jesus sent his disciples out to continue his mission, and in the spirit of Pentecost that is the foundation stone of our school, each group of Transition Year students are given a blessing by the school chaplain and formally 'sent out' on their mission to live our ethos within the wider community where they are challenged to learn a new language, the language of loving service.

SERVICE

> Service learning courses requires students to dislocate and disorientate themselves from the familiar and to give themselves fully to the experience guided by community experts.[6]

The 12 pastoral centres that the students visited cater for physical, intellectual, emotional and sensory disability and the school does its best to match each student with a placement that will encourage their skills and talents to flourish. There is also a member of staff within each centre who has agreed to act as liaison officer with the school and to monitor and offer guidance to the students for the duration of the placement.

Of the 22 participants, 12 worked in day-care centres; six were placed in long-term residential facilities and four spent their pastoral placement in special needs schools. Alzheimer's/dementia, wheelchair users, intellectual disability, autism, Down syndrome, multiple sclerosis and blindness were some of the specific disabilities encountered by the students on their pastoral placement. As only six of the participants had worked directly with people in need before, this was a new learning experience for most of them. For example, one student on completing the questionnaire said. 'Where I was, it was quite a mix of severe disabilities. One that stuck with me was Angelman Syndrome. The person who has it is always smiling and laughing and they are really, really touch sensitive … I hadn't heard of most of the issues that were in my centre before.'

In each placement situation, the students had direct engagement with people in need. One student described his typical day as follows: 'I made tea and coffee for all and also fed the clients that were unable to drink by themselves. I assisted with the art class every morning by helping the clients paint and also by washing brushes and palettes. I helped one individual develop her typing skills on the computer. I played games with the clients. I organised crosswords for the clients and I was always there for conversation.' A summary of the duties performed by the group produced a most interesting word cloud from www.wordle.net. (See previous page.)

Many of the verbs point to active engagement with another person: *e.g.*, 'accompany', 'talk', 'assist', 'play' and 'bring', while the dominant nouns give a sense of the service activities undertaken by the students: *e.g.*, 'tea', 'art', 'crosswords' and 'games'.

This word-cloud confirmed the wonderful engagement between the TY students and the clients, both young and old, that I witnessed during my visits to the placements. Regularly I would find students sitting and chatting with elderly residents as they completed puzzles, with others sprawled on a classroom floor helping children complete educational projects. On one memorable occasion I arrived at a day centre to find a strapping rugby player being taught how to waltz by a tiny elderly resident of a nursing home! On his return he referred to that afternoon as the highlight of his placement.

Students wrote of the joy and sense of inner well-being that they were experiencing while on placement and many noted that, for the first time in their lives, they felt they were making a positive difference in the lives of others. A participant wrote that 'one day I brought a girl out in a wheelchair for a walk. She was really, really happy and laughing the whole time. I felt like a good person, that I had done something good and worthwhile. You get a good self-image'. Another discovered a particular joy and generosity of spirit in completing a jigsaw puzzle with a client: 'we both really enjoyed it and I bought them a box of puzzles before I left. The person whom I gave it to was overjoyed.'

IMPACT

Students in the course of their formation, must let the gritty reality of this world into their lives, so they can learn to feel it, think about it critically, respond to its suffering and engage it constructively.[7]

When students returned from pastoral placement the chaplain and I met with them for a period of reflection on their experience. At this gathering students spoke of their experiences and shared both the challenges they faced and the insights they gained. It became clear that in the course of the two weeks these students were not just giving of their time and talents to others, they were also receiving a huge amount in return. Three particular areas of impact emerged.

The first impact on the student's lives was seen in the admiration they expressed for the full-time staff and volunteers working in the centres. This particular summary reflects the experience of the students: 'I think that the staff do unbelievable work in this centre. I genuinely don't know how they do it every day. They come in before 7 a.m., prepare the centre for the ladies, wake them up, wash them, dress them and bring them to breakfast. Throughout the day, they cater for the ladies' needs, getting them a cup of tea, reading or talking to them or feeding them at meals.' He concluded with the mature insight that the staff in his placement made the residents feel like 'they're living the lives they're used to'. The time spent in the company of the staff and volunteers also led a number of students to reflect on whether or not they could pursue a career that involved the service of others. One noted that it 'takes an impressive person to do something like that' while another felt that the pastoral placement has 'made me more likely to pursue a career in something like teaching'. There was plenty of evidence to show that students experienced at first hand the value and sense of meaning that a person can find in living a life in service of others and found in the staff and volunteers wonderful role models.

The second major impact that pastoral placement had on the participants was a newfound respect for the clients and their daily lives. In the course of the two weeks, the students not only got to learn about various types of disability, they also got to know the person living with the disability. One student remarked: 'A person is not their disability. I did not view it like this before my placement.' This getting to know people was particularly evident among the students who worked side by side with the elderly. After his 10 days in a residential centre, another wrote: 'I have more of a respect and admiration for the elderly, who in their lifetime achieved so much and deserve to be treated well and remembered for that ... A lot of them have amazing experience and insights and should be valued for it.' Working with these people led to a deeper appreciation and heightened respect for the elderly clients. Another observed that 'these people have led amazing lives' and offered the wonderful insight of the elderly 'as the glue that holds a family together'. Many participants also committed themselves to spending more time in the company of their grandparents as a result of their pastoral placement experience.

While staff and clients impacted the lives of the participants from the outside, the third common impact occurred 'within' the students themselves. Eighteen of the students wrote that they had acquired new skills as a result of their placement experience. Most of these revolved around learning how to communicate with people and how to care for those in need. Some spoke of simple things like the value of learning how to make a good cup of tea while another delighted in his new skill of learning how to fold and operate wheelchairs because 'my granny uses a wheelchair, so if she is ever in need of some assistance, I will be able to help her with whatever problem she faces'.

As well as these new skills learned, the students also wrote of discovering within themselves a depth to life or what many referred to as 'more' in their lives than they were previously unaware of. In reply to the question: 'Do you think the pastoral placement will have any long-term impact on your life?' participants wrote that in future, they would be 'more' aware or thoughtful of others in need; they would be 'more' likely to help a stranger, be 'more' grateful for their lives, be 'more' understanding of disability and be 'more' likely to volunteer. A typical summary of their experience was that; 'As a result of my placement, I am <u>more</u> grateful for my health and I take <u>more</u> out of every day. I also try to do <u>more</u> for others'. A heightened awareness of the value of daily life was also noted by another TY student who wrote that his two weeks of service 'made me understand how fortunate I am and how easily the smallest things can make huge differences in someone's life and that I should do everything I can to make those differences'.

CONCLUSION

It would be misleading to suggest that a service learning programme designed to foster the living of Christian ethos in the community is not without its challenges and complexities. As Alan S. Waterman notes 'Because service experiences often take place in contexts with which the students do not have prior experience, and calls for activities that they will not have previously performed, there is often a noticeable level of anxiety present prior to the start of a service project'.[8]

Despite the period of preparation spent with the participants many students wrote of first day nerves. For instance, one said he 'felt like a fish out of water' while another wrote of being 'very nervous' throughout his first day. Some wrote about being 'uncertain what to do' and there were those who found the placement to be 'quite overwhelming' on their first day.

In the course of the survey other powerful and difficult emotions were acknowledged. One spoke of feeling 'kind of useless' at times and another was 'frightened' when a day care centre user spoke candidly of the accident that left him paralysed. Also, since many of the centres deal with the elderly, the issue of bereavement was a challenge faced by participants and one student referred to a deep sense of 'hopelessness' when he discovered that one of the residents on his ward had died.

As well as these challenging, personal issues facing the participants, Health Information and Quality Authority (HIQA) guidelines for those working with vulnerable clients and Garda vetting requirements are certainly making it more complicated both for schools to design community based service learning programmes and for pastoral centres to welcome TY school students into their communities. However, in a world increasingly characterised by teenagers struggling with depression, stress and mental health issues, the experience of pastoral placement has convinced me that any educational programme that helps participants understand and express faith values, engage in community service, develop a deep sense of self-worth, re-enforce life as positive, confirm young people in their understanding that they are good people and that they have an important contribution to make to society is worth persevering with no matter what obstacles are placed in its way.

When writing about his time since he has returned to school from pastoral placement, one student commented: 'Whenever I see someone is need, I am thinking about them. I wonder if they are OK or if they need a hand. I have even done the cliché of helping an old woman across the road a few times. It's becoming second nature, I don't even have to think about it'.

If this does not show the value of living a Christian ethos in the wider community ...what can?

19 Being Stewards of Creation: Ethos and Caring for the Earth

PAUL WHEARTY

A PLANET IN CRISIS

It is common knowledge that the earth is suffering. Humanity is currently witnessing a planetary crisis because we have systematically plundered the planet, desecrated the natural landscape and selfishly exploited its habitats. Since the emergence of humankind, people have done more damage to the planet than has been done by any other species since the primordial flaring forth. This damage has had a disastrous effect on the planet and a destructive impact on its flora and fauna. Extinction, global warming and climate change have become the lexicon of present-day reality.

A planet in crisis is a people in crisis. The history of humankind can be observed in the sad state of the earth. The current narrative asserts that human activity is responsible for global warming. Carbon dioxide emissions and the desecration of the earth's flora have been responsible for a change in the chemistry of the air. This crime against nature and humanity exacerbates the effects of the greenhouse effect. The melting of the ice-caps and desertification are a real threat to all life-forms. In examining these adverse consequences, one may identify that it is not only flora and fauna that are impacted negatively; humankind itself is also under threat. Currently, the number of environmental refugees is predicted to rise significantly and the desecration of natural habitats will threaten more of the planet's flora and fauna with extinction.

People have always created myths and stories to try to understand the reason and meaning for existence, and their place in it. These stories and myths are now obsolete. A new story is needed. It must be an inclusive story that no longer places humankind as superior to creation or to each other. The present-day individualistic and anthropocentric-based narrative needs amendment. As Thomas Berry proposes, it is necessary to place 'the human within the dynamics of the planet rather than place the planet within the dynamics of the human'.[1] Socially, scientifically, technically, educationally, medically, legally and spiritually an entire overhaul of the current anthropocentric paradigm is necessary.

A local example reflects this desire to dominate our environment. In 2014 BioAtlantis was granted a licence to mechanically harvest kelp in Bantry Bay. This process will negatively impact seals, guillemots, oyster catchers, other marine life and their food chain. Despite being granted this licence, neither an independent environmental impact assessment nor independent monitoring programmes have taken place. The impact on the local human population also needs to be considered. This illustrates the fact that we have 'a moral sense of suicide, homicide and genocide but no moral sense of biocide or geocide'.[2]

The cry of the earth is audible and we lament the devastation that is causing its demise. There is urgent need to counteract the deep-seated social, cultural, environmental, religious and anthropological beliefs that are at the root of this tragedy. The solution depends on a radical reinterpretation of what it means to be human, what it means to be Christian, and what it means to be an earth citizen. Many agree that there is now an unambiguous onus on humankind to care for the earth as never before. Likewise, Christians will recognise that alongside the necessary technological or scientific responses to safeguard the earth, a fundamental change of heart is required. It is in heeding the cry of the earth that Christian ethos and Catholic social teaching are seen as positive means to advocate the importance of environmental care and a reorientation of our thinking about our relationship with the earth.

Christianity is faith- and action-based; it is a response to and participation in the life and mission of Christ. It asks for intentional discipleship and not mere observance of rules and regulations.³ How is this applicable to caring for the earth today? Being in communion with Christ predisposes disciples to see and experience life through the mind and heart of the Creator, which is to love and care for all existence, but most especially for anyone, or anything, that is neglected, deprived, marginalised, or under threat. The impending impoverishment of the earth calls on all to protect what is an essential part of who and what we are, and a critical part of the presence of God to us.

This discipleship is two-fold. It may be thought of in terms of 'mission and ministry'.⁴ This mission and ministry orientation provides us with a sense of relationship with the world which, for most people, is where we first encounter the reality of God in wonder and awe. It helps us become aware of the connectedness of all living things, the mutual interdependence of all life. We strive for humanity to become a 'communion of subjects' as opposed to a 'collection of objects'.⁵ This mission, when combined with ministry, creates a strong desire for change, for the protection of what is sacred, what is life-giving for us and for the world. Schools provide excellent fora in which this discipleship can be fostered.

ENVIRONMENTAL LITERACY – LEARNING TO WRITE A NEW STORY

Education is a positive tool that may be used to enable a more eco-friendly paradigm to emerge. The need for improved environmental education has been recognised internationally for some time. In 1975 in Belgrade, UNESCO determined that

> The goal of environmental education is to develop a world population that is aware of, and concerned about the environment and its associated problems, and which has the knowledge skills, attitudes, motivations, and commitment to work individually and collectively toward solutions of current problems and prevention of new ones.⁶

From 2005 to 2014, the United Nation's Decade of Education for Sustainable Development continued to stress the necessity of environmental education and to reiterate the importance of the role of education in curbing and combatting the environmental crisis. These environmental education programmes are meant to increase awareness and develop an environmental literacy that provides students with knowledge of ecological issues, how best to reduce one's environmental footprint, and tackle climate change. These programmes were also intended to promote active engagement in decision-making processes and endeavours to make students appreciate sustainability as it relates to biodiversity, and the necessity for quality of human life in the biosphere through understanding that 'all things in the ecosphere have equal rights to live and blossom and to reach their own individual forms of unfolding and self-realization. To harm nature is to harm ourselves, and to defend earth is self-defence'.[7]

Knowledge is the keystone on which environmental sensitivities and changed attitudes are built. Environmental literacy is essential to the process of change for it provides the language, stimulates inspiration and promotes a response that is in the best interest of the planet, and ourselves. Accurate environmental knowledge enables children, as the future guardians of the planet, to make informed decisions and to act appropriately. This has a knock-on effect. Children influence the homestead. Adults learn through the enthusiasm of children. Through their children, a community is more likely to circumvent complacency and apathy and actively participate in environmental protection and conservation.

Participation in environmental conservation has been something that has been widely promoted by the Ecological School Plan. Whilst the green school concept originated in an Ecological School Plan proposed by the Foundation for Environmental Education in Europe (FEEE) in 1994, it was not until 1997 that An Taisce designed the Green School programme for Ireland. An Taisce remained true to the vision that FEEE had conceived. They ensured that it was broad, structured, systematic, and permeated both the educational curricula and the management of the schools. The programme is also devised to ensure that a child's knowledge about environmental protection would be brought home.

The programme has proved to be successful. It has positively influenced the behaviour of parents and is a major factor influencing people's decision to recycle. While one may agree that the Green School Programme contributes positively to the environment, it can also be suggested that environmental education programmes have a propensity to fall on deaf ears. Irish society may be proud of its recycling figures, yet we are still behind our German and French counterparts. What causes so many people to ignore the harmful consequences of their actions? It may be that a deeper relationship with nature and a more thorough knowledge of faith could change one's viewpoint to maximise the impact of environmental education and the need to care for the earth.

LEARNING TO LIVE AS ONE

The Christian ethos is summarised by the Love Commandment (Mark 12:30). To love our neighbours as ourselves is at the core of our response to the love of God and the life and human flourishing this brings. It is this commandment that may be the first step in inspiring the school community to care for the earth.

In observing the planet today, poverty is evident. This poverty is born of greed. Humanity's imperfect nature leaves us susceptible to self-indulgence and the endless desire for more. The epidemic of consumerism in many cultures makes it difficult to detach self from a materialistic mentality. The desire for more ensures that maintaining a proper relationship with the earth is all the more difficult. The mutuality and integrity of a self-earth relationship can so easily be disregarded, leading to indifference to the plight of the earth and the negative effects this has on people.

This indifference is a type of theft. 'The climate is a common good belonging to all and meant for all'.[8] We know all too well that climate change leads to loss: the loss of habitat, material resources create a consciousness that the loss of fresh air leads to a lower quality of life. In diminishing the quality of life of the earth community, one assumes the role of a thief – stealing from others the source of life. We cannot be unaware of the global poverty that exists as a result of this theft. The persistence of this type of poverty is one of the great scandals of our world today. This fact is documented daily in the media.

Pope Francis emphasises that our faith and action should move from a passive to an active mode. A cultural as well as a spiritual conversion is needed. He calls for our willingness to change our thinking and develop an open, renewed relationship with creation that reaches beyond the boundaries of Church to include all peoples, all cultures, and all faiths.[9] For, undoubtedly, a united global effort is required to change our collective mentality.

One of the significant places such a cultural conversion can take place is within the school. If this is so what then does cultural conversion look like in a Christian school? It is for all; not just students, but staff and, by extension, the wider community. A new way of thinking is needed to permeate the entire school curricula that encourages a sense of responsibility for the earth and the development of a morality sensitive to the harm humanity is inflicting on our common home. The protection of God's handiwork, our common birthplace, is a duty of care for us all. This is a way of interpreting and proclaiming the Good News and the Gospel values that invite humankind to respect all of creation, and all who are dependent on it. The Christian understanding of love is holistic and inclusive, it understands that our love for God and neighbour should include our love of the earth and the life it provides for us.

Laudato Si' illustrates the importance of a trinitarian approach to humanity's relationship with God, the earth and all people. It is this sense of mutuality and interconnectedness that educators need to promote within the school to help identify a broader, more inclusive understanding of community and the significance of our common humanity, being dependent as we are on the same planet and each other. Just as in everyday life we experience various forms of exploitation in our communities, we can see the same happening in our relationship with the earth. The earth has been, and continues to be, exploited. Gospel values and Christian social teaching provides us with an understanding of how and why we exploit the earth, and in what ways we might begin to remedy this injustice and restore the life-giving relationship that is meant to exist between God, creation and ourselves. We should not leave to future generations the ecological and social problems we have created. We need to realise that '[t]he earth is finite and we must live in a way that is fair and just toward future generations of humans and other creatures'.[10] We have to remain cognizant of the needs of our planet and future generations. Such intergenerational solidarity is a crucial part of good stewardship of the earth, it reflects our concern for future generations, and is an indication of a genuine relationship with God that sees the reality and presence of God reflected in nature. And so, '[t]he restoration of various levels of ecological equilibrium'[11] must be central to the school culture and ethos. God, humanity and the earth are meant to exist in an intimate and closely intertwined relationship. Since '[t]hese three vital relationships have been broken, both outwardly and within us'.[12] Catholic social teaching calls on the community to repair these relationships. This goal is very much in harmony with the Catholic school ethos.

A Christian ethos of care for the earth focuses on the empowerment of pupils as active agents for change, change based on being able to recognise God's presence and activity in the world and in us, and be concerned about the current and future inhabitants of the world. The world, in all its physical, human and spiritual reality is the arena through which we encounter, dialogue with, and relate to God and each other in the home we call earth. This is the locus where we exist, find identity, discover, search for meaning, love, dream, hope, and relate to all that exists. Understanding this relationship is the basis of an integral ecology centred on the right understanding of an essential, mutual, interdependent relationship. This type of dynamic participation combines faith and action in an attempt to solve the environmental crises at a personal and global level, it embraces the interconnections crucial for the survival of the planet and the prospering of humanity at all levels of human existence.

The school context is a good place to inaugurate the sought after cultural conversion, it is a good place to teach about the centrality of an interdependent relationship between humanity, nature and God. Imagine the impact of students coming to the stage of recognising the relationship between God, humanity and the planet as sacrosanct, as inviolable? This can be the source of the motivation and inspiration to change.

SCHOOLS AND THE PROMOTION OF ENVIRONMENTAL CARE

From a school ethos perspective, an active participation and cultural conversion may begin with an understanding of Jesus, who epitomises the importance and transforming power of trustworthy relationships, moral behaviour and caring attitudes. Just like Jesus, our lives and actions are meant to signify the presence of the Kingdom of God – where our lives unfold as they were meant to; where we love, care, grow, protect and nurture each other, and the world, in the light of our relationship with the Divine. It is said that we become like those we love and admire – because they reveal possibilities in and for us, they are pointers to what we can become, and show us potential we could never have discovered by ourselves.

A Catholic school ethos is meant to parallel this process, calling on contemporary disciples to reflect on their attitudes and values see the environment as an integral aspect of their relationship with God and others. Such dialogue may also make the school community aware of the negative aspects of our culture and economy that have been internalised and, consequently, discourages them from being environmentally conscious and globally caring. Environmental solutions cannot be separated from the human story, or God's story, or the story of the earth.

In recognising that creation is God's handiwork and is entrusted to the stewardship of humanity, the school community has the opportunity to recognise the earth and its community are 'of God'. Indeed, sacramental preparation for the reception of the Eucharist can provide the pupils with an insight into Jesus becoming one with creation. This heightens the triune relationship of humanity, nature and God and perhaps will inspire the response of gratitude, love and respect. No doubt, it can be difficult to remain aware amid the noise of modernity and the constant pull of advertising and the media. The overstimulation of the modern world can be lessened by the contemplation and stillness. A prayerful and appreciative Christian ethos can enable the seeds of environmental knowledge, and right relationship with God and people to germinate at an individual and community level and become the source of change.

It is obvious that a community response is crucial to genuinely care for the earth. Schools have an opportunity to play a significant role in counteracting climate change. The time for humankind to begin 'burden sharing' and 'paying our ecological debt'[13] requires an education system which promotes a new way of thinking about human beings. The Catholic school may provide the ideal context and be able to focus on the solution, the mission and the ministry. This highlights the importance of a deep sense of belonging and the necessity of 'the mutuality, interrelatedness and interdependence of human beings'.[14] Perhaps, then, the evolution of a new eco-justice is possible and a desire to treat others as equals may develop. Casual pedagogies will not suffice. A goal-based approach is important to counteract the 'critique of the myths of modernity grounded in a utilitarian mind-set'.[15] The entire school community can be initiated into how planetary care is integral to faith, faith in God, faith in people, and faith in the essential goodness of creation.

We understand quite clearly that reconciliation between ourselves and God is an integral aspect of a life-giving relationship, and essential to becoming who and what we are meant to be as sons and daughters of God. Now we recognise that a similar type of reconciliation between humankind and the earth is necessary. Developing an environmental awareness and promoting an ecological morality is the best means to renewal, to a better future, and advancing a sense of solidarity with and responsibility for the well-being of the earth. The school is perhaps the appropriate place to begin this renewal. It is the place of great influence which can powerfully advocate and passionately nurture the paradigm which sees good relationships as central to a graced, humane and authentic way of being for all.

Mindfulness and Christian meditation have increased in popularity within Irish schools. This provides the opportunity for students to sit in silence and allow their awareness to deepen. They have time to meditate and reflect. Silence allows a deeper faith and inner peace to permeate the curricula for Social, Environmental and Scientific Education (SESE), Social, Personal and Health Education (SPHE) and Religious Education (RE). As sources for active engagement in faith development and ecological awareness, this may facilitate students becoming more discerning citizens of the world and more intentional partners in global renewal. Faith development and environmental education are meant to complement each other and help promote a collective consciousness that encourages the school community to come together to take responsibility for the home which has been entrusted to them. For these reasons, and more, the Catholic school is an excellent forum in which the journey towards a renewed understanding of relationship can be a positive force for change and the care of the earth.

20 Politics and Ethos in Irish Primary Schools

CLARE MALONEY

On February 17, 2007, following a period of consultation with all of the main education partners and Church groups, the Minister for Education announced an additional model of primary school patronage to accompany those already in existence in Ireland. Announcing details of the new schools, Minister Hanafin said:

> The changing shape of Irish society places new demands on the education system in responding to the needs of emerging communities. The role of the traditional churches in managing and providing schools is enormously valued and appreciated as is the growing role of other patronage bodies. In many of our new communities, however, there is a need for *an additional choice that can accommodate the diverse preferences of parents for varying forms of religious education and faith formation during the school day, in a single school environment that includes and respects children of all religions and none.* This new model of community national school provides that option and can be a rich addition to the range of primary school provision already offered by the existing patronage bodies.[1] [Emphasis added]

This new school model – Community National School (CNS) – is now under the patronage of the state's Education and Training Boards (ETB) and as such is the first state-patronage model of primary school in Ireland. Previously primary schools had been state-aided but not state-owned. Now, years later, it is worth reflecting on the issues

involved in being a state school, seeking to honour the spirit of the state's primary educational aim:
- to enable the child to live a full life as a child and to realise his or her potential as a unique individual;
- to enable the child to develop as a social being through living and cooperating with others and so contribute to the good of society;
- to prepare the child for further education and lifelong learning.

Historically, the question of allowing for the education of children of a faith, within the state's commitment to a holistic, child-centred education evolved through the provision in Irish primary schools of two different curricula: a state curriculum that took account of everything except faith education; and a faith education curriculum (for historical and cultural reasons, faith was until now, synonymous with Christianity) provided by the schools' patron. Though neither of these education providers – State or patron – crossed over into the other's curricular domain, it is important to note that Irish primary education has been rooted in their mutual recognition of each other's role and the necessity for both curricula in educating the whole child. Paradoxically, the arrangement has also imposed clear but – given the educational emphasis on integration across all subject areas – increasingly problematic demarcation between religious education and 'the rest' of education. However, the sharing of roles and responsibilities in this formal setting is an important indicator of how each of these legitimate institutions viewed the other's presence in the public square of the Irish educational system. Indeed the State in its *Primary School Curriculum 1999* confirms this legitimacy:

> In seeking to develop the full potential of the individual, the curriculum takes into account the child's affective, aesthetic, spiritual, moral and religious needs. The spiritual dimension is a fundamental aspect of individual experience, and its religious and cultural expression is an inextricable part of Irish culture and history. Religious education specifically enables the child to develop spiritual and moral values and to come to a knowledge of God.[2]

In emphasising breadth and balance in its pedagogic practices the state curriculum also seeks to reflect 'the many dimensions of human experience, activity and expression, and is directed towards the development of the full potential of every child'.[3]

The cooperation that evolved between faith education and state education has become contentious of late, in a context in which Christianity is no longer the sole occupant of the religious educational domain in primary education. Perhaps, more significantly, this is taking place against a backdrop of cultural shifts that question the role of any and all religions in the public square, some citing the French model of Church-State separation as the ideal 'solution'. It is worth noting that it is not only in religion that shifts have been experienced. Declan Kiberd in his book *After Ireland*[4] sums up the wider cultural and political Ireland out of which the CNS model grew, as an Ireland 'suffering a crisis of authority'. Scandals in the Churches, in the banking sector as well as political corruption and economic collapse, mismanagement in health services and in the Garda have shaken Irish peoples' faith in institutions in general. Today, it is not only the institutions of religions – whether Christianity, Islam or any other – that have come under suspicion and are being questioned. Recent political and economic events in America, Europe and the United Kingdom, suggest that the Richter scale is still registering shock waves.

Francis Campbell provides a useful sample of questions arising in the context of our contemporary culture, faith and education today:

> What kind of polity do we live in or want and how does it relate to faith? Is our culture a secular one that sees only a private role for faith in the wider society? Is it something that is confined to one particular day in the week? Is it an individual freedom to worship but without a collective dimension that is allowed to manifest itself in society? Will it be a world in which the state emerges with a monopoly on service provision in education at the expense of the wider society? Will it be a world in which providers can offer a service but will not be able to call on official funds to do so? Or is our world comfortable with a number of

service providers with the state regulating the space to sustain acceptable standards in service delivery and content? In such a world regulator and service provider must find ways to cooperate respecting the proper role and remit of the other.[5]

It is somewhat ironic that in the present cultural milieu with its growing diversity of education provision and apparent secularism, the Department of Education and Science (DES), and schools themselves, have continued to classify the growing diversity of primary school types according to a religious schemata – denominational, non-denominational, multi-denominational and in some cases, inter-denominational.[6] Ironically also, despite these supposed demarcations, one could visit any school type in Ireland today and be unsurprised to find children of any faith or life-stance enrolled. Denominational schools may have children who are not of their denomination or who do not subscribe to any religious belief; schools such as Educate Together, who offer a non-religious ethics programme, may have children from across the spectrum of world faith communities. In this evolving situation, the new Community National School model, is more interesting still, since the Education and Training Boards are in effect state agency and patron in one, carrying sole responsibility for two previously separate curricular areas, if they are to offer education of the whole child.

The challenge facing CNS is complex. Traditionally the focus of attention with regard to educating children of all faiths and none begun by focusing on competing absolutist questions about God – does God exist; which God is which; are they all ultimately the same; what exactly does this or that religion 'believe', what does atheism 'not believe'? Do religions have a place in primary education today seeking social cohesion? Often the focus is on the intellectualisation of faith so that it becomes little more than a philosophical thought process, translated into primary classroom practice as 'circle time'. To take one example, educational engagement with the majority Roman Catholic faith is reduced to compliance in facilitating 'delivery' of two sacraments – Eucharist and Confirmation (a compliance made possible by the relevant Church authority as well as the education and training boards). To approach faith education from such a discourse is to regress to an educational position in which content had priority over the child's experience, a priority that even as far back as the 1971 state curriculum and post-Vatican II Christian religious education programmes, had been abandoned. Today, primary school curricula worldwide, whether in faith or in general education, give priority to the child and her/his experience rather than the question of curriculum content and learning approach. A survey of ethos statements of any school type in Ireland will evidence depth, breadth and generosity of vision in relation to the child and his/her full humanity. Both philosophically and theologically, agreement on child-centredness is unanimous. Indeed it is so to the extent that there is the risk of no longer pausing to consider what we mean by 'the child'; or what it means to be human. It may be that the pendulum has swung so completely from content priority to making the child the priority that what we mean by 'the child' tends to be taken as self-evident. This can pose a certain risk, pointed to by Rowan Williams in his book *Being Human: Bodies, Minds, Persons*:

> There are grounds for being a bit concerned about our current models of human life and human well-being. No need to panic; but if we are to think and act in a way that helps to make the world more rather than less human – and humane – we need more clarity than our culture usually gives us as to what we think is 'more' human.' Unless we have a coherent view of what sort of humanity we want to nurture in our society, we will be at sea over how we teach, how we vote, how we save and buy and sell, how we entertain ourselves, how we think about the beginning and end of life… If there is one great intellectual challenge for our day, it is the pervasive sense that we are in danger of losing our sense of the human. [7]

Taking just one area of concern that Williams mentions, that of teaching, if his concern is valid, then we may need more clarity than our educational culture usually gives us as to how we are to understand 'the child'. How we think about the wholeness of the human child will influence what and how we teach. A faith-based appreciation of the human child can have much in common with a non-faith-based appreciation but they will not coincide completely. All of the world faiths understand the human as being in relation with the divine, a relationship mediated through tradition, experience, significant story, rituals and texts, and lived out in the practice of a community in the everyday reality of our shared world. A non-faith-based view of the human person will see no such relationship with divinity and is therefore lived in a different context. If the CNS state school is to operate in line with the state's current PSC and seek to educate the whole child, and every child, then the child's experience of faith which is infused in being human, in being this particular person, must be afforded the same educational rigour and integrity as that afforded to any other subject on the curriculum. The point here is that the starting point for development of a curriculum suitable for children of a faith in a state school such as CNS must be the state schools own basic educational aim, not because of a responsibility to any particular Church or faith community, but because the state puts the child, the whole child, at the centre of educational discourse and planning.

As CNS faces its complex task certain features on the Irish cultural landscape are worth noting. For example, an oft quoted statistic that shapes our sense of the reality of the Ireland we live in, comes from the National Census: 'While Ireland remains a predominantly Catholic country, the percentage of the population who identified as Catholic on the census has fallen sharply from 84.2 per cent in 2011 to 78.3 per cent in 2016. There has been a corresponding rise in the number with no religion, which grew by 73.6 per cent.'[8] It is vitally important to note the statistic in the same census showing that 89 per cent of the population of Ireland identify with a faith. Reflecting this statistic, pupil intake in the CNS sector in 2014 showed that 92 per cent of pupils enrolled declared a faith identity.[9]

The 2022 census reveals that, while there has been a decrease in the percentage of the population claiming to be Roman Catholic, there is an increase in those claiming to be Islamic, Greek Orthodox, and Hindu. This rise is such that the percentage of the population claiming no religion has also fallen.

Extract from the Census Report 2022

Religion

A question on religion has been a part of the Irish census for many years which creates a long historical time series charting the relative growth and decline in the number of people identifying with various religions and also with no religion. The question on religion used in Census 2022 differed from the Census 2016 version which may impact comparabliity.

- The percentage of the population who identified as Roman Catholic fell from 3,696,644 (79%) in 2016 to 3,515,861 (69%) in 2022.
- The total number of Roman Catholics fell by 180,783.
- The figure for people with no religion increased by 284,269 and stood at 736,210.
- The Church of Ireland category showed little change but remained the second largest religious category with 124,749 people.
- Other categories with large numbers included Orthodox (100,165) and Islam (81,930).
- The number of Hindus more than doubled from 13,729 to 33,043.

These statistics are challenging. They raise the question for CNS schools of how to educate equally, how to do justice to the life stances of the 8 per cent of their children who declare as being humanist, atheist or agnostic (or do not declare at all) but it cannot be at the expense of the 92 per cent of their pupils who declare a faith, and *vice versa*. Nor can quality of content and learning process be at the expense of the integrity of what a faith education must involve by way of its content – shared texts, stories, rituals, practices and experiences. To offer a child of faith a religious education that does not provide opportunities to pray is like offering a child an education in music without the opportunity to sing. Nor can it – even with the assent of a faith community – simply consign faith education to a space 'outside' or excluded from the much vaunted 'inclusivity' of the school day.

The challenge facing CNS is significant and will require innovative and imaginative thinking. Accommodation for the equal educational rights and full humanity of all their children is unlikely to be found in one programme alone. Real engagement with diversity and difference will require real diversity and difference in learning structures as well as in organisation and routine. Accommodation unlikely to be found in flattening faith education into a learning about my own and others' faith, however well intentioned. Such an approach has long since been discredited, as 'educationally thin'. And, to draw on the 'soft' option of a combination of spirituality/mindfulness/wellbeing, is to sap the robustness of faith education's learning opportunities. Within a state school, faith education can ask for no more than the integrity of approach that is afforded other curricular areas on the basis of their contribution to the full life of the child. But neither must it settle for any less.

CNS and its complex task of evolving and shaping a new school model is, hopefully, still a work in progress – though it is one that study of its curriculum and teaching learning structures suggests may have taken a misguided turn of late. However, it should also be said that the challenge of educating all children, in all their humanity is one that faces all primary schools, not just CNS. How does the denominational school educate the whole child whom they have enrolled and accepted, but who is not of their faith especially since they too seek to educate all of every child? If a school removes faith education for its children of faith to a time outside of school hours – education which they must pay for, privately – those schools may believe themselves to be 'inclusive' in accepting all children into their school, but they must also accept that it is at a cost to the integrity and characteristic spirit of the state's understanding of education. Both the child and education are compromised. Clearly the child whose faith education must take place outside school hours, must carry the burden of dis-integrating a part of the self that is not deemed educable within the school's ethos. Clearly she is learning that a vital part of her humanity does not belong in her school, that she and her family must exclude part of herself from her living out of her day in her 'inclusive' school. Clearly, in doing so, the child must lessen her 'self', a reductive self-denying process more aptly described as 'de-humanising'. Where this happens it is by way of a process that is anti-educational and contrary to the ethos and characteristic spirit of the state's own basic educational aim.

Williams' concerns, about the nature of what it means to be human, begin to echo.

Epilogue
Love Comes first:
Reflections on Catholic School Ethos

DENIS ROBINSON

This book has explored many significant aspects of school ethos to provide a sense of the profound vision and distinguishing aspects of Catholic education. In doing so it has provided an overview of the anthropology, theology, philosophy, pedagogy, psychology and sociology that describes what is most distinctive about the teaching and learning experience in first and second level Catholic education.

What is, for me, an obvious observation to make in this final chapter is the absence of a specific mandate that love, the Christian understanding of love, be presented as a named, identifiable goal and integral aspect of Catholic school ethos. The idea of love is most definitely implied in all Catholic schools but a focus on an intentional, practical implementation of Christian love is never directly addressed. School mission statements are based on the life and teaching of Jesus, on Gospel values, Christian ideals, or a specific charism as the foundational inspiration for a school ethos. Of course, this is laudable and implies that the students will be loved, nurtured and respected. But I wonder is this specific enough, do we really practise what it means to love in an educational setting from a Christian perspective?

Without doubt, the ideal of Christian love is ever present and presumed but the language never states explicitly how this will be implemented or what values and actions will be used to communicate and express this love. We are familiar with the language that describes the relationship between school leaders, teachers and their students. This is generally expressed in terms of a duty of care, an ethic of care, teacher love or professional love. These terms tend to reflect a more ethical or legalistic understanding of the school relationship. However, is the language of care or ethics sufficient enough to articulate what it means to love and educate from a Christian perspective? My feeling is that care is not the same as Christian love. It may be an aspect of love but doesn't capture the same level of conviction, personal commitment, nor the depth of vision, openness or the fearlessness of genuine Christian love.

Perhaps it is necessary to re-examine what Christian love is, and outline its various components, to discover how is can be expressed and what impact it might have on teaching and learning in a school environment. This process might help provide a fuller approximation of what is the heart and soul of Catholic education and how it might be realised.

THE PRIMACY OF LOVE

Love is an intrinsic human value. The power and necessity of love is understood by everyone. It is the one universal need required to promote a full and flourishing life since it, more than anything else, touches one's innermost being to permeate, enrich and positively influence the unfolding of our individual and community life. Nothing constitutes or completes us so much as love.

So it comes as no surprise that we as Christians experience the nature of God as love. The primary mission of Jesus was to reveal the unquestionable, transforming and faithful love God has for all humankind. In Jesus the presence of God is personified. He came to live within the limits of human existence, became visible and tangible to confirm this love, to demonstrate his identification and solidarity with us, and to touch the minds and hearts of all with his love, truth and compassion. In Jesus, people experienced God's desire to share himself completely with us, to love and heal, to save us from ourselves, to give life as no one else can, to raise us to the dignity of sons and daughters of God, and make us like himself. The experience and acceptance of this transforming love has the ability to make divine what is human. This is a truly metamorphic love story. Nothing compares to it, nothing captivates or enlightens as it does, and, as we have seen throughout the ages, nothing has the power to transform as the love of God because it, more than any other type of love, can touch the heart, soul, mind and body to infiltrate our consciousness and every fibre of our being to reflect the wonder of God within us.

God's love is not exclusive to the good or a lucky few; it is extended to all human beings so that we are all equally and infinitely loved. It is a love that makes no distinctions. It is so inclusive that in God's eyes we are all one, we are family, we are brothers and sisters. We are bound by this love as nothing else binds us. God is love, it is his nature, it is what best describes God in human terms. As Christians we are invited to reflect and live this love as an integral part of our lives in order to fulfil our nature and achieve our deepest, transcendent potential as *imago Dei*.

It is important to understand that the instinct and capacity to love is not something which is added on to our human nature, it is a given, a constituent part of being human. This makes love an essential characteristic of what it means to be authentically human. Perhaps it is this very capacity to love that makes being human so special since it reflects the inner nature of God in us. Just as there are no exceptions to God's love, there should be no exception to our love. The foundation of our obligation to love makes everyone we encounter our neighbour and part of ourselves. As we see in the parable of the Good Samaritan (Luke 10:25-37), this even applies to those who are considered different or even enemies. One's neighbours are not those who live close by, or those we like and choose to associate with, they are not chosen, they are

> .... not created by accident of birth, or nationality, or religion, or law; they are discovered through love... this love far exceeds some minimal respect for our neighbour's legal rights and liberties and instead requires us to seek their full flourishing and

belonging with every fibre of our being. Modern law, of course, cannot demand such dedicated commitment from its citizenry. But biblical law does. Nor can public policy generate such love in the hearts of people. But the Spirit of Jesus can and always seeks to do so primarily amongst those who are consciously open to his presence and power.[1]

Relationship with God and neighbour, and what it means to be truly human, is most convincingly demonstrated by our love. Jesus teaches that what is most necessary is to love first and always, that each in our own unique way reflect God's love, making it evident in our lives, our values and actions. To live and communicate this love necessarily epitomises and expresses the essential bond between the divine and human, and between all human beings. This love is a lot more than a word or a feeling, it is a relationship which involves intention and action, participation and involvement, it means wanting the best for the other, helping each other reach our full potential. It is about mutuality and reciprocity. It is personal and communal. It is a union and communion. It is an inclusive way of being. The primary focus is on loving rather than seeking to be loved.

In Jesus we see God's love expressed, not just in words, but in deeds such as compassion, forgiveness, self-giving, mercy, service, perseverance, sacrifice, respect, generosity, solidarity, hope, faith, commitment and much more. It is only when we experience the depth, quality and consistency of God's love that we can really begin to appreciate the power of his love for us and then, perhaps, we might be confident enough to be open to share this love and seek to be this love with others. Needless to say, such love requires a commitment, it makes real demands, it necessarily involves our personalities, emotions, thoughts and motivations. Love is the critical lens through which we encounter, experience and engage with God and people who are to be loved with one's heart, mind, soul and strength. This is non-negotiable. This is what it means to be Christian. If Catholic schools do not explicitly include and express this primary obligation to love then they lack something essential to Christianity. Daniel O'Leary is of the view that:

> Maybe it is time to recover the language of love in the work of education... I sometimes wonder whether we get lost too easily in the persistent search for rational clarity; whether we confuse religious knowledge (and religious behaviour) with a heart-felt sense of belonging to God; whether we lose sight of falling in love with God in pursuit of a more doctrinally explicit creed of beliefs.[2]

CHALLENGES

It can be difficult and even daunting to speak of the invitation to embody the intentional practice of Christian love, in imitation of God's love, with its emphasis on respect, sacrifice, empathy, courage, forgiveness, justice, humility, kindness, unity, service and compassion in a learning and teaching environment. While it is undoubtedly central to the ethos of a Catholic school we, more often than not, neglect the task of living intentional love because its implementation is challenging.

We are confident in educating the mind, teaching critical reasoning, imparting knowledge, empowering students with information and learning strategies. Good and necessary as this is, the human heart needs more to flourish and discover the phenomenal potential within. No matter how beneficial it is, learning remains partial if we do not deliberately develop and give expression to the transcendent love that is a constituent part of our nature. John O'Donohue captured the essence of this when he wrote:

> [L]ife itself is the prime sacrament; that life is the home of the eternal, albeit in veiled form; that the life of each person is a sacrament, wherein the eternal seeks to become tangible and active; that each individual is chosen for a creative destiny in this world; that each one incarnates a different dimension of God; that at death, life is not ended, but elevated and transfigured into another form; that we are not outside, but, within God.[3]

In the light of this understanding, the acquisition of knowledge alone is insufficient without the intentional inclusion and praxis of what is foundational to Christian life - the understanding and practice of Gospel love. God's love for us reveals the meaning, beauty and potential of our humanity. As St Paul tells us – we can have everything but without love there is an empty hollowness about us; without love something essential to our humanity is missing, without love we can never begin to understand and appreciate the nature of God, or what it means to be truly human (1 Corinthians 13).

Embodying Christian love it is not about a warm, romantic, emotional sentimentality. It is not about wishful thinking, or an idealistic understanding of student-teacher relationships; nor is it just about being nice and well intentioned. Neither can it be considered a refuge, a way of shielding ourselves or students from the pain and evil that exists in the world. It is not a love that promises to alleviate all difficulties and suffering, it does not deny our many inadequate approximations of love or the powerful and often challenging contrary emotions such as hatred, fear, shame, anger, and despair, that befall us.

Rather than viewing Christian love as a way to avoid or overcome the harsh realities of life, it is a means to respond to it.[4] This type of love necessarily needs to be expressed as a decision more than a sentiment, a practical involvement more than a good intention, it is an action more than a mind-set. When we choose to love as Christians we choose to confront whatever dehumanises, to face the fears that incapacitate, challenge the alienation that separates, resist the hopelessness that destroys, and meet all the other little and large tragedies that befall and diminish our humanity - inside and outside the classroom. Christian love is always grounded in reality, it both questions and inspires, it teaches and empowers; it helps us to know how to be a good neighbour, and inspires us to love in good times and bad.

It may be somewhat controversial to speak about how to intentionally love one another in the *zeitgeist* of education in contemporary Ireland. The Church sexual abuse scandals, and the incidences of paedophilia in schools, has cast a long shadow and generated a crisis of faith for many. Perhaps this is all the more reason for us to try to understand the type of relationship that is genuinely loving, from a Christian perspective, and appropriate in the context of a school environment. This process has already begun in the Grow in Love programme taught in RE, and the Relationship and Sex Education classes. These are at the forefront of addressing the meaning and implications of Christian love in life, relationships and intimacy. The task is now to build on, integrate, and make what is already happening in some classrooms a whole school reality so as to cultivate the praxis of Christian love as an integral part of education and school ethos.

THE PRAXIS OF LOVE

One of the more renowned proponents of pedagogical practice, Paulo Freire, emphasised in his writings that education is fundamentally an act of love. He wrote: 'it is impossible to teach without a forged, invented, and well thought-out capacity to love,'[5] and that 'Loving is not enough; one must know how to love'.[6] The mere intention or desire to love is inadequate, maintaining it as an ideal to be aspired to is ineffectual, nor should it remain something that is presumed but not actively cultivated. Just as we cannot take for granted that love is expressed in the act of educating, we cannot take for granted that the praxis of Christian love will happen automatically in a Catholic school. It needs to be intentionally promoted.

Perhaps the most distinctive contribution that a Catholic school can provide their students is to help them develop the capacity to become loving human beings, patterned after the love God and the example of Jesus. It is the process of internalising God's love, making it our own, that creates the conditions for developing the confidence, personal convictions and social motivation to want to make Gospel love an integral part of our lives.

Gospel love cannot be separated from action, the action that seeks to liberate from what is unfinished about us and repudiate any form of oppression or injustice. This love can be an indignation that seeks change and redress; it can serve as a moral and strategic compass for action; it is what teaches, enlightens and guides; it can be expressed as compassion, patience, tolerance, mercy, gentleness, service, and the right use of power. A speech given by Martin Luther King Jr. to the Southern Christian Leadership Conference in 1967, during the Civil Rights Movement, provides an example of how the Gospel love enlightens and emancipates our values. Speaking of his understanding of the relationship between love and power, he said:

> One of the great problems of history is that the concepts of love and power have usually been contrasted as opposites – polar opposites – so that love is identified with a resignation of power, and power with a denial of love.... What is needed is the realization that power without love is reckless and abusive, and that love without power is sentimental and anaemic. Power at its best is love implementing the demands of justice, and justice at its best is love correcting everything that stands against love.[7]

The praxis of love emerges out of the union of reflection and action when Gospel love, Gospel values, inform and guide a person's thinking and decisions to promote genuine and effective relationships with God and neighbour. This kind of love, these Gospel values, change the way we interpret the world and is a potent catalyst for inner and outer change. However, to speak of love is never enough. It is essential to understand that

> How one loves matters; it has effects on the texture of everyday life. Love is as love does. It is both an intention and an action... by always thinking of love as an action rather than a feeling is one way in which anyone using the word in this manner automatically assumes accountability and responsibility.[8]

Jesus, in his actions, shows us how to fully embrace the good and bad in life, and continue to love. Love was the reason for his life, the meaning of his life. He shows us what humanity looks like and what it can achieve when we try to reflect the transforming love of God. As the standard and model for a fulfilled human existence, his actions provide us with a set of very distinct Gospel values which demonstrate how Christian love is expressed. Implementing these Gospel values shapes our lives and empowers us to act responsibly in the way we love and give life to one another. Yet, most of us find it difficult to express such life-giving Gospel love. Marianne Williamson speaks about this reluctance to really embrace our capacity for such love. She suggests that we feel more at ease with our weaknesses, our sinful, self-pre-occupied shadow side because it relieves us of the challenge to really love, to live fully, to move out of our comfort zone, be more other-centred and accept the risk that such Gospel love requires:

> Our deepest fear is not that we are inadequate. Our deepest fear is that we are powerful beyond measure. It is our light, not our darkness that most frightens us. We ask ourselves, 'Who am I to be brilliant, gorgeous, talented, fabulous?' Actually, who are you not to be? You are a child of God. Your playing small does not serve the world. There is nothing enlightened about shrinking so that other people won't feel insecure around you. We are all meant to shine, as children do. We were born to make manifest the glory of God that is within us. It's not just in some of us; it's in everyone. And as we let our own light shine, we unconsciously give other people permission to do the same. As we are liberated from our own fear, our presence automatically liberates others.[9]

Perhaps we shrink from expressing Gospel love because we feel inadequate to the task, or anxious about being responsible for such love. We can feel overwhelmed by the invitation to love as God loves. This fear is understandable; that is why it is important to see love in its different aspects to help us to understand how love can be expressed and communicated through Gospel values and their consequent actions.

AN EXAMPLE

We all know that for love to be real it has to be acted out in the things we say and do. The Gospel love we are speaking of is expressed as compassion, forgiveness, patience, generosity, kindness, patience, reverence and in many other ways. Let's take a brief look at one of the important Gospel values that teaches us how to love. We do not often consider how humility reflects and expresses love, we rarely explore the implications it can have in cultivating good relationships and helping us deal with the tendency to be proud or arrogant, or how it can improve the quality of relationships between school leaders, teachers and students and validate the praxis of intentional Christian love.

Humility as a concrete expression of love calls on us to respect others, it allows us to listen beyond our differences, not to act in arrogance, and accept that people can have other points of view about life and the world. Humility means that we are willing to be less self-centred or self-absorbed in order to be open to others and God; it means letting go of pre-conceived notions of who we are, of what we believe to be certain, and even who God is. Genuine dialogue, and meaningful relationships, cannot take place without humility. The practice of humility prevents us from becoming entrenched in our own perceptions of reality, it helps us recognise that our understanding can be narrow and limited. Humility takes account of the limitations and weaknesses of people. It tries, with sensitivity, to identify bias and prejudice; it acknowledges the darker side of our nature and accepts there are things, people, and occasions that make us feel uncomfortable and insecure. Humility accepts that we are incomplete, and that no one knows it all. It encourages us to accept that we may be less knowledgeable than we think we are and, therefore, be more open to learn and change. Truth cannot be discovered without humility, and with truth comes wisdom.

Some may think of humility means being indecisive and weak, lacking in confidence, or to mean we have a low opinion of ourselves. On the contrary, Christian humility is about respect for self, and while being modest and unpretentious, acknowledges our strengths and weaknesses, and equally acknowledge the gifts and talents we have that can be nurtured, developed and put at the service of others.[10] There are many other ways in which Gospel love is expressed such as commitment, service, solidarity, hope, faith, mercy, justice, fortitude, gentleness and kindness. Having the opportunity to explore these, as different ways of understanding and expressing love, even as briefly as this, gives a sense of how each Gospel value complements and builds on the others to help us become an open and conscientious sacrament of God's love.

It might now be possible to understand why Jesus commanded us to love (John 15:12). Towards the end of his life this new commandment emerged, 'to love one another as I have loved you' (John 13:34). It was not a suggestion, a wish or recommendation. Rather, it represents the imperative to love as he loved, to be and act as he did. This commandment is considered indispensable because he knew, better than anyone, that we could only truly learn, be nurtured, fulfilled and transformed by such love. How else can we grow from being a gifted image to a more real likeness of God, or change from the inside out to reflect the very nature of God?

CONCLUSION

At this stage in the evolution of Catholic education there is an obvious need to balance the systematic development of the mind with the careful cultivation of the heart. There is no doubt that love is an intrinsic value, central to what it means to be human and Christian and, therefore, must be an integral part of Catholic education. Determining how we go about intentionally loving in a school context entails asking difficult questions about why and how we are to purposefully love one another. It will be a challenge to deliberately incorporate Christian values into our established ways of learning and being a school community.

Regardless of the challenges, we need to acknowledge the enormous contribution it will bring to education when it is primarily driven by love. This entails engaging in a discourse with school leaders and teachers, boards of management, parents, and school volunteers around progressing the concept and practice of Christian love as an integral part of education. No doubt there are teachers and school leaders who are doing the best they can to care; there are those who could not love their students more, just as there are those who have little interest in promoting Christian love as an integral part of Catholic education.

We also need to remember that there are many children enrolled in schools with a Christian ethos who have a different faith tradition or none at all and these must be respected and be part of the dialogue. Being aware of the anxieties and complexities of such a challenge does not absolve us from beginning the process of moving toward what seems to be the next stage in the evolution of Catholic schools – where it is understood that love must come first, love is the priority, the critical lens through we learn and grow.

Notes

Prologue:
Where There Is No Vision the People Perish

1 Thomas Groome, *Educating for Life: A Spiritual Vision for Every Teacher and Parent.* 1998, New York: The Crossroad Publishing Co.
2 Donald de Raadt, Donald R. and Veronica D. de Raddt. 'Where There is No Vision, The People Perish: Ethical Vision and Community Sustainability'. *Systems Research and Behavioral Science*, Vol 22, 2005, pp.233-247.
3 Eithne Woulfe and James Cassin (eds). *From Present to Future: Catholic education in Ireland from the new century.* 2006, Dublin: Veritas.
4 Conor Reidy, *The Challenges Facing the Maintenance of the Catholic Ethos in Primary Schools in the Republic of Ireland.* A Research paper presented at Mount St Anne's Conference Centre, Portarlington, 23 February 2019.

1. Basic Convictions: Faith in God and Faith in People

1 For a wonderful treatment of the tragic and evolutionary interpretations of the garden story see Kess Frey, *Human Ground Spiritual Ground*, Great Barrington. MA, 2012, Portal Books.
2 Bruce Sanguin, *The Way of the Wind.* 2015, Vancouver, Viriditas Press, pp.15-16.
3 Denis Gleeson, *Unbinding Christian Faith: Free to Be.* 2015, Dublin, Cluain Mhuire Press, p.110.
4 Marcus J. Borg, *Jesus: Uncovering the Life, Teachings and Relevance of a Religious Revolutionary.* 2006, New York, HarperOne, p.91.
5 Gleeson, *Unbinding Christian Faith*, pp.112ff.
6 For the classic treatment of human growth and transformation that I draw heavily upon here, see Thomas Keating, *The Human Condition: Contemplation and Transformation.* 1999, New York, Paulist Press.
7 Thomas Keating, *Foundations for Centering Prayer and the Christian Contemplative Life: Open Mind Open Heart.* 2002 London, Continuum International Publishing, p.41.
8 Keating, *The Human Condition*, p.15.
9 Keating, *The Human Condition*, p.11.
10 Frey, *Human Ground Spiritual Ground*, p.85.
11 Keating, *The Human Condition*, p.35.
12 Kathleen Deignan (ed), *Thomas Merton: A Book of Hours.* 2007, Notre Dame IN, Sorin Books, p.95, quoted from Thomas Merton's *The Waters of Siloe*, pp.349-350.
13 Sanguin, *The Way of the Wind*, p.63.
14 Sanguin, *The Way of the Wind*, p.39-40.
15 Jack Mahoney, *Christianity in Evolution.* 2011, Washington DC, Georgetown University Press, p. 161.
16 Mahoney, *Christianity in Evolution*, p.66.

17 Teihard de Chardin, *Toward the Future* (from the essay on The Evolution of Chastity, pp. 86-87). Trans. René Hague. 1936, London: A Harvet Press.

2. Leading from within: The Inner Dynamics of School Leadership

1 Diarmuid O'Murchu *Quantum Theology: Spiritual Implications of the New Physics*. (2004) New York: Crossroad Publishing Company, p.91.
2 Michael Onyebuchi Eze. *Intellectual history in contemporary South Africa*. (2010) UK: Palgrave Macmillan. pp. 190–191.
3 Ilia Delio, 'Clare of Assisi and the mysticism of motherhood, *Franciscans at Prayer*, (2007) ed. Timothy J. Johnson, Medieval Franciscans 4. Leiden and Boston: Brill, 54, 47 (31-62).
4 Nick Cowley & Nigal Purse. *5 Conversations: how to transform trust, engagement and performance at work*. (2019) UK: Panoma Press, pp.9 & 18..
5 Lee Bolman and Terrence Deal. *Reframing the path to school leadership: a guide for teachers and principals*. (2019) USA: Corwin, p.22.
6 Parker Palmer. *The Courage to Teach*. (2007) San Francisco: Jossey-Bass, p.3.
7 Leonard Doohan, *Spiritual Leadership: The quest for integrity*. (2007) New York: Paulist Press. p.37.
8 Simon Dolan and Yochanan Altman. 'Managing by values: the leadership spirituality connection', in *People & Strategy*, (2012) 35 (4), at 24, pp.21-26.
9 Frank Anderson. *Making the Eucharist Matter*. (1998) Notre Dame, IN: Ave Maria Press. pp36-38
10 Richard Kearney. *Anatheism: returning to God after God*. (2010) New York: Columbia University Press. p.165.
11 John J Shea. *Finding God Again*. (2005), Maryland: Rowman & Littlefield Publishers, Inc. pp. 57-59.
12 Leonard Doohan. *op. cit.*, p.29.
13 Cuiying Gao. *A narrative inquiry into contemplative leadership: concepts, characteristics, challenges, opportunities*. (2018) PhD thesis, Dublin City University. pp.174-185.
14 Ned Prendergast, 'The Terms of our Affiliation.' In *Strategies for Building Faith Communities in Schools*. (2005) ed. Tony Hanna, Dublin: Centre for Education Services, p.71 (59-72).

3. Leadership, Ethos and Catholic Social Teaching

1 Attributed to Louise Bush-Brown. Reported in *Respectfully Quoted: A Dictionary of Quotations*. Suzy Platt (Ed) USA: Library of Congress, 1989.
2 Tony Bush. *Theories of Educational Leadership and Management*, 4th ed. London: Sage, 2011, 5-8.
3 I am further distilling the categorisations of Tony Bush. What I call a conventional model, he refers to as the Formal Model. He proposes three descriptive models: political, subjective and ambiguous. Finally, he outlines two normative models: collegial and moral.
4 *Catechism of the Catholic Church*, 1718-1719.
5 What is being described here is known as the natural law.
6 Thomas Aquinas. *Summa Theologica*, IIa IIae, q. 57, a. 2.
7 *Popolurom Progressio*, (1967), 15.
8 *Compendium of the Catholic Social Doctrine*. Pontifical Commission for Justice and Peace, 2004.
9 Daniel Groody in *Globalisation, Spirituality and Justice: Navigating a Path to Peace*. New

York: Orbis Books, 2007.They are: A-nalysis of social reality; G-ratuity of God; O-rdering of society towards the common good; D-ignity of the human person; O-ption for the poor; F-reedom as rights and responsibilities; L-ife as a sacred gift; I-nvolvement of all in creation of a new order; F-amily of blood and family of mankind E-nvironment and ecological stewardship. *Globalization, Spirituality, and Justice* (Orbis Books, 2007), 101-120. See also the United States Bishops for a list at http://www.usccb.org/beliefs-and-teachings/what-we-believe/catholic-social-teaching/seven-themes-of-catholic-social-teaching.cfm.

10 *Centesimus Annus*, (1991), 43.
11 Donal Dorr, *Option for the Poor and the Earth*. New York: Orbis Books, 2012, p. 157.
12 *Veritatis Splendor* (1993) 7-8.
13 *Populorum Progressio*, 15-16.
14 *Gaudium et Spes* (1965), n. 26 (Austin Flannery, ed., *Vatican Council II: Constitutions, Decrees, Declarations*, 1996, Dublin: Dominican Publications, p.191.
15 *Rerum Novarum*, (1891), 19.
16 Latin American Bishops, *Poverty of the Church*. Medellin, Columbia, 1968, 9.
17 *Sollicitudo Rei Socialis* (1987), 38.
18 *Centesimus Annus* (1991), 48.
19 *Caritas in Vertiate* (2009), 34.
20 *Evangelii Gaudium* (2013) 8.

4. Building Bridges: Inter-religious Dialogue, Inclusion and Diversity

1 Congregation for Catholic Education. *Educating to Intercultural Dialogue in Catholic Schools, 2013, par 57*
2 For example: *Nostra Aetate*, 1965; *Redemptoris Missio*, 1990; *Dialogue and Proclamation*, 1991; *Educating for Intercultural Dialogue in Catholic Schools*, 2013
3 Second Vatican Council. *Nostra Aetate* (1965), n. 2, in Austin Flannery (editor), *Vatican Council II: Constiutions, Decrees, Declarations*, 1996, Dublin: Dominican Publications, pp. 570-571
4 Congregation for Catholic Education. *The Catholic School on the Threshold of the Third Millennium.* 1997, Vatican City: Libreria Editrice.
5 *The Catholic School,* par 85.
6 Congregation for Catholic Education. *The Religious Dimension of Education in a Catholic School.* 1988, Vatican City: Libreria Editrice, par 6
7 Congregation for Catholic Education. *Lay Catholics in Schools: Witnesses to Faith.* 1982, Vatican City: Libreria Editrice, par. 42
8 *Educating to Intercultural Dialogue in Catholic Schools,* par 55
9 Ibid
10 Ibid, par 83
11 Pope Prancis, *Global Compact on Education*, Congregation for Catholic Education, p. 21.
12 *Educating to Intercultural Dialogue in Catholic Schools,,* par 54
13 Second Vatican Council, *Dignitatis Humanae.* 1965, n. 5 in Austin Flannery (ed.), *op. cit.* p. 551-568; also Holy See document, *Charter of the Rights of the Family,*1983, par 5
14 Alison Mawhinney, Ulrike Niens, Norman Richardson, and Yuko Chiba. *Opting Out of Religious Education: The Views of Young People from Minority Belief Backgrounds.* 2010, Belfast: Queens University,
15 Manal Hamzel and Kimberly Oliver, 'Because I Am Muslim, I Cannot Wear a Swimsuit' *Research Quarterly for Exercise and Sport*, 83(2), (2012), pp. 330 – 339. See also Elnour, A. and Bashir-Ali, K. 'Teaching Muslim Girls in American Schools' *Social Education*, 67, (2003), pp. 62-66;

16 *Educating to Intercultural Dialogue in Catholic Schools, par 83*
17 Audrey Bryan. 'Corporate Multiculturalism, Diversity Management and Positive Interculturalism in Irish Schools and Society' *Irish Educational Studies*, 29(3), (2010), pp. 253 – 269. See also Aiveen Mullally. '*We are Inclusive but are we being Equal?*': *Challenges to Community National Schools Regarding Religious Diversity*', Ed D Thesis, Dublin City University, 2018.
18 *The Religious Dimension of Education in Catholic Schools*, par.6.
19 Adrienne Rich. *Bread, Blood and Poetry*, NY: Norton & Co, 1994.

5. The Role of Ethos In Relationship and Sexuality Education

1 Paula Mayock, Karl Kitching, Mark Morgan. *Relationships and sexuality education: An Assessment of the challenges to full implementation in post-primary schools* (Dublin: Crisis Pregnancy Agency, 2007), 171.
2 Department of Education. *Report of the Expert Advisory Group on Relationships and Sexuality Education* (Dublin: The Stationery Office, 1995), 6.
3 Pontifical Council for the Family. *The Truth and Meaning of Human Sexuality* (Vatican City: Libreria Editrice Vaticana, 1995) 11-12.
4 Ronald Rolheiser. *Seeking Spirituality; Guidelines for a Christian Spirituality for the Twenty First Century* (London: Hodder and Stoughton, 1998).
5 Diarmuid O'Murchu. *Reclaiming Spirituality* (New York: Crossroad Publishing Co, 1998).
6 Michel Foucault. The History of Sexuality. Translated by R. Hurley in 3 Volumes (New York: Pantheon, 1978, 1985, 1986).
7 Dáil Éireann. Debate on Provision of Objective Sex Education Bill 2018, March – April 2018.
8 Carl O'Brien. *The Irish Times*, January 8, 2019; Kenneally, Shane. *The Irish Times*, May 28, 2019.
9 Catholic Schools Partnership (CSP). *Catholic Education at Second Level in the Republic of Ireland – Looking to the Future* (Dublin: Veritas, 2014).
10 David Angel. 'The Four Types of Conversations: Debate, Dialogue, Discourse, and Diatribe.' (davidangel.com, 28/12/2016).
11 Leo Varadkar. Address on the occasion of the Visit of Pope Francis. Dublin Castle, August 2018.
12 Congregation for Catholic Education. *The Religious Dimension of Education in a Catholic School: Guidelines for Reflection and Renewal* (Vatican City: Libreria Editrice Vaticana, 1988).
13 Religious Institute on Sexual Morality, Justice, and Healing. *Open Letter to Religious Leaders About Sex Education* (religiousinstitute.org, 2002).
14 Dermot Lane. *Catholic Education: In the light of Vatican II and Laudato Si* (Dublin: Veritas, 2015), 33, 59.
15 World Health Organisation (WHO). Regional Office for Europe and BZgA. *Standards for Sexuality Education in Europe: Guidance for Implementation* (Köln: BZgA, 2012).
16 Synod of Bishops. *Final Document on Young People, The Faith and Vocational Discernment* (Vatican, 2019), 39.
17 John Paul II. *Veritatis Splendor, Encyclical Letter* (Vatican City: Libreria Editrice Vaticana, 1993), 95.
18 Paul VI. *Gravissimum Educationis, Declaration on Christian Education* (Vatican City: Libreria Editrice Vaticana, 1965), 8.
19 Fida Sanjakdar. 'Can difference make a difference? A critical theory discussion of religion in sexuality education.' *Discourse: Studies in the Cultural Politics of Education*, 39, no.3 (2018): 393-407.

20 Department of Children and Youth Affairs. *LGBTI+ National Youth Strategy 2018-2020 – LGBTI+ Young People: visible, valued and included* (dcya.gov.ie, 2018), 16.
21 Pope Francis. *No Longer Slaves but Brothers and Sisters, World Day of Peace Message*, 2015.
22 Paul Meany. 'Catholic Education – The International Context.' *Studies*, 108, no.429 (2019), 42.
23 Pope Francis. *Address to participants in the plenary session of the Congregation for Catholic Education.* Clementine Hall, 13 February 2014.
24 Mayock, Kitching, Morgan. *Relationships and sexuality education: An Assessment of the challenges to full implementation in post-primary schools* (Dublin: Crisis Pregnancy Agency, 2007), 120.
25 Lieven Boeve. 'Religion after Detraditionalization: Christian Faith in a Post Secular Europe.' *Theological Quarterly*, 123, no. 70 (2005): 99 – 122.
26 James Martin. *Building a Bridge: How the Catholic Church and the LGBT Community Can Enter into a Relationship of Respect, Compassion, and Sensitivity* (New York: Harper One, 2018).
27 Congregation for Catholic Education. *Male and Female He Created Them – Towards a Path of Dialogue on the Question of Gender Theory in Education* (Vatican City: Libreria Editrice Vaticana, 2019), 55.
28 Pope Francis. *Christus Vivit, Post Synodal Apostolic Exhortation* (Vatican City: Libreria Editrice Vaticana, 2019), 222.
29 Joan Chittister. *The Time Is Now, A Call to Uncommon Courage* (New York: Penguin Random House, 2019), 50.

6. School Ethos: A Sign of Hope and Uncompromising Love

1 Joseph Ratzinger. *Jesus of Nazareth, The Infancy Narratives.* London: Bloomsbury, 2012, pp. 32-33.
2 Seán Goan. *Gospel Values and the Catholic School.* Article for Le Cheile, A Catholic School Trust. 2014, p.1.
3 John R. Sachs. *The Christian Vision of Humanity: Basic Christian Anthropology.* Collegeville, MN: Michael Glazier Press, 1991, p.28.
4 Eamonn Conway. *The Splintered Heart: Conversations with a Church in Crisis.* Dublin: Veritas, 1998, p.1.
5 Barbara Brochu and Penny Baragar-Brcic. 'Engaging the Young to Experience God', *Religious Education*, Vol.102, Fall 2007, No.04, p.352.
6 Editorial, 'Is The End of Christianity in Sight?', *The Guardian*, 28 May, 2016, p. 34.
7 Fred P. Edie, 'Liturgy and Faith Formation: Reimagining a Partnership for the Sake of Youth'. *Liturgy*, 29:1, 2014, pp.3 4-44 at p. 35.
8 Jayne Mondoy. 'Liturgy Education in the Curriculum', *Liturgical Ministry*, Winter, 2009.-18, 26-29 at p.29.
9 Eamonn Conway. 'The Commodification of Religion and the Challenges for Theology: Reflections from the Irish Experience' *Bulletin ET Journal of the European Society for Catholic Theology*, Vol.17, 2006/1, pp.143-151. Special Issue, *Consuming Religion in Europe? Christian faith Challenged by Consumer Culture*, L. Boeve and K. Justaert (Eds), Peeters: Leuven.
10 Lieven Boeve. 'Religion after Detraditionalisation: Christian Faith in a Post-Secular Europe.' *Irish Theological Quarterly* (70), No. 2, 2005, 99-122 at p.107.
11 Michael Paul Gallagher. 'Religious Readings of our Culture,' *Studies: Irish Quarterly Review*, Vol 94, 2005, 141-150 at p.144.
12 Ibid., p.148.
13 Merylann J. Schuttloffel. 'Catholic Identity: The Heart of Catholic Education', *Catholic*

Education: A Journal of Inquiry and Practice Vol. 16/ Issue 1, 2012, pp. 148-154 at p. 152.
14 Sachs. *The Christian Vision of Humanity*, p. 11.
15 David Matzko McCarthy. *The Heart of Catholic Teaching: Its Origins and Contemporary Significance*. Grand Rapids, MI: Brazos Press, 2009, p. 28.
16 Goan. *Gospel Values and the Catholic School*, pp. 2-3.
17 John Bollan. *The Light of His Face, Spirituality for Catholic Teachers*. Dublin: Veritas Publications, 2007, p. 131.
18 Sachs. *The Christian Vision of Humanity*, pp.28-32.
19 D. Vincent Twomey. *The End of Irish Catholicism?* Dublin: Veritas, 2003, p.140.
20 Brochu and Baragar-Brcic. *Engaging the Young to Experience God*, p.355.
21 Don N. Howell, Jr. *Servants of the Servant: A Biblical Theology of Leadership*. Eugene OR: Wipf & Stock, 2003, p.3.
22 Sachs. *The Christian Vision of Humanity*, p. 23.

7. It's Everyone's Business: A Whole-school Approach to Ethos

1 Catholic Schools Partnership. *Catholic Education at Second-Level in the Republic of Ireland – Looking to the Future*. 2015, Dublin, p. 9.
2 Terence Deal and Kent Peterson, *Shaping School Culture: The Heart of Leadership*. 1999, San Francisco: Jossey-Bass, p. 2.
3 Gareth Byrne, *Why religious education has an important role to play in our society*, 2014. https://www.irishtimes.com/news/education/why-religious-education-has-an-important-role-to-play-in-our-society-1.1853105
4 Gareth Byrne, *Why religious education has an important role to play in our society*.
5 Department of Education and Skills, *Religious Education Syllabus*. 2003, Dublin: The Stationary Office.
6 Catholic Schools Partnership, *Catholic Education at Second-Level in the Republic of Ireland*, p. 35.
7 University of Notre Dame, *ACE - Ireland About*, 2018. https://ace.nd.edu/ireland/mission).
8 Warren Bennis, *On Becoming a Leader*. 1996, Pearson Education Canada, p. 57.
9 Patrick Duignan, *Educational Leadership: Together Creating Ethical Learning Environments*. 2012, Melbourne: Cambridge University Press, p 53.
10 Department of Education and Skills, *Looking at Our School 2016: A Quality Framework for Post-Primary Schools*. 2016, Dublin: The Inspectorate, p. 7.
11 Department of Education and Skills, *Looking at Our School 2016*, p. 7.
12 Catholic Schools Partnership. *Catholic Education at Second-Level in the Republic of Ireland*, p. 24.
13 Parker J. Palmer, 'Evoking the Spirit in Public Education', *Educational Leadership*, December 1998 /January 1999, http://www.couragerenewal.org/parker/writings/evoking-the-spirit/
14 Parker Palmer, 'Evoking the Spirit in Public Education'.
15 Archbishop J. Michael Miller, 'On Renewal in our Time.' In *Renewing the Mind : A Reader in the Philosophy of Catholic Education*, edited by Ryan N.S. Topping. 2015, The Catholic University of America Press, p375.
16 Donal McKeown, 'The Goals of Education and the Catholic School in Context', *Why Send Your Child to a Catholic School?*, edited by Maura Hyland, 2014, Dublin: Veritas, p. 26.
17 Dermot. Lane, *Catholic Education and the School: Some Theological Reflections*. 1991, Dublin: Veritas, p. 15.

8. A Question of Identity: The Contribution of Teachers to Living Ethos

1. Carl G. Jung and Anieta Jaffe, A. *Memories, Dreams, Reflections*, New York: Vintage Books, 1989, p. 361.
2. Ibid. p.362.
3. John D. Caputo, *Hermeneutics: Facts and Interpretation in the Age of Information*, London: Pelican, 2018.
4. William A. Proefriedt, *How Teachers Learn: Toward a More Liberal Teacher Education*, New York: Teachers College Press, 1994, p. 33.
5. Ibid. p. 5.
6. Paulo Freire, *Cultural action for freedom*, Harmondsworth: Penguin, 1972. p. 21.
7. Parker P. Palmer, *The Courage to Teach: Exploring the Inner Landscape of a Teacher's Life*, San Francisco: Jossey-Bass, 1998, p. ix.
8. Ibid. p. 10.
9. Ibid. p. 11.
10. Wilfred Carr, 'What is an educational practice?' in M Hammersley (ed) *Educational Research: Current Issues Volume 1*, London: Paul Chapman, 1993, p. 168.
11. Dan C. Lortie, *Schoolteacher: a sociological study*, Chicago: The University of Chicago Press, 1975, p. 61.
12. Linda Haggarty, Keith Postlethwaite, Kim Dent, and Jean Ellins, 'An Examination of Beginning Teacher Learning during the Induction Year', paper presented at the British Educational Research Association Annual Conference, University of Manchester, 2-5 September 2009.
13. Myles Horton and Paulo Freire, *We Make the Road by Walking: Conversations on Education and Social Change*, Philadelphia: Temple University Press, 1990, p. 98.
14. Paulo Freire, *Pedagogy of Freedom: Ethics, Democracy and Civic Courage*, Lanham, MD: Rowman and Littlefield, 1998, p. 126.
15. Ibid.
16. Caputo, op. cit., p. 13.
17. Kevin Williams, 'Education and the Catholic Tradition', in Bailey, R., Barrow, R., Carr, D. and McCarthy, C. (eds.), *The SAGE Handbook of Philosophy of Education*, London: SAGE, 2013, p. 170.
18. Jacques Derrida, 'The Villanova Roundtable: A Conversation with Jacques Derrida' in JD Caputo (ed) *Deconstruction in a Nutshell: A Conversation with Jacques Derrida*, New York, Fordham University Press, 1997, p. 5.
19. Ibid. p. 6.
20. Ibid.

9. A Culture of Care: Ethos and the Quality of Relationships

1. Henry Giroux. *America on Edge: Giroux on Politics, Culture and Education* (New York: Palgrave Machmillan, 2006).
2. Charles Taylor. *The Malaise of Modernity* (Concord, ON: Anansi, 1991)
3. Nel Noddings. 'Caring'. *Justice and Caring: Essential Readings in Feminist Ethics.* (New York: Routledge, 1995). p. 16.
4. Alison Jagger. 'Caring as a feminist practice'. *Justice and Caring: Essential Readings in Feminist Ethics.* (New York: Routledge, 1995, p.180).
5. Selma Sevenhuijen. *Citizenship and the Ethic of Care.* (London: Routledge, 1998).
6. Nel Noddings, ibid.
7. Jennifer Nias. *Primary Teachers Talking: a Study of Teaching as Work.* (Continuum International publishing group, 1989).

8 Kathleen Lynch. 'Carelessness: a hidden doxa in higher education'. *Arts and Humanity in Higher Education* (California: Sage Publications, 2007).
9 John Baker; Kathleen Lynch; Sara Cantillon and Judy Walsh. *Equality: from Theory to Action.* (England, Basinstoke: Palgrave Macmillan, 2004).
10 Andy Hargreaves. 'The emotional practice of teaching.' *Teachers and Teacher Education* (Great Britain: Elsevier Science, 14 (8), 1998, pp. 835-854 at p.835).
11 Deborah McLennan. 'The concept of co-option: why evolution often looks miraculous.' *Evolution, Education and Outreach* (1, 2008, pp. 247-258). Https://doi.org/10.1007/s12052-008-0053-8
12 Anna Kuna and Matti Rimpela. 'Well-being in schools: a conceptual model.' *Health Promotion International* (17, 1, 2002, pp.79-87.)
13 Amartya Sen. 'Introduction questions and themes.' *Inequality Re-examined* (Oxford academic, 1995, online edition). https://doi.org/10.1093/0198289286.003.0001
14 Stephen Ball. 'The teacher's soul and the terror of performativity.' *Journal of Education Policy* (2001)
15 Jo Warrin. 'Creating a whole school ethos of care.' *Emotional and Behavioral Difficulties* (22, 3, 2017, pp.188-199).
16 Amitai Etzioni. 'The responsive community: a communitarian perspective.' *American Sociological Review* (61, 1, 1995, pp.1-11).

10. From the Floorboards up: Ethos and Adolescent Faith Formation

1 Paul Weller. 'From the Floorboards Up'. From the album, *As it is now,* released in 2005. Universal Music Publishing Group.
2 James Fowler. *Stages of Faith Development: The Psychology of Human Development.* New York: Harper Collins, 1981, pp. iii-5,
3 Ibid. p. 5.
4 Ibid.
5 Maria Harris and Gabriel Moran. *Reshaping Religious Education: Conversations on Contemporary Practice,* Louisville, KY: Westminster John Knox Press, 1996, p.109.
6 Dermot Lane. *The Experience of God: an Invitation to do Theology.* Dublin: Veritas, 2003. p. 75.
7 Fowler. *Stages of Faith Development.* p. 24.
8 Laurence Steinberg. *Adolescence.* Sixth International edition. New York: McGraw-Hill Higher Education, 2002, p. 313.
9 David Tuohy and Penny Cairns. *Youth 2K: Threat or Promise to a Religious Culture.* Dublin: Marino Institute of Education, 2000
10 Steinberg, *Adolescence. p.284.*
11 Joanne Hendrick. 'Learning by Doing', *NACTA Journal,* 2011. 55(3), p. 98.
12 Mark Patrick Hederman. *The Boy in the Bubble.* Dublin: Veritas Publications, 2012.
13 Martin Buber. *I and Thou.* New York: Charles Scribner's Sons.1923. *Reprint* Continuum International Publishing Group, 2004.
14 Hederman, *The Boy in the Bubble.* p. 56.
15 Michael Hryniuk. 'Creating space for God: toward a Spirituality of Youth Ministry'. *Religious Education: The official journal of the Religious Education Association,* 2005. 100(2), pp.139-156.
16 Harris and Moran, *Reshaping Religious Education.* p. 109.
17 Tuohy and Cairns. *Youth 2K. p.59.*
18 William Kay and Leslie Francis. *Drift from the Churches: Attitude toward Christianity during Childhood and Adolescence.* Cardiff: University of Wales Press, 1996, p. 32.
19 Roy Baumeister and Mark Leary. 'The Need to Belong: Desire for Interpersonal At-

tachments as a Fundamental Human Motivation'. *Psychological Bulletin*, 1995, 117(3), pp. 497-529.
20 Michael Drumm and Tom Gunning. A *Sacramental People*, volume I. First ed. Dublin: Columba Press, 1999, p. 30.
21 Marian De Souza, Patricia Cartwright and E. Jacqueline McGilp. 'An Investigation into the Perceptions of the Spiritual Wellbeing of 16-20 year-old Young People in a Regional Centre in Victoria', in: Norman, J. (ed.) *At the Heart of Education: School Chaplaincy and Pastoral Care*, Dublin: Veritas, 2002, pp.122-134.
22 Tuohy and Cairns. *Youth 2K.* p. 56.
23 Beverly Faircloth. 'Making the Most of Adolescence: Harnessing the Search for Identity to Understand Classroom Belonging', *Journal of Adolescent Research*, Sage Publications, 2009, 24(3), pp. 321-348 at p. 327.
24 Cheryl Ellerbrock and Sarah Kiefer. 'School based Interpersonal Relationships: Setting the Foundation for Young Adolescents' Belonging in Middle School, *Middle Grades Research Journal*, 2014, 9(2), pp. 1-17.
25 Hryniuk, 'Creating Space for God', p. 147.

11. Ethos Supports Learning for Life and Lifelong Learning

1 Louise Watson. *Lifelong Learning in Australia.* 2003, Canberra, Department of Education, Science and Training, p. 3.
2 Ruth Deakin Crick, Patricia Broadfoot and Guy Claxton. *Developing an Effective Lifelong Learning Inventory.* 2002, Bristol: Graduate School of Education, University of Bristol, Lifelong Learning Foundation.
3 Kathleen Lynch. *The Hidden Curriculum: Reproduction in Education, a Reappraisal.* 1989, London: Falmer.
4 Terence McLaughlin. 'The Educative Importance of Ethos'. *British Journal of Educational Studies.* 53 (3), 2005, pp. 306-325.
5 Noel Canavan and Luke Monahan. *School Culture and Ethos. Releasing the Potential. A Resource Pack to Enable Schools to Access, Articulate and Apply Ethos Values.* 2000, Dublin: Marino Institute of Education.
6 Caitkin Donnelly. 'In Pursuit of School Ethos'. *British Journal of Educational Studies.* 48, 2000, pp. 134-154.
7 Terrence Deal and Kent D. Peterson. *Shaping School Culture.* 1999, San Francisco, CA, Jossey-Bass, p. 2.
8 Pamala Munn, Mairi Ann Cullen, Margarete Johnstone, and Gwynedd Lloyd. 'Exclusion From School: A View From Scotland of Policy and Practice'. *Research Papers in Education.* 16(1), 2001, pp. 23-42.
9 Ibid.
10 Frederick Schmitt and Reza Lahroodi. 'The Epistemic Value of Curiosity'. *Educational Theory.* 8, 2008, 125-48. University of Illinois.
11 Ingrid Larkin and Amanda Beatson. 'Blended Delivery and Online Assessment: Scaffolding Student Reflections in Work- Integrated Learning'. *Marketing Education Review.* 24(1), 2014, p. 914.
12 Parker Palmer. *The Courage to Teach.* 1999, San Francisco: Jossey-Bass.

12. Creating Good Memories: Ethos and School Gardens

1 Robert Macfarlane. *Landmarks.* London: Penguin, 2015, p. 135.
2 Edward O. Wilson. *Biophilia.* USA: Harvard University Press, 1984, p. 43.

3   Sandra Austin. 'Garden-based Learning in Primary Schools: Meeting the Challenges and Reaping the Benefits'. *Education*, 3-13, 50:6, 707-72, 2022.
4   Rowena Passy. 'School Gardens: Teaching and Learning outside the Front Door'. *Education*, 2014, 42(1), pp. 23-38. See also Dilafruz R. Williams and P. Scott Dixon. 'Impact of Garden-based Learning on Academic Outcomes in Schools: Synthesis of Research between 1990 and 2010'. *Review of Educational Research*, 2013, 83(2), pp. 211-235.
5   Paula Owens. 'Creative Fieldwork: Whose Place Is It Anyway?' In S. Pickering (ed.) *Teaching Outdoors Creatively* (first edition). Oxford: Routledge, 2017. pp. 42-58
6   Justin Dillon, Mark Richinson, Kelly Teamey, Marian Morros, Mee Young Choi, Dawn Sanders, and Pauline Benefield. 'The Value of Outdoor Learning: Evidence from Research in the UK and Elsewhere', *School Science Review*, 2006, 87(320), p. 107.
7   Dorothy Blair. 'The Child in the Garden: An Evaluative Review of the Benefits of School Gardening.' *The Journal of Environmental Education*, 2009, 40(2), pp. 15-38.
8   Simon Catling, Richard Greenwood, Fran Martin and Paula Owens. 'Formative Experiences of Primary Geography Educators'. *International Research in Geographical and Environmental Education*, 2010, 19(4), 341-350. See also David Sobel. *Place-based Education: Connecting Classrooms and Communities*. Massachusetts: Orion 2013.
9   Sandra Austin, 'Garden-based learning in primary schools'. This research tapped into the experience of teachers in six primary school in the Dublin area about the experience of using a school garden. The names of the schools and teachers are pseudonyms to protect their identity.
10 Dilafruz R. Williams and P. Scott Dixon. *Art. cit.*
11 Heather Ohly, Sarah Gentry, Rachel Wigglesworth, Alison Bethel, Rebecca Lovell and Ruth Garside. *A Systematic Review of the Health and Well-being Aspects of School Gardening: Synthesis of Quantitative and Qualitative Evidence*. BMC Public Health, 2016, 16, p. 286.
12 Diane Reay. 'Sociology, Social Class and Education'. *Routledge International Handbook of the Sociology of Education*, 2010, pp. 396-404.
13 Passy, Ibid.

13. Ethos in School Traditions, Symbols and Rituals

1   Congregation for Catholic Education, *The Religious Dimension of Education in a Catholic School Children* (Vatican City, Editio Typoglotica Vaticana, 1988), n. 50.
2   Ibid., n. 69.
3   And they devoted themselves to the apostles' teaching and fellowship, to the breaking of bread and the prayers. And fear came upon every soul; and many wonders and signs were done through the apostles. And all who believed were together and had all things in common; and they sold their possessions and goods and distributed them to all, as any had need. And day by day, attending the temple together and breaking bread in their homes, they partook of food with glad and generous hearts, praising God and having favour with all the people. And the Lord added to their number day by day those who were being saved. (RSV)
4   Pope St. John-Paul II *Catechesi Tradendae*, n. 37.
5   *Directory for Masses with Children*, Sacred Congregation for Divine Worship, Rome 1973, n. 21.
6   Jeremy Gallet, 'Documents of Formation: The Directory for Masses with Children and the Lectionary for Masses with Children – Another Look,' *Liturgical Ministry*, number 9, Summer 2000, p. 141.
7   Jeremy Gallet, *art. cit.*, p. 142.
8   *Directory for Masses with Children*, n. 12.
9   *Directory for Masses with Children*, n. 9.

10 Coming from the writing of the educationalist, Jerome Bruner, the spiral curriculum is one where learning begins with simple concepts and ideas in order to instil a particular subject. As time progresses and children grow, these concepts and ideas are revisited and can become more sophisticated and difficult in their presentation. Teaching children about the Last Supper begins with an understanding of meals and food and celebrations, before moving on to an explanation of Eucharist.
11 *Directory for Masses with Children*, n. 29.
12 Louis Weil, 'Children and Worship,' in *The Sacred Play of Children*, ed. Diane Apostolos-Cappdona (New York: Seabury Press, 1983), p. 58.
13 *Directory for Masses with Children*, nn. 2, 12.
14 Edward Matthews, *Celebrating Mass with Children – A Commentary on the Directory for Masses with Children*, (New York: Paulist Press, 1975), p. 37. While this source is very old, it was written only two years after the Directory was published. The commentary is full of enthusiasm for the potential of the Directory in the life of the Church.
15 *Directory for Masses with Children*, n. 10.
16 *Directory for Masses with Children*, n. 1.
17 *Directory for Masses with Children*, n. 10.
18 Congregation for Catholic Education, *The Catholic School* (Vatican City, Editio Typoglotica Vaticana, 1977), n. 54.
19 *Directory for Masses with Children*, n. 11.
20 Weil, p. 58.

14. Creating a Sacred Space: Reflective Practice

1 David Whyte, 'Cultivating the Imagination in Children' *Leadership*, March/April, 2004, pp.20-21.
2 Leslie McClain, Rose Ylimaki, and Michael P. Ford, 'Sustaining the heart of education: finding space for wisdom and compassion', *International Journal of Children's Spirituality*, Vol. 15, No. 4, 2010, pp.307-16.
3 Judy Brown, *The Sea Accepts All Rivers & Other Poems*. 2016, Bloomington, Indiana: Trafford.
4 Daniel Goleman, *Social Intelligence: The New Science of Human Relationships*. 2006, London: Hutchinson, pp.282-284.
5 Rainer Maria Rilke, *Poems*. 1934, London, Hogarth Press, p.27.
6 Parker Palmer, *To Know As We Are Known: Education as a Spiritual Journey*. 1993, New York: HarperOne, pp.71-72.
7 Aostre Johnson and Marilyn Webb Neagley, (Eds) *Educating From The Heart*. 2011, Plymouth: Rowman & Littlefield, p.11.

15. Parents as Partners: Ethos at Home

1 Joyce Epstein, Mavis Sanders, Beth Simons, Karren Clark Salinas, Natalie Rodriguez Jansorn, and Frances Van Voorhis, *School, Family and Community Partnerships*. 2002, Thousand Oaks, CA: Corwin Press, pp. 85-102.
2 Garry Hornby., and Rayleen Lafaele. 'Barriers to Parental Involvement in Education: An Explanatory Model. *Educational Review*, 63(1), 2011, pp. 37-52. R
3 Concepta Conaty. *Including All: Home, School and Community United in Education*. 2002, Veritas Publications, Dublin, p.108.
4 Rosaleen Doherty, 'The Experience of Parental Involvement in a DEIS-based Secondary School in Dublin', MA Thesis, Mary Immaculate College Limerick, 2016.

5 Austin Flannery, O.P. (ed.), *Vatican Council II: Constitutions, Decrees, Declarations*, 1996, Dublin, Dominican Publications, pp, 573-592.

16. Ethos at Play: Extra-curricular Activities

1 Daniel O'Leary. 'Pursuing Purest Gold', *The Tablet*, 19-26 August 2017, p. 10.
2 Stephen Laumakis, Peter Laumakis, Paul Laumakis. 'Playing to Win vs. Playing for Meaningful Victories', *Journal of the Philosophy of Sport*, Volume 44, Issue 2, 2017, Abstract published online: 13 February 2017.
3 Ronnie Delany. *Staying the Distance*, 2006, Dublin: O'Brien Press, p. 14.
4 Ibid. p. 24.
5 Ibid. p. 27.
6 Ibid. p. 81.
7 Ibid. p. 102.
8 Sigmund Loland and Mike Namee. 'Fair Play and Ethos in Sports: An Eclectic Philosophical Framework'. *Journal of the Philosophy of Sport*. Vol. 27, 1, 2000, pp, 64.
9 Delany, *Staying the Distance*, p. 86.

17. Going the Extra Mile: After-school Support

1 Department of Education and Skills. *Statistical Bulletin: Enrolments September 2023– Preliminary Results*. http://www.gov.ie/en/publication055810-education-statistics/
2 TUSLA - Child and Family Agency. *Developing the Statement of Strategy for School Attendance-Guidelines for Schools*. Dublin: TUSLA, 2015.
3 Ibid p.16.
4 Ibid p. 13.
5 Siobhán Shovlin. *The Role of Initiatives in Promoting and Improving Attendance in DEIS Band 1 Primary Schools*. An MA dissertation submitted to Mary Immaculate College, Limerick in June 2017.
6 Ibid p.26.
7 Seán Ruth. 'Leadership and Liberation', *Doctrine & Life*, vol. 57, no. 2, 2007,15-24. p.16.
8 Healthy Food for All. *A Good Practice Guide for Breakfast Clubs*. Dublin: Healthy Food for All, 2012. p.11.
9 Noreen Flynn. Tackling Educational Disadvantage: Home and School in *Beyond Educational Disadvantage*. Eds. Paul Downes and Louise Gilligan. Dublin: Institute of Public Administration, 2007, p. 91.
10 Sharon Friel and Catherine Conlon. *Food Poverty and Policy*. Dublin: Combat Poverty Agency, 2004. p. 23.
11 TUSLA, *The Core Elements of the School Completion Programme*, National Co-ordination Team, 2009, p. 12.
12 'DEIS: Delivering Equality of Opportunity in Schools'. *Department of Education and Skills*.

18. Ethos in the Wider Community: Community Service

1 Pope Francis to Catholic students, teachers: It takes a village to raise a child. 2014 May 12. Accessed March 27, 2018. https://www.romereports.com/en/2014/05/12/pope-francis-to-catholic-students-teachers-it-takes-a-village-to-raise-a-child/
2 Myles Horton, and Paulo Freire. *We make the road by walking: Conversations on education and social change*. (Philadelphia: Temple University Press, 1990)
3 Shelley H. Billig, 'Research on K-12 school-based service-learning.' *Phi Delta Kappan*

81, no. 9: (2000)658-664 at 661.
4   Maryse H. Richards, Rebecca Cornelli Sanderson, Christine I. Celio, Jane E. Grant, Inhe Choi, Christine C. George, and Kyle Deane. 'Service-Learning in Early Adolescence Results of a School-Based Curriculum.' *Journal of Experiential Education* 36, no. 1 (2013) 5-21 at 6.
5   Susan Benigni Cipolle. *Service-learning and social justice: Engaging students in social change.* Plymouth, UK: Rowman & Littlefield Publishers, 2010.
6   Nicholas A. Bowman, Jay W. Brandenberger, Connie Snyder Mick, and Cynthia Toms Smedley. 'Sustained Immersion Courses and Student Orientations to Equality, Justice, and Social Responsibility: The Role of Short-Term Service-Learning.' *Michigan Journal of Community Service Learning* 17, no. 1 (2010) 20-31.
7   Thomas G. Plante, Katy Lackey, and Jeong Yeon Hwang. 'The impact of immersion trips on development of compassion among college students.' *Journal of Experiential Education* 32, no. 1 (2009) 28-43.
8   Alan S. Waterman, 'An overview of Service Learning and the Role of Research and Evaluation in Service Learning Programs.' In *Service-learning: Applications from the Research*, edited by Alan S. Waterman, 1-11. New York, NY: Psychology Press, 2013, Kindle.

19. Being Stewards of Creation: Ethos and the Care of the Earth

1   Thomas Berry. *The Great Work: Our Way Into The Future.* New York: Bell Tower, 1999.
2   Thomas Berry. *Creative Energy: Bearing Witness for the Earth.* San Francisco: Sierra Club Books, 1996.
3   Brian Swimme and Thomas Berry. *The Universe Story.* San Francisco: Harper, 1992, p.43.
4   John Sachs *The Christian Vision of Humanity: Basic Christian Anthropology.* London: Michael Glazier Books, 1991, p.104.
5   Ibid.
6   Gregor Torkar. 'Learning experiences that produce environmentally active and informed minds', *NJAS – Washington Journal of Life Sciences.* 2014, Vol. 69, pp. 49-45 at p. 49.
7   Brigid Reynolds and Seán Healy, '*Laudato Si*' and Social Justice' in *Laudato Si': An Irish Response.* ed. Sean McDonagh,. Dublin: Veritas, 2017, pp.105-125.
8   Pope Francis *Laudato Si'.* Vatican Website. 2016, Paragraph 23.
9   *Laudato Si'.* Paragraph 66.
10 Seán Mc Donagh *Laudato Si – A Prophetic Challenge for the 21st Century.* Lecture given at Dromantine Retreat and Conference Centre, Newry. June 25th 2016.
11 Dermot A. Lane. *Catholic Education: In the Light of Vatican 11 and Laudato Si.* Dublin Veritas, 2015, p. 48.
12 *Laudato Si'.* Paragraph 66.
13 Lorna Gold (2016) *Laudato Si – A Prophetic Challenge for the 21st Century.* Lecture given at Dromantine Retreat and Conference Centre, Newry. June 25, 2016.
14 Lane *Catholic Education.* p. 50.
15 Ibid.p. 48.

20. Politics and Ethos in Irish Primary Schools

1   https://www.education.ie/en/Press-Events/Press-Releases/2007-Press-Releases/PR07-12-13.htgl
2   Department of Education and Science, *Primary School Curriculum,* 1999, Chapter 5 Curriculum areas, p. 58

3 Primary School Curriculum, Introduction Chap 1 Aims Principles and Features, p. 10
4 Declan Kiberd. *After Ireland: writing the nation from Beckett to the present*. (London: Head of Zeus Ltd., 2017).
5 Francis Campbell. *The Future of Faith Based Schools in a Pluralist Society*. Keynote address 2016 National Education Conference https://www.icatholic.ie/edconf-2016-francis-campbell/
6 Department of Education and S, *A Guide to the Irish Education System Primary*, 2014. The primary education sector includes state-funded primary schools, special schools and private primary schools. State-funded primary schools used to be known as national schools and include religious schools, such as Roman Catholic, Church of Ireland Muslim, non-denominational schools; multi-denominational schools; and Gaelscoileanna (schools that teach through the Irish language).
7 Rowan Williams. *Being Human: Bodies, Minds, Persons*. 2018, London: SPCK.
8 National Census 2016: Chapter 8 Religion https://www.cso.ie/en/media/csoie/releasespublications/documents/population/2017/Chapter_8_Religion.pdf
9 See National Council for Curriculum and Assessment, *Goodness Me Goodness You General Rationale* 2015.

Epilogue
Love Comes first: Reflections on Catholic School Ethos

1 Christopher Marshall (2013) 'Eternal life and the common good: why loving one's neighbour matters in the long run'. *Victoria University of Wellington Law Review*, 44(2), 403-412 at 411.
2 Daniel O'Leary, (2008) *Begin with the heart: recovering a sacramental vision*. Dublin: Columba Press. pp. 159-160.
3 John O'Donohue. To awaken the divinity within. *The Way*, July 1996. p. 267.
4 Sean Chabot. (2008). 'Love and Revolution'. *Critical Sociology*, 34(6) 803–828 at p.816
5 Paulo Freire. (1998) *Teachers as cultural workers: letters to those who dare to teach*. Boulder, CO: Westview, p. 3.
6 Op. cit., p. 126.
7 Martin Luther King. (1990 [1967]). 'Where do we go from here?' In J. M. Washington (Ed.), *A testament of hope: The essential writings and speeches of Martin Luther King, Jr*. New York: Harper, pp. 245–252 at p. 247.
8 Bell Hooks. (2000). *All about love: new visions*. New York: William Morrow and Company, Inc. pp.4-5 and p.13.
9 Marianne Williamson. (1992). *A return to love: reflections on the principle of 'A course of miracles'*. New York: Harper Collins, p.190 (in some editions p.165).
10 Antonia Darder. (2003). 'Teaching as an act of love: Reflections on Paulo Freire and his contributions to our lives and our work'. In Antonia Darder, Marta Baltodano, & Rodolfo D. Torres (Eds.), *The critical pedagogy reader*. New York: Routledge Falmer, pp. 497–510.